# THE ADDED DIMENSION:

*The art and mind of Flannery O'Connor*

# THE ADDED DIMENSION
## The art and mind of Flannery O'Connor

*Edited by*

MELVIN J. FRIEDMAN *and* LEWIS A. LAWSON

FORDHAM UNIVERSITY PRESS
*New York*

A belief in fixed dogma cannot fix what goes on in life or blind the believer to it. It will, of course, add to the writer's observation a dimension which many cannot, in conscience, acknowledge; but as long as what they *can* acknowledge is present in the work, they cannot claim that any freedom has been denied the artist. A dimension taken away is one thing; a dimension added is another, and what the Catholic writer and reader will have to remember is that the reality of the added dimension will be judged in a work of fiction by the truthfulness and wholeness of the literal level of the natural events presented. If the Catholic writer hopes to reveal mysteries, he will have to do it by describing truthfully what he sees from where he is. A purely affirmative vision cannot be demanded of him without limiting his freedom to observe what man has done with the things of God.

FLANNERY O'CONNOR
"The Church and the Fiction Writer"
*America,* March 30, 1957.

# Acknowledgments

Farrar, Straus & Giroux, Inc. for permission to quote from
*Everything That Rises Must Converge* by Flannery O'Connor.
Copyright © 1956, 1957, 1958, 1960, 1961, 1962, 1964, 1965 by
the Estate of Mary Flannery O'Connor.
*A Memoir of Mary Ann* by Flannery O'Connor. Copyright ©
1961 by Farrar, Straus & Cudahy, Inc.
*The Violent Bear It Away* by Flannery O'Connor. Copyright
© 1955, 1960 by Flannery O'Connor.
*Wise Blood* by Flannery O'Connor. Copyright © 1949, 1952,
1962 by Flannery O'Connor.

Harcourt Brace Jovanovich, Inc. for permission to quote from
*A Good Man Is Hard to Find* by Flannery O'Connor. Copyright © 1955 by Flannery O'Connor.

# Note

*Three* (New York: New American Library, 1964) contains
*Wise Blood, A Good Man Is Hard to Find,* and *The Violent
Bear It Away.* Since this edition is so readily available, all page
references in the present volume have been standardized to
refer to *Three*; they are incorporated in the text and placed
within parentheses. The page references to the stories which
appear in *Everything That Rises Must Converge* (New York:
Farrar, Straus & Giroux, 1965) likewise appear in the text, preceded by *Everything*.

# Contents

# *Preface*

THIS COLLECTION is intended as an *omnium gatherum* of critical opinions about a writer who died in her "early prime." The editors and contributors, however much they may disagree in their interpretation of the work Flannery O'Connor has left behind, are firmly agreed on their estimation of her achievement.

It is always difficult to appraise the writing of one's contemporaries. The classic blunders of the great nineteenth-century critics Sainte-Beuve and Taine are unpleasant reminders for anyone who treads on the still sacred remains of recently deceased writers. With this caution in mind the present volume can be no more than a tentative series of judgments.

In this instance the contributors were further handicapped by the unavailability of a posthumous collection of stories, *Everything That Rises Must Converge*, which was not as yet in print when they wrote their essays. Early reviews of this volume have pointed to its containing the most mature work of Flannery O'Connor. This remark in Theodore Solotaroff's review (*Book Week*, May 30, 1965) is fairly typical: "All in all they comprise the best collection of shorter fiction to have been published in America during the past 20 years."

This volume must then stand more on the spontaneity of its *aperçus* than on the finality of its judgments. The collection was conceived more as a representation of many points of view than as a unified approach to Flannery O'Connor's fiction. Thus an attempt was made to gather together a group of critics who would, by their own persuasions, place her in the various categories suggested by her work.

The paradox of the Roman Catholic in a Protestant South had suggested to us immediately the names of most of our contributors. Harold C. Gardiner, S.J., and Sister M. Bernetta Quinn, O.S.F., were among the earliest who revealed serious interest in Flannery O'Connor; they are also among the most persuasive Roman Catholic commentators on recent American fiction (Father Gardiner is now serving as literary editor of *The New Catholic Encyclopedia*). P. Albert Duhamel, who has written perceptively on her before, has always expressed an enlightened lay Catholic point of view. Nathan Scott, with an approach partly shaped by Reinhold Niebuhr and Paul Tillich, has labored more faithfully than anyone else in a discipline which has profitably turned to Protestant theology to interpret twentieth-century literature. His books on Camus, Beckett, and Niebuhr, have offered us exciting new optics for viewing many of our contemporaries.

The other five contributors express no particular religious bias. In Louis Rubin and Hugh Holman we have two of the most gifted commentators on recent Southern literature. Rubin's *The Faraway Country* is the most brilliant study of twentieth-century Southern literature now in print. When *Harper's* published its special supplement, "The South Today" (April, 1965), Rubin did the "Notes on the Literary Scene." Holman has devoted a good deal of his attention to Southern writing and is generally considered to have done the best work on Thomas Wolfe.

Caroline Gordon is among the most accomplished of Southern fiction writers and also a most remarkable literary critic. College students have read her "Old Red" with enthusiasm for several decades, but she will probably in the end be remembered as much for her novels as for her stories. The order of her achievement can be partly measured by the first issue of *Critique* (Winter, 1956) which was entirely given over to estimations of her work.

Among the contributors to this special issue on Caroline Gordon was Frederick J. Hoffman. There is no sustained body of critical writing more impressive than his many books from *Freudianism and the Literary Mind* (1945) to *The Mortal No* (1964). Irving Malin has written studies on many phases of recent American fiction, including a new book on the contemporary Jewish novel which received front-page coverage in *The New York Times Book Review* (May 30, 1965).

The editors have been properly awed by the impressive credentials of the contributors to this volume. No attempt has been made to control the direction of the essays (although general subjects were assigned to each essayist) or to edit the point of view or style of the contributors. Uniformity has been sacrificed to diversity. Thus there is a certain amount of overlapping, *e.g.*, Duhamel has written an entire essay on Flannery O'Connor's possible debt to the Fugitives and Holman has reiterated, in passing, some of the same convictions. When faced with a relatively slight body of work—two novels, a collection of short stories, and scattered stories and essays— duplication of some sort is almost unavoidable.

The introduction has tried to present a sustained, coherent estimation of Flannery O'Connor's work, from her earliest story, "The Geranium," through the posthumous volume, *Everything That Rises Must Converge*. It attempts to travel a middle road and offer an *entrée* to the more specialized studies which follow.

# Preface to the Second Edition

IT HAS BEEN more than a decade since the appearance of the first edition of *The Added Dimension*. The book has fared well with reviewers and with authors of other studies on Flannery O'Connor. The generous responses of many O'Connor critics and readers have suggested to Fordham University Press the need for a second edition of *The Added Dimension,* in its paperback series.

The editors have felt no necessity to make substantial changes in any of the essays: minor corrections and adjustments, however, have been worked into the text. The bibliography has not been updated because of the many reliable bibliographical sources now available. There is a quite complete listing of works by and about Flannery O'Connor at the end of Leon V. Driskell's and Joan T. Brittain's *The Eternal Crossroads: The Art of Flannery O'Connor* (The University Press of Kentucky, 1971). Allen D. Lackey's "Flannery O'Connor: A Supplemental Bibliography" (*Bulletin of Bibliography,* October–December 1973, pp. 170–175) is complete through 1972. Aside from standard sources—like the annual *MLA International Bibliography,* with the accompanying *MLA Abstracts,* and the checklist at the end of each issue of *American*

*Literature*—there is the relatively new annual bibliography of Southern literature in the spring number of *Mississippi Quarterly* and the imposing annual bibliographical issue of *Journal of Modern Literature*. *Mississippi Quarterly* has been offering its invaluable annotated listing since the spring of 1969 in an attempt to update *A Bibliographical Guide to the Study of Southern Literature*, ed. Louis D. Rubin, Jr. (Louisiana State University Press, 1969; Melvin J. Friedman did the entry on Flannery O'Connor in the *Guide*—see pp. 250–253).

Clearly the most important bibliographical source for critical writing about Flannery O'Connor is Robert Golden's and Mary Sullivan's *Flannery O'Connor and Caroline Gordon: A Reference Guide* (G. K. Hall, 1977). At this writing the book has not been published, but Robert Golden (who is responsible for the O'Connor sections) and Mary Grace Smith (an editor at G. K. Hall) have kindly allowed us to examine parts of the typescript. Golden's annotations are "descriptive" rather than "evaluative" and the material is arranged chronologically—with each year divided into two sections: the first listing books and monographs; the second listing articles, sections of books, and review essays. A sampling of Golden's annotations reveals that he is a careful, judicious, and knowledgeable scholar. The book is intelligently set up to allow for frequent new editions when necessary.

Another bibliographical item of considerable value is David Farmer's *A Descriptive Bibliography of the Works of Flannery O'Connor*, scheduled for fall 1977 publication by Burt Franklin. Mr. Farmer generously allowed us to examine sections of it. The introduction clearly states the need for such a work: "It is often difficult to observe trends in an author's publishing career until a descriptive bibliography has been completed, for only then are certain patterns organized and perceptible, and only then is a complete overview of a career possible." Mr. Farmer more than fulfills our expectations. He not only describes the well-known parts of the O'Connor canon but also systematically examines the previously unknown undergraduate writing and the linoleum block cartoons she contributed to various campus publications at Georgia State College for Women. There are also sections devoted to translations of O'Connor's work and to adaptations, films, and parodies of it. Farmer's book is a labor of love, the happy result of living in close proximity to the Georgia writer's work for many years.

\* \* \*

Copyright considerations have prevented the reprinting of the "Flannery O'Connor in Her Own Words" section of the first edition of *The Added Dimension*. Fortunately, much of this material has since become available in Sally and Robert Fitzgerald's collection, *Mystery and Manners: Occasional Prose* (Farrar, Straus & Giroux, 1969).

The new material offered in this second edition includes " 'The Perplex Business': Flannery O'Connor and Her Critics Enter the 1970s," which offers an overview of recent developments in O'Connor criticism and editing; the emphasis is on book-length studies of her work. Portions of this essay have appeared in different form in *Journal of Modern Literature, American Literature, Southern Literary Journal,* and *Studies in American Fiction.* We should like to thank the editors of these journals for allowing us to use this material. Since the completion of " 'The Perplex Business' " two new books have appeared—which should at least receive a mention here: Dorothy Tuck McFarland's *Flannery O'Connor* (Frederick Ungar, 1976) and John R. May's *The Pruning Word: The Parables of Flannery O'Connor* (University of Notre Dame Press, 1976). Mr. Golden, in the introduction to his bibliography, offers the following astounding information about the present status of writing about Flannery O'Connor: "There are now eighteen books devoted exclusively to her fiction and sixty-five Ph.D. dissertations that discuss her works."

After all this encouraging news, it is our painful duty to mention the deaths of two of the contributors to the first edition of *The Added Dimension*: Frederick J. Hoffman and Harold C. Gardiner, s.j. Crescunt eundo.

*The University of Wisconsin–Milwaukee* MELVIN J. FRIEDMAN
*The University of Maryland* LEWIS A. LAWSON

# Postscript: A Personal Note

After the second edition of *The Added Dimension* was far advanced I had the kind of privileged experience which should not go unrecorded. During a Fulbright semester in Belgium in 1976 I was invited to give a series of lectures on Flannery O'Connor at a variety of French universities, including Nice, Aix-en-Provence, Lyon, Montpellier, and Paris. It turned out that O'Connor was required reading for "agrégatifs" (advanced graduate students) in France during this period. The reaction to her work was heartening: students and professors alike responded to the finer tunings of her language and the subtleties of her craft. My own response to her *oeuvre* seems to have been sharpened and even refashioned. I began to see the "French face" of Flannery O'Connor with the same clarity as I once saw the French face of William Faulkner through the optics of Valery Larbaud, André Malraux, and Jean-Paul Sartre. The French seem on the way to appropriating Flannery O'Connor in the same agreeable way they once appropriated Poe and Faulkner.

Virtually all of Flannery O'Connor is now available in French translation. Maurice-Edgar Coindreau has sensitively translated both *Wise Blood* and *The Violent Bear It Away* and Henri Morisset has given us French versions of *A Good Man Is Hard to Find* and *Everything That Rises Must Converge*. *Mystery and Manners* is now available in André Simon's 1975 translation. The most recent addition to the French canon is a volume entitled *Pourquoi ces nations en tumulte?* which contains translations of five of the M.A. thesis stories ("The Geranium," "The Barber," "The Wildcat," "The Crop," and "The Turkey") as well as "The Partridge Festival" and "Why Do the Heathens Rage?". Thus all of the stories which make up *The Complete Stories of Flannery O'Connor* are available in French except for the early versions of chapters of *Wise Blood* and *The Violent Bear It Away*. One could scarcely ask for more.

O'Connor country is almost predictably the Midi, the south of France. Enthusiasm for her there runs very high. Indeed the Université Paul Valéry in Montpellier has a Centre d'Étude et de Recherches sur les écrivains du Sud aux États-Unis and publishes a journal called *Delta*. The second issue of *Delta*, published in March 1976, is entirely devoted to Flannery O'Connor. It contains an interesting exchange on the Georgia writer between Coindreau and Michel Gresset, previously unpublished letters of Flannery O'Connor to Coindreau, a series of critical articles (several using structuralist techniques to good advantage), and an invaluable bibliography of works by and about Flannery O'Connor drawn up by Gresset and Claude Richard. The bibliography is especially useful for its listing of all French translations of O'Connor's work and of the critical writing done about her in France. The dynamic presence of Claude Richard, who directs the Centre and edits *Delta*, makes Montpellier a kind of adopted homeland for Flannery O'Connor and for other Southern writers.

So all is clearly well with Flannery O'Connor in France. Her reputation there seems firmly assured only a dozen years after her death.

MELVIN J. FRIEDMAN

# Introduction

MELVIN J. FRIEDMAN

GORE VIDAL recalled to us, several years ago, with some nostalgia the period when Carson McCullers "was *the* young writer." Reviewing *Clock Without Hands* for the September 28, 1961 *Reporter*, Mr. Vidal seemed to feel that something very special was lost during the twenty-one years which separated *The Heart Is a Lonely Hunter* from Carson McCullers' last novel.

> She was an American legend from the beginning, which is to say that her fame was as much a creation of publicity as of talent. The publicity was the work of those fashion magazines where a dish of black-eyed peas can be made to seem the roe of some rare fish, photographed by Avedon; yet McCullers' dreaming androgynous face, looking out at us from glossy pages, in its ikon elegance subtly confounded the chic of the lingerie ads all about her.
>
> Unlike too many other "legends," her talent was as real as her face. . . . Her prose was chaste and severe and realistic in its working out of narrative.

This could have been written with similar appropriateness about Flannery O'Connor before her untimely death on August 3, 1964. In a certain sense Flannery O'Connor had re-

1

placed Carson McCullers as the image of the young writer and
the reception accorded *The Violent Bear It Away* in many
ways resembled the earlier critical response which greeted *The
Heart Is a Lonely Hunter.* Although Flannery O'Connor's face
was perhaps more rounded and less "dreaming androgynous"
than that of her older contemporary, she still managed a talent
"as real as her face" and a prose both "chaste and severe." She
had always been the darling of *Kenyon Review* and *Sewanee
Review* on the one hand, of *Commonweal* and *The Critic* on
the other. She has proved agreeable to most of the literary and
quasi-literary factions which pass judgment on contemporary
literature. She has failed to please only the most ultra-conserva-
tive Catholics who find her brand of Catholicism not orthodox
enough and the most "textual" literary critics who find her
language too bare and her experiments with structure not eccentric enough. The reviews of every one of her books have been
overwhelmingly favorable with critics as distinguished as
Caroline Gordon, Granville Hicks, Louis D. Rubin, Jr., and
R. W. B. Lewis passing sympathetic judgment.


Her death prompted more than the usual number of literary
obituaries. Only Hemingway and Faulkner, in recent memory,
managed a more elaborate elegiac farewell. We recall, for example, the Faulkner memorial issue of *Saturday Review* and
William Styron's fine testimonial in *Life*, "As He Lay Dead,
a Bitter Grief." Flannery O'Connor's tributes were more modest
and less commercial. In the same way as she avoided placing
her best work in the glossier weeklies in favor of the less fashionable monthlies and quarterlies so the response to her death
has been limited to the smaller circulation journals. The best
obituaries appeared in *Sewanee Review, Commonweal, The
Christian Century* and *Jubilee.* (The memorial piece by Thomas
Merton in the November, 1964 *Jubilee* is one of the most in-
cisive discussions of her that we have.) There are two remark-

able brief prose elegies by Elizabeth Bishop and Elizabeth Hardwick in *The New York Review of Books*. The most ambitious of the testimonials by far is the special Winter 1964 issue of *Esprit* (published by the University of Scranton). This contains an impressive number of short statements by a wide variety of people—mainly writers and clergymen—who knew her and her work. The most intriguing perhaps is the wonderfully appreciative piece by Katherine Anne Porter which ends so fitly: "I want to thank you for giving me the opportunity to tell you about the Flannery O'Connor I know. I loved and valued her dearly, her work and her strange unworldly radiance of spirit in a human being so intelligent and so undeceived by the appearance of things. I would feel too badly if I did not honor myself by saying a word in her honor: it is a great loss."

Flannery O'Connor was born in Savannah in 1925. She died near Milledgeville, Georgia thirty-nine years later. Except for a creative writing session at the University of Iowa, a short stay in New York, a sojourn in the Connecticut home of the Robert Fitzgeralds', and a trip to Lourdes, she spent most of her life in her native Georgia. She has shown the same devotion to birthplace as so many other Southern writers. Hers is one of the rare literary instances in which the life and the work are clearly indivisible. Even Cleanth Brooks felt obliged to desert his accustomed "new critical" stance when he said of her in the memorial issue of *Esprit*: "In her instance, I find it hard to separate the person from the artist."

The settings of her stories and novels are in the area she knew so well—Georgia or the part of Tennessee which borders on north Georgia; often backwoods or rural areas. She has never tried to superimpose on these settings a mythical or ritualistic importance; she seems to have no interest in creating a Yoknapatawpha County or a Port Warwick (the city which recurs in William Styron's fiction) as a symbolical Southern landscape. She seems content to write about the region she knew best in its own "Southern gothic" terms with a disarming modesty unknown in most writers of similar reputation.

One phase of this modesty was reflected in her unwillingness to make pronouncements about her craft. Granville Hicks asked her to contribute to his 1957 symposium on the future of the novel, *The Living Novel* (Macmillan). Hers is the only essay in the collection which does not speak ex cathedra about how a novel is or should be written and why it is a dynamic form. (All of the contributors are practicing novelists and their remarks usually reveal the self-confidence and assurance of successful craftsmen who are certain the novel has a future because they are still writing fiction.) She credits a good deal of her success as a novelist to the region she comes from ("It's generally suggested that the Southern writer has some advantage here.") and to her position as a practicing Catholic ("It affects his writing primarily by guaranteeing his respect for mystery."). Her most telling statements in this essay link the novelist's plight with spiritual and moral purpose:

> In the greatest fiction, the writer's moral sense coincides with his dramatic sense, and I see no way for it to do this unless his moral judgment is part of the very act of seeing, and he is free to use it. I have heard it said that belief in Christian dogma is a hindrance to the writer, but I myself have found nothing further from the truth.

This essay, somewhat ambiguously called "The Fiction Writer and His Country," is interesting not only for what it does not say about the craft of novel-writing—ascribing the novelist's gifts to what resembles divine intervention—but also for the suggestion of certain elements which commentators have been quick to find in her fiction. Words like "grotesque," "redemption," and "violence" appear with astonishing regularity and appear to be essential to Miss O'Connor's critical vocabulary. She insists on a delicacy "for the grotesque, for the perverse, and for the unacceptable" in the kind of fiction she writes. This would seem to be paradoxical until one examines her novels and short stories which abound in sordidness and poverty and yet maintain a delicate aesthetic balance on the side of gentility and religious affirmation.

In an essay Flannery O'Connor wrote in the March 30, 1957 issue of *America* we get a similar notion that the practicing Catholic and the creative writer can be temperate bedfellows. In this article, "The Church and the Fiction Writer" (another title which sounds too much like a sermon), she asks for humility in the writer—a quality which she more than amply possessed. She resolves again the seeming difficulty about being a religious writer with a clever turn of phrase: "When people have told me that because I am a Catholic, I cannot be an artist, I have had to reply, ruefully, that because I am a Catholic I cannot afford to be less than an artist." (If one were to gather together Flannery O'Connor's maxims this could serve as an epigraph to the collection.) She ends on a positive note with her usual affirmative tone: "If we intend to encourage Catholic fiction writers, we must convince those coming along that the Church does not restrict their freedom to be artists but ensures it (the restrictions of art are another matter)." This could be taken as a call to literary arms to a new generation of Catholic novelists who are sure to benefit from the enlightened Vatican reigns of Pope John XXIII and Paul VI.

Another sampling of her talents as essayist is the charming piece which appeared in the September, 1961 *Holiday*, "Living with a Peacock."* On the surface this seems to be nothing more than a pleasant digression on the art of peacock raising, a favorite hobby of Flannery O'Connor. A closer reading reveals an oblique glance at the artistic process—perhaps not consciously intended. A statement like the following could easily be applied to characters in her fiction: "Those that withstand illnesses and predators (the hawk, the fox, and the opossum) over the winter seem impossible to destroy, except by violence." One should especially notice the word "violence" which is so essential a part of her literary vocabulary. It becomes clear after a while that raising peacocks is almost an addendum to

*Rechristened "The King of the Birds" in *Mystery and Manners*.

her fictional practices. Sister M. Joselyn, O.S.B., writing in the special issue of *Esprit*, has this to say about it: "Perhaps it is because the peacocks freed so much for our delight that was in Flannery O'Connor, helped her so greatly to show us what she was, became her 'objective correlative,' if one wants to be literary about it."

Flannery O'Connor is never very far from literature as we see again in her introduction to *A Memoir of Mary Ann* (1961). This work, which is dedicated "To the memory of Nathaniel Hawthorne," is a recounting of the life of an afflicted child—with remarkable reserves of strength, who managed to survive until the age of twelve—by the Dominican nuns who cared for her so devotedly. Flannery O'Connor's preface, neatly avoiding the temptation of sentimentality, introduces a very intriguing quasi-literary equation. She remarks that Mary Ann was born with a disfiguring tumor on her face. This recalls to Miss O'Connor Hawthorne's story "The Birthmark," which is rendered doubly appropriate on this occasion because of the dedication of the volume to Hawthorne and because of his daughter's unique relevance: "The Dominican Congregation to which the nuns belong who had taken care of Mary Ann had been founded by Hawthorne's daughter, Rose." The literary judgments clearly begin to take over and we are invited to an appraisal of another Hawthorne work, *Our Old Home*. Later we are reminded: "Death is the theme of much modern literature. There is *Death in Venice, Death of a Salesman, Death in the Afternoon, Death of a Man*." The names of Ivan Karamazov and Albert Camus are introduced in a still later context. Flannery O'Connor's vocabulary is again reinforced on a variety of occasions by the appearance of her favorite word, "grotesque"; for example ". . . one of them asked me during the course of the visit why I wrote about such grotesque characters, why the grotesque (of all things) was my vocation."

The temptation is to dwell even more on this introduction —which offers us so many interesting approaches to her work

—but Father Gardiner has already done the job in his essay in our collection.

All of her essays and critical writing convince us that everything with Flannery O'Connor is related to her career as a writer. Her place (the South), her religion (Catholicism), her hobby (peacock-raising) reinforce her novels and stories at every turn. One can even attach the three words most appropriate to her fiction to each: "grotesque" to the South; "redemption" to Catholicism; and "violence" to peacock-raising. Yet the vocabulary is interchangeable, and the words act as movable parts in an aesthetic which is dynamic and vital. All of her qualities, however, spring from the humility which she asks for in the creative writer. This virtue is everywhere in evidence in her interviews and in her appearances as part of a symposium or panel discussion.

When Herbert Gold set down the views on writing of the various contributors to his anthology *Fiction of the Fifties,* the shortest statement by far was made by Flannery O'Connor. Hers was the refreshingly uncomplicated remark that it is difficult to write in any age; her comment had the double virtue of reading like an apothegm and destroying the notion which Gold's anthology intended to convey that fiction writing was quite different in the fifties from what it had been at any other period. The interviews which appeared in the June 12, 1955 *New York Times Book Review,* in the Winter 1959 issue of *Esprit,* in the November 1, 1959 and July 22, 1962 issues of the *Atlanta Journal and Atlanta Constitution,* in the Spring, 1960 *The Motley,* in the Fall, 1960 *The Censer,* in the May 12, 1962 *Saturday Review,* and in the August-September, 1962 and June-July, 1963 numbers of *The Critic,* all had the same virtues of brevity and good sense.

Flannery O'Connor participated in the Vanderbilt Literary Symposium on April 23, 1959. The results, which appear in the February, 1960 issue of *Vagabond* as "An Interview with Flannery O'Connor and Robert Penn Warren," again reveal a disarming modesty and an urgency about hiding behind the literary coattails of her older contemporary. (She is perhaps somewhat in awe of Warren's "Fugitive" origins, if we are to accept the suggestions offered by Professors Duhamel and Holman in their essays in our collection.) She is content to point out, "I never think in terms of fable or myth. Those things are far removed from anything that I know when I write"; and to make certain observations about her region and its demands.

Her participation in a symposium at Wesleyan College, Macon, Georgia, on October 28, 1960 gave much the same impression. She was in the good company this time of two established Southern writers, Katherine Anne Porter and Caroline Gordon, of a younger Southern writer, Madison Jones, and of the principal commentator on recent Southern writing, Louis D. Rubin, Jr. Her quantitative contribution, as it was earlier at Vanderbilt, was slight indeed. She allowed the others the long, anecdotal digressions. When called upon to contribute comments about her own working habits or fictional problems she was content with something as unpretentious and self-effacing as "I sit there before the typewriter for three hours every day and if anything comes I am there waiting to receive it" or "I really didn't know what a symbol was until I started reading about them. It seemed I was going to have to know about them if I was going to be a respectable literary person. Now I have the notion that a symbol is sort of like the engine in a story and I usually discover as I write something in the story that is taking on more and more meaning so that as I go along, before long, that something is turning or working the story." The latter may sound too consciously homespun but it is fairly typical of her refusal to enlist the aid of critical jargon when setting down an artistic notion.

Her public lectures, usually delivered at small Southern or Catholic colleges, were tactfully brief and pleasantly modest. The Catholic magazines which printed them usually prefaced the lecture with a statement attesting to its refreshing simplicity and honesty; a personal statement such as the fairly typical "soft-spoken, reserved" usually accompanied the remarks about the speech.

It is not surprising, then, that her fiction should be filled with the same modesty and self-effacement. In a sense, the most revealing statement she has made about her techniques as a story and novel writer is found in her essay about peacocks: "I intend to stand firm and let the peacocks multiply, for I am sure that, in the end, the last word will be theirs." Indeed the last word is always that of one of her characters as Flannery O'Connor manages in each of her successive works to (in Joyce's words) "refine herself out of existence."

A Flannery O'Connor story or novel is always the slowly paced, leisurely uncovering of a series of unusual people and circumstances. She seems always intent on at first disenchanting us—mainly through a systematic puncturing of the myth of Southern gallantry and gentility—and then restoring our confidence when she has forced us to view her world on her own terms. She forces us to go through a complete Cartesian purgation; our minds are cleansed of all previous notions. When we have forgotten the other books we have read, we can then allow for the existence of Hazel Motes (*Wise Blood*), Rayber (*The Violent Bear It Away*), The Misfit ("A Good Man Is Hard to Find") and Mary Grace ("Revelation"). We almost willingly "suspend disbelief" in the face of impossible happenings to unlikely people. This is part of what we must go through when we read most fiction writers. But never have I so acutely felt the compulsion to reject everything and start over again that I feel with Flannery O'Connor.

This is all the more curious because the demands she makes are not in the direction of new techniques or startling dislocations of structure. Her novels and stories are in every sense traditionally constructed and make no use of the experimental suggestions of a Joyce, a Proust, a Faulkner, or even a Styron. Her work is usually completely faithful to chronology, with no attempt at reproducing an atmosphere of psychological time.

In short, her fiction bears no relation whatever to the so-called "art novel."

Professor John J. Clarke made somewhat the same point in his longish contribution to the special issue of *Esprit,* concluding his comments with the apt statement: ". . . [her stories] contain neither stream-of-consciousness narration nor existentialist brooding upon the world's ills." It is clear that Flannery O'Connor has never dovetailed to current fashion. She has been able to write in the age of the *nouveau roman* without being at all affected by the technical innovations of Alain Robbe-Grillet, Nathalie Sarraute, or Michel Butor.

She has made clear her position on the subject in her interview with Gerard Sherry in *The Critic* (June-July, 1963): "So-called experimental fiction always bores me. If it looks peculiar I don't read it. . . . I'm a very traditional sort of writer and I'm content to try to tell a good story as I've just defined it." It seems to me that François Mauriac is her master here. (She admitted a debt to Mauriac in the lecture she gave at the College of St. Teresa and referred to him again in "The Church and the Fiction Writer." Both William Van O'Connor and Allen Tate, writing in the special issue of *Esprit,* notice a kinship with Mauriac's Jansenism. William Sessions in the October 28, 1964 *National Catholic Reporter* recalled an afternoon in Lourdes with Flannery O'Connor when she "remarked at lunch how so many Mauriac faces seemed to be around. . . .") Mauriac made clear his position on the experimental novel, Joyce-style, in his essay "Le Romancier et ses personnages":

> One should recognize that the art of the novel is, primarily, a *transposition* of reality and not a *reproduction* of it. It is apparent that the greater pains a writer takes to sacrifice nothing of the complexity of life, the more he renders the impression of artifice. What is less natural and more arbitrary than the association of ideas in the technique of interior monologue as Joyce uses it? *

* The translation is my own. The original is found in François Mauriac's *Oeuvres complètes,* vol. 8 (Paris, no date), p. 306.

Not only is this essay a sharp warning against the "new" stream-of-consciousness fiction but Mauriac's own novels reveal a systematic distrust of experimentation. Mauriac's words in "Le Romancier et ses personnages" could never be Flannery O'Connor's (she always expresses herself with less critical sophistication) but the sentiments could easily be hers. We can say, indeed, that she transposes rather than reproduces reality. Her work is always far removed from the twin sins of artifice and arbitrariness. And her statements about her craft are very close to her practice.

Where Flannery O'Connor is closest to Mauriac's "*transposition* of reality" is probably in her notion of character. She has a kind of Dickensian devotion to oddity. While so many recent novelists have begged for anonymity in their notion of character—a letter of the alphabet or a strange pun like Watt often suffice as names—Flannery O'Connor insists on precise and detailed delineation. Her creatures are usually rounded personalities, believable if only on their own terms. Caroline Gordon has already made this abundantly clear: "In Miss O'Connor's vision of modern man—a vision not limited to Southern rural humanity—all her characters are 'displaced persons,' not merely the people in the story of that name. They are 'off center,' out of place. . . ." (*Critique*, Fall, 1958). This does not mean that they are "outsiders" in Colin Wilson's sense or "absurd" men in Albert Camus' sense. They are not introspective types who brood about metaphysical problems, nor are they very concerned with the existentialist notion of self-identification. They go about their business in a workaday manner, but it is the "business" which is usually unorthodox or, in Caroline Gordon's words, "off center." Flannery O'Connor's characters are almost all fanatics, suffering from what we might diagnose as an acute sense of dislocation of place.

Almost everywhere in her fiction some person is trying to fulfill a mission in unfamiliar surroundings. The mission is usually self-imposed and the role assumed is invariably self-appointed. Most of Flannery O'Connor's characters suffer from what Sir Maurice Bowra has described in quite a different context as "the troubling and unloved responsibilities of prophecy." Hazel Motes is on a train at the beginning of *Wise Blood,* Flannery O'Connor's first novel, in the act of leaving his native Eastrod, Tennessee, on his way to Taulkinham. He has decided to reject the traditional Jesus figure and preach a new "Church Without Christ." He has first to go through the ritual of dislocation before he can fulfill the terms of his prophecy, thus leaving a known area to travel to an unknown one. The prophecy and dislocation end in disaster and death. The same formula may explain Mr. Head's and Nelson's trip to Atlanta in "The Artificial Nigger" and Calhoun's trip to Partridge in "The Partridge Festival." The mission is unsuccessful in each case. The Guizacs' sojourn on the McIntyre farm in "The Displaced Person" ends in disaster for all concerned; Polish immigrants fail to transplant their Catholicism and old-world morality to the Bible Belt South. Finally, Tarwater, in *The Violent Bear It Away,* does not successfully carry the prophecy of his great-uncle to the big city in an attempt to convert his remaining relatives; he too returns to his native Powderhead after a succession of failures.

The transplantation-prophecy-return motif is as old as the Greeks. (One is tempted to link it with Toynbee's "withdrawal and return.") We find it in Homer. But more important, we find it in most of the contemporary Southern school. William Styron's characters often leave their native surroundings with a prophetic urge to renew themselves; they either return unsuccessfully like Mr. Head, Nelson, and Tarwater, or die horribly like Hazel Motes or Mr. Guizac. In the first category we would place Cass Kinsolving of *Set This House on Fire* and Captain Mannix of *The Long March*; in the second Peyton Loftis of *Lie Down in Darkness* and Mason Flagg of *Set This House on Fire.* The theme also recurs in Faulkner and Carson McCullers. But nowhere is it as strenuously present as in the fiction of Flannery O'Connor. One feels that her entire notion of character depends on the fictional creature's leaving his native habitat with an evangelical urge and then returning in defeat or else dying in defeat. The peculiarities and oddities (Mauriac's "*transposition* of reality") seem a part of the whole plan; the working out of a mythical situation in modern terms forces the odd behavior and credos of a group of people who are often ironic counterparts of classically-defined heroes.

It is probably safest to leave this kind of interpretation as a marginal suggestion. Flannery O'Connor is no believer in mythical parallels ("I never think in terms of fable or myth") and certainly offers no outward concern with archetypal patterns in her fiction. One cannot insist often enough that she depends on traditional procedures to the almost complete exclusion of technical experimentation. It is probably no accident, however, that the motif which we have discovered running through almost all of her writing is of great antiquity—Homerically conventional.

To look more closely at her fiction, one finds her publishing stories as early as 1946 in the prestige "little magazines." She has occasionally published in *Harper's Bazaar* and *Esquire* but has generally favored the smaller circulation journals, with the *Sewanee Review, Partisan Review, Kenyon Review,* and *New World Writing* as her preferred outlets (at least, early in her career). Her stories have won an uncommon number of O. Henry and Martha Foley awards. She has never published in *The New Yorker* which distinguishes her from many other successful story writers of her tradition, like Peter Taylor and Eudora Welty.

It is clear that Flannery O'Connor has been rarely if ever the victim of commercialism. When one of her stories, "The Life You Save May Be Your Own" (collected in *A Good Man Is Hard to Find*), was produced on television she could only comment wryly: "I didn't recognize the television version. . . . Gene Kelly played Mr. Shiftlet and for the idiot daughter they got some young actress who had just been voted one of the

ten most beautiful women in the world, and they changed the
ending just a bit by having Shiftlet suddenly get a conscience
and come back for the girl" (*The Critic*, August-September,
1962). Her remarks lack the outraged paternalism which William Styron expressed in *The New Republic* (April 6, 1959) on
the occasion of the television version (distortion) of his *The
Long March,* but they more convincingly and even devastat-
ingly point out the futility of commercialism. Her quiet under-
statement, noticeable here, is also an essential of her short
stories.

Still Flannery O'Connor held on to a limited commercial
sense through most of her career; this may partly explain the
fact that segments of her two novels, *Wise Blood* and *The
Violent Bear It Away,* originally appeared separately in magazines before they were recast as sections of the longer works.
(She perhaps had something of the nineteenth-century feuille-
tonist, like Dickens or Dostoevsky, in her blood.) Essential
changes were generally made during the transference. Probably
closer to the point than commercialism, however, is that the easy
rhythm of writing shorter fiction and then, on occasions, re-
shaping it so as to suit the needs of a novel and, on others,
allowing it to remain intact gives one the impression (and this
has frequently been said before about her) that she is essentially a story writer who twice strayed into the novel form.
Even when she is clearly giving an installment from a novel-in-
progress, as with the piece entitled "Why Do the Heathens
Rage?" (*Esquire*, July, 1963), the pieces fall neatly into place
as they do in the well-made short story. The final sentence of
this supposedly fragmentary piece has her usual conclusive
note: "Then it came to her, with an unpleasant jolt, that the
General with the sword in his mouth, marching to do violence,
was Jesus."

With this assumption in mind, it is probably best to look first
at her short stories. Her first published story "The Geranium"
sets the tone for the transplantation and dislocation of place
theme. Old Dudley has been forced to leave his accustomed

Southern setting in favor of the squalor and confinement of New York City. His one pleasure is watching through his window, with studied interest, a neighbor's geranium plant during long periods of the day. By the end of the story he has been deprived of this single diversion and understands, with so many other Flannery O'Connor characters, how stifling displacement can be. He is a part of that Southern diaspora who has experienced the bitter taste of exile. Flannery O'Connor's unpretentious style is already noticeable in this early story.

> He shuffled to the chair by the window and sank down in it. His throat was going to pop. His throat was going to pop on account of a nigger—a damn nigger that patted him on the back and called him "old timer." Him that knew such as that couldn't be. Him that had come from a good place. A good place. A place where such as that couldn't be. His eyes felt strange in their sockets. They were swelling in them and in a minute there wouldn't be any room left for them there. He was trapped in this place where niggers could call you "old timer." He wouldn't be trapped. He wouldn't be. He rolled his head on the back of the chair to stretch his neck that was too full.

Although the entire passage is in the third person, some of it is detached narrative, the rest the characteristic manner of Old Dudley. The first two sentences, with their grammatical and syntactical regularity, are the words of the omniscient author. In the third sentence we already feel the pressure of Dudley's mind which takes over entirely in the ungrammatical and incomplete fourth through seventh sentences. The rhythm starts again in the eighth sentence with almost exactly the same pattern of objective narrative turning into Dudley's idiom. Flannery O'Connor in this passage avoids the more experimental possibilities of stream-of-consciousness fiction, as she does everywhere else in her work, but does try to approximate the workings of the character's mind if only through the indirect third person.

"The Partridge Festival," published fifteen years later, has quite a different setting from "The Geranium" but the story-telling techniques remain the same. The writing is perhaps richer and more metaphorically suggestive in the more recent story. Calhoun, with his touch of "the rebel-artist-mystic," arrives in the uncongenial setting of Partridge, the hometown of his two great-aunts ("box-jawed old ladies"), in order to view in the flesh a crazed killer who had recently shot down six of the townspeople. He has turned Singleton, the murderer, into a prophet whose message has remained unheeded; Calhoun, we might say, has his own curious vision of dry bones, with Singleton as a latter-day Ezekiel passing the judgment of doom on the fallen inhabitants of Partridge. The more verbal Mary Elizabeth, who shares Calhoun's sentiments, borrowing a term from modern literary criticism, prefers to call him a "Christ-figure." The two depart on their pilgrimage to the state asylum to see Singleton. The transplantation-prophecy-return motif sets in; the mission ends disastrously. Singleton, another of Miss O'Connor's false prophets, betrays the trust Calhoun and Mary Elizabeth placed in him.

The best of Flannery O'Connor's stories appeared either in *A Good Man Is Hard to Find* (1955) or in the posthumous collection *Everything That Rises Must Converge* (1965). The ten stories in the 1955 volume have fairly similar Southern settings and exploit the problems of violence, redemption, and grotesquerie which have always obsessed her. *A Good Man Is Hard to Find*, however, lacks the essential unity and organization of another book which it occasionally resembles, *Winesburg, Ohio*. Flannery O'Connor's "grotesques" seem to have gone through the same kind of disturbing experiences as Sherwood Anderson's characters (with an added religious weight). Most of them have had classical "moments of illumination" which have revealed special "truths" to them; it was the truths, as Sherwood Anderson would say, which made them grotesques.

Hulga's artificial leg in "Good Country People," The Misfit's misplaced Jesus complex in "A Good Man Is Hard to Find," Bevel's need for baptism in "The River," Ruby's fear of pregnancy in "A Stroke of Good Fortune," have made them all, in Flaubert's words, "grotesques tristes." Almost every critic who has written about Flannery O'Connor has suggested the presence of grotesques surrounded by a gothic eeriness. Very few of the characters in *A Good Man Is Hard to Find* are free from this charge. But Flannery O'Connor is always patient enough to explain the source of the moral, physical, or spiritual discomfort and has a way of building her story upon it. Her prime concern, as we mentioned earlier, seems to be with oddity of character but always within the demands of narrative expression.

As a good example of all this, we might take "Good Country People." Flannery O'Connor introduces us to Hulga's infirmity on the first page. She is careful to surround her with two other women, Mrs. Hopewell, her mother, and Mrs. Freeman, "a good country person." In a way, the grossness and insensitivity of these two women clash with the hypersensitivity of Hulga; without their presence in the story we could not appreciate her aloneness and frustration. Flannery O'Connor persists in referring to three things about Hulga which have a way of recurring like leitmotives: her artificial leg, the symbolical change of her name from Joy to Hulga, and her Ph.D. When the Bible salesman appears and makes ready his seduction of the young lady, we have been aesthetically prepared for what is to happen. The "grotesque" scene in the barn when the salesman makes off with the artificial leg and mockingly shows his irreverence does not shock the reader who has already been warned of impending ironical twists and turns by an elaborate series of clues.

Thus the grotesqueness and oddity of character are not suspended in a vacuum. Flannery O'Connor painstakingly prepares us for all her effects. In a fictional world where everyone is some kind of false prophet one is prepared for fake Bible salesmen making off with artificial legs that belong to female Ph.D.'s. The delicate moral balance on which all the stories in

*A Good Man Is Hard to Find* are built is similarly understandable. We tend to suspend disbelief in the presence of a young
boy who cannot get enough of baptism ("The River"), of a
murderer who likens himself to Jesus ("A Good Man Is Hard
to Find"), of a 104-year-old Civil War veteran who drops dead
on a graduation platform watching his sixty-two-year-old granddaughter receive a bachelor's degree ("A Late Encounter with
the Enemy"), or of a tramp with a philosophical turn who
abandons a deaf-mute he has just married in a roadside restaurant ("The Life You Save May Be Your Own"). Prose paraphrase does no justice to Flannery O'Connor's plots and characters. She convinces us of things which are quite outside our experience through means which require considerable aesthetic
reorientation.

The second collection, *Everything That Rises Must Converge,* also suffers from an absence of unity; the richness of
texture of most of the individual stories, however, helps us
forget the discomforts of a miscellany. If we can generalize
about a group of stories written between 1956 and the time of
her death, we can say that her work has assumed greater
metaphysical awareness in the last years of her life. The vision
which Mrs. Turpin has at the end of "Revelation" is an example of what I mean. Sarah Ruth's reaction to Parker's tattoo
of a Byzantine Christ is another. Asbury's sense of "purifying
terror" at the end of "The Enduring Chill" is the most meta-
physically chilling of all. (Sister Bernetta's article has some
relevance here.)

"Greenleaf" (which originally appeared in the Summer, 1956,
*Kenyon Review*) is the earliest story in the volume. The "Southern gothic" tone is as authentically felt as in most of the stories
in *A Good Man Is Hard to Find.* In a way, "Greenleaf" affords
a very natural bridge between the two collections of Flannery
O'Connor's stories. The ingredients of revivalism and violence
are a functional part of the narrative. Mrs. Greenleaf has a
curious avocation which she calls "prayer healing."

Every day she cut all the morbid stories out of the newspaper—
the accounts of women who had been raped and criminals who
had escaped and children who had been burned and of train
wrecks and plane crashes and the divorces of movie stars. She
took these to the woods and dug a hole and buried them and then
she fell on the ground over them and mumbled and groaned for
an hour or so, moving her huge arms back and forth under her
and out again and finally just lying down flat and, Mrs. May sus-
pected, going to sleep in the dirt.

The story moves slowly until the very end when it erupts in
sudden and unexpected violence. The ending clearly favors the
"grotesque" as it turns on a simple but rather dreadful stroke of
irony.

Flannery O'Connor's later stories seem to depend more on
obviously disturbed types. There is considerable introspection
in stories like "The Enduring Chill" and "The Comforts of
Home." The first of these reads almost like a Southern caricature of late Salinger. There are the Salinger overtones of Bud-
dhist orientalism, of the impending nervous breakdown. Flannery O'Connor manages to get inside the mind of Asbury who
suffers from the spiritual irresolution of so many of the Glass
clan. The final words of the story cast a mood of religious terror:

Asbury blanched and the last film of illusion was torn as if by a
whirlwind from his eyes. He saw that for the rest of his days, frail,
racked, but enduring, he would live in the face of a purifying
terror. A feeble cry, a last impossible protest escaped him. But
the Holy Ghost, emblazoned in ice instead of fire, continued, im-
placable, to descend.

"Enduring" is a favorite part of William Faulkner's vocabulary
and is especially noticeable in his Nobel Prize address. There
is also a suspicion of the existential in this passage (one of the
rare moments in her work when this fashionable creed is at all
apparent).

"The Comforts of Home" exploits irony as tellingly as anything else in her fiction. The title, the character relationships,
the style itself depend heavily on ironical juxtapositions. The
"psychopathic personality" of the girl, who is the unwilling and
inactive protagonist of the story, is not quite advanced enough
for the asylum; her nymphomaniac tendencies, on the other
hand, do not quite suit her for the ways of Southern gentility.
This is all explained in an appropriately ironical passage which
has some of the cleverest turns of phrase in all of Flannery
O'Connor:

> The lawyer found that the story of the repeated atrocities was for
> the most part untrue, but when he explained to her that the girl
> was a psychopathic personality, not insane enough for the asylum
> . . . not stable enough for society, Thomas's mother was more
> deeply affected than ever. The girl readily admitted that her story
> was untrue on account of her being a congenital liar; she lied,
> she said, because she was insecure. She had passed through the
> hands of several psychiatrists who had put the finishing touches
> to her education. She knew there was no hope for her. In the
> presence of such an affliction as this, his mother seemed bowed
> down by some painful mystery that nothing would make endur-
> able but a redoubling of effort. To his annoyance, she appeared to
> look on *him* with compassion, as if her hazy charity no longer
> made distinctions.

"Hazy charity" heightens the effect which has been steadily
built up in the passage; it is well placed in the final sentence to
underscore the irony, the same kind of irony which Katherine
Anne Porter achieves with a phrase like "sour gloom."

"Revelation" also depends on an obviously disturbed type.
This time we have a return to the Hulga of "Good Country
People," but to a Hulga-type with a vengeance. Mary Grace,
on vacation from Wellesley College, sits quietly with a book in
hand, in a doctor's waiting room. Most of the story is seen
through the eyes of Mrs. Turpin, another of the "good country

people." Mary Grace is scornful of what she hears, especially of the succession of platitudes which erupt from Mrs. Turpin; we get such silent reactions from her as: "The girl's eyes seemed lit all of a sudden with a peculiar light, an unnatural light like night road signs give." Midway through the story comes Mary Grace's moment of violence, as she hurls the book at Mrs. Turpin and thoroughly loses control. As she is tied down and carried off to an ambulance, Mary Grace shouts the words which will always haunt Mrs. Turpin: "Go back to hell where you came from, you old wart hog." Flannery O'Connor stays with Mrs. Turpin's point of view until the end of the story and minutely describes her almost mystical experience as she stands observing the hogs in their enclosure.

"Everything That Rises Must Converge" is faithful to the pattern of transplantation-prophecy-return. It offers many reminders of the earlier "The Artificial Nigger." Julian accompanies his mother on Wednesday nights to the downtown "Y" for her reducing classes. Julian is of the company of Mary Elizabeth, Hulga, and Mary Grace; as he rode the bus with his mother on her weekly mission, ". . . Julian was withdrawing into the inner compartment of his mind where he spent most of his time." Julian observes his mother's gestures of condescension toward a Negro child with disturbed embarrassment. The bus ride downtown, which occupies much of the story, is saturated with the silent conflict between mother and son—mainly on the racial issue. The moment of violence occurs when Julian's mother tries to give the Negro child the traditional "bright new penny"; the reaction of the child's mother is vintage O'Connor:

> The huge woman turned and for a moment stood, her shoulders lifted and her face frozen with frustrated rage, and stared at Julian's mother. Then all at once she seemed to explode like a piece of machinery that had been given one ounce of pressure too much. Julian saw the black fist swing out with the red pocketbook. He shut his eyes and cringed as he heard the woman shout, "He don't take nobody's pennies!"

"Everything That Rises Must Converge" is another attempt to chronicle the disproportion between the Hulgas and the "good country people." Julian's mother's clichéd formulas ("Rome wasn't built in a day," "and the world is in such a mess," "I at least won't meet myself coming and going,") have the marks of the prophetic tone. Her remarks, to quote Sir Maurice Bowra again out of context, "assumed all the airs of prophecy and sought to speak with the voice of thunder from Sinai." The gesture with the penny and its rejection are part of the pattern of "hazy charity" which we have seen so often in Flannery O'Connor's work.

The principal characters in "Parker's Back" have ironically appropriate Biblical names; the husband's name is Obadiah Elihue (although he insists on O. E.), the wife's Sarah Ruth. The tone of Biblical pastiche is apparent through the story. O. E. Parker is intent on pleasing his wife, the daughter of a "Straight Gospel preacher," by adding to the impressive collection of tattoos on his chest and arms a huge Byzantine Christ on his back. Sarah Ruth's response to her husband's elaborate gesture is the deflating: "Idolatry. Enflaming yourself with idols under every green tree! I can put up with lies and vanity but I don't want no idolator in this house!" The story ends on a mock-Biblical note: "There he was—who called himself Obadiah Elihue—leaning against the tree, crying like a baby." Flannery O'Connor sets up here an incongruous mixing of styles: the Biblical turning into the vernacular.

"The Lame Shall Enter First," labeled a novella when it first appeared in the *Sewanee Review* (Summer, 1962), is the most finished piece in *Everything That Rises Must Converge*. It bears an uncommon likeness to the second part of *The Violent Bear It Away*—as Robert Fitzgerald has already suggested in his remarkable introduction to *Everything That Rises Must Converge*. It's almost as if Flannery O'Connor still had further commentary to make on the Rayber–Tarwater conflict. Rayber is replaced by Sheppard, Tarwater by Rufus Johnson, Bishop by Norton. Rayber's hearing aid has given way to the telescope as a central metaphor for the work. Somewhere in the background is Rufus Johnson's grandfather, who, very much like Tarwater's great-uncle, engages in ceaseless "religious" activities: "He's gone with a remnant to the hills. . . . Him and some others. They're going to bury some Bibles in a cave and take two of different kinds of animals and all like that. Like Noah. Only this time it's going to be fire, not flood."

Sheppard, like Rayber before him, has taken over the secular education of a young boy. He tries to disenchant Rufus Johnson with the narrow religion of his grandfather in favor of the challenges of modern science. The telescope which he buys for Rufus becomes the measure of the Newtonian universe which he must oppose to the preaching of the Gospel. There are several exchanges between the two in which Sheppard opposes the world of the telescope to Rufus' Holy Bible. On one occasion Sheppard suggests, "It's at least possible to get to the moon. . . . We can see it. We know it's there. Nobody has given any reliable evidence there's a hell." Rufus counters, "The Bible has give the evidence . . . and if you die and go there you burn forever."

While Sheppard concentrates on Rufus' education he sorely neglects his son Norton. The novella ends on a note of tragic irony.

> The light was on in Norton's room but the bed was empty. He [Sheppard] turned and dashed up the attic stairs and at the top reeled back like a man on the edge of a pit. The tripod had fallen and the telescope lay on the floor. A few feet over it, the child hung in the jungle of shadows, just below the beam from which he had launched his flight into space.

Norton's death neatly parallels the baptism-drowning of Bishop at the end of the second part of *The Violent Bear It Away*. The mechanical worlds of Rayber and Sheppard have failed their sons in their moments of desperate need. *The Violent Bear It Away* continues on to an affirmative ending while "The Lame

Shall Enter First" ends with a world-view which approximates looking at the world through the wrong end of a telescope.

Flannery O'Connor's first novel *Wise Blood* (1952) is not the apparent success of either of the two collections of stories. Her talents seem to lie so clearly in the direction of short fiction that we should not be surprised that her first attempt at the longer form should be episodic and fragmentary. The first edition, published by Harcourt, Brace, in fact leaves blank pages between chapters, almost begging that we come to a complete end-stop before proceeding to the next division.

Nathanael West and Franz Kafka are the writers most often suggested as inspirations for *Wise Blood*. Hazel Motes, the central figure of the novel, has the crusading zeal of a Miss Lonelyhearts and the blind steadfastness of a Kafka hero, but it is probably unwise to carry the connection further. When he arrives in Taulkinham to preach the gospel of the Church Without Christ he receives his redemption and purification in a way which seems unorthodox: he frequents the bed of a well-known prostitute whose address he found on a lavatory wall. This establishes the tone of unconventional prophecy and evangelism which runs through the novel. Hazel Motes meets a succession of false religionists and we are intended to measure the sincerity of his convictions against the hypocrisy of theirs. One of these figures, Asa Hawks, has pretended to blind himself to enhance his career as an itinerant beggar. Another, Hoover Shoats, has made a profitable career of espousing new religions: "You watch out, friend. I'm going to run you out of business. I can get my own new jesus and I can get Prophets for peanuts, you hear?" A third, Enoch Emery (blessed with the hereditary faculty of "wise blood"), steals a shriveled-up mummy from a museum to oblige Hazel Motes with a new jesus for his religion. Hazel makes his way through this corrupt universe of false prophets to advance the sincere cause of his new cult. (Flannery O'Connor interestingly calls him "a Christian *malgré lui*" in the preface to the 1962 edition of *Wise Blood*.) When he realizes that all has failed he blinds himself with quicklime and proceeds to subject himself to every variety of torture (like a latter-day Oedipus as one critic has suggested). In accustomed fashion for Flannery O'Connor's characters, Hazel Motes has had his moments of religious feeling and violence. He has experienced a series of surrealistic horrors and has worked out his destiny in terms of the rigid transplantation-prophecy-return (death) pattern. There is one observer of all this action who supplies the final irony to Hazel Motes's "achievement." This is his landlady (another of the host of "good country people") who represents the common sense of the unenlightened and uninitiated; Flannery O'Connor is fond of giving this type the final say:

The landlady sat there for a while longer. She was not a woman who felt more violence in one word than in another; she took every word at its face value but all the faces were the same. Still, instead of blinding herself, if she had felt that bad, she would have killed herself and she wondered why anybody wouldn't do that. She would simply have put her head in an oven or maybe have given herself too many painless sleeping pills and that would have been that. Perhaps Mr. Motes was only being ugly, for what possible reason could a person have for wanting to destroy their sight? A woman like her, who was so clear-sighted, could never stand to be blind. If she had to be blind she would rather be dead. It occurred to her suddenly that when she was dead she would be blind too. She stared in front of her intensely, facing this for the first time. She recalled the phrase, "eternal death," that preachers used, but she cleared it out of her mind immediately, with no more change of expression than the cat. She was not religious or morbid, for which every day she thanked her stars. She would credit a person who had that streak with anything, though, and Mr. Motes had it or he wouldn't be a preacher. He might put lime in his eyes and she wouldn't doubt it a bit, because they were all, if the truth was only known, a little bit off in their heads. What possible reason could a sane person have for wanting to not enjoy himself any more?

She certainly couldn't say.

One notices how this passage shifts from objective narrative to the landlady's idiom. The change probably occurs in the third sentence. The irony of the second sentence is the one didactic attempt on the part of the narrator to ridicule the landlady. From then on Flannery O'Connor allows the landlady herself to complete the caricatured portrait of Bible Belt morality.

Hazel Motes and the other oddly named eccentrics in *Wise Blood* seem quite without precedent until one recalls again the Sherwood Anderson of *Winesburg, Ohio.* A possible model for Motes's Church Without Christ could be Dr. Parcival's strange crucifixion notion: everyone is Christ and we are all crucified. At least the sense of violence and metaphysical grotesqueness attached to each are vintage fanaticism.

*The Violent Bear It Away* (1960) is a much better novel. Unlike *Wise Blood* it is more than a tightly knit collection of stories. It is the best example in Flannery O'Connor's work of the transplantation-prophecy-return motif; in fact, the novel is divided into three parts which correspond neatly to the three phases. In the first section, Tarwater prepares to leave home, after the death of his great-uncle, to join his Uncle Rayber. The long middle section is the strange working out of the prophecy which ends in Tarwater's baptism-drowning of Rayber's idiot son, Bishop. The final section is the return to Powderhead. The picaresque element in the novel has already been suggested, but more important probably is the *Bildungsroman* aspect. Tarwater is another authentically American boy, in the tradition of Huck Finn and the young Ike McCaslin (with the added dimension of being religiously displaced), who goes through a typically American initiation before he can become a man. His "education" and character formation are intimately linked to Flannery O'Connor's South, which Arthur Mizener has characterized as "a breeding ground for prophets." Tarwater's confused attempts at turning the tables on Rayber and baptizing Bishop can easily be likened to Ike McCaslin's ambivalent feelings about the bear hunt in Faulkner's "The Bear" or more cautiously to Huck's uncertainty about Jim's destiny in Twain's novel. In each case the spiritual resolution which turns the boy into a man is crucial.

The link with Faulkner has already been pointed out by several reviewers of *The Violent Bear It Away*. Vivian Mercier writing in the *Hudson Review* (Autumn, 1960) has said that "all the characters are Faulknerian grotesques, including the idiot's atheist father." Louis D. Rubin, Jr. had earlier pointed out similarities between the Bundrens of *As I Lay Dying* and Flannery O'Connor's characters in the Autumn, 1955 issue of the *Sewanee Review*. It can be pointed out convincingly, I think, that the burial complications in *The Violent Bear It Away* are at least related to the funeral procession in *As I Lay Dying*. Tarwater's great-uncle had insisted that he be given Christian burial rites. Tarwater, prompted by a voice which follows him around almost like his conscience in reverse, decides to set fire to the house which contains the great-uncle's corpse. Upon his return to Powderhead in the third part of the novel, he discovers that despite his efforts the uncle was granted proper burial through the unexpected intervention of a Negro, Buford. In a curious way the novel gains a kind of structure through the repeated references to the burial in much the same way that *As I Lay Dying* is constructed about the journey to Jefferson with the corpse of Addie Bundren. In both novels there is also an elaborate series of observers who pass judgment on the proceedings and form a *consensus gentium* to counterbalance the eccentricities of the participants in the action. Tarwater's behavior is viewed with some surprise by a salesman who offers him a ride on his way to Rayber's house. A truck driver serves a similar function as Tarwater makes his way back to Powderhead. Another observer, Buford, is waiting for him there to condemn him for failing to give his great-uncle Christian burial. We get this balance between the "grotesques" and the workaday world which Flannery O'Connor fails to give us convincingly in *Wise Blood*.

We notice also in *The Violent Bear It Away* what P. Albert Duhamel has called "a 'violent' view of reality." This seems also to be unmistakably Faulknerian. Faulkner's novels rarely harbor false prophets but they are almost always filled with every variety of violence: suicide, rape, lynching. Tarwater's pyromania beautifully qualifies him for an elite position in Yoknapatawpha County.

Lest we carry the Faulkner parallel too far, we should make clear that Flannery O'Connor has learned nothing from Faulkner's prolix style, from his experiments with structure and technique, from his frequent use of the devices of stream-of-consciousness fiction. Her chaste, unimposing sentences, her fairly strict chronological narratives, her refusal to tamper with consciousness, place her at the other extreme from the Faulkner of *As I Lay Dying, The Sound and the Fury, Absalom, Absalom!*, and "The Bear." The third person is scrupulously maintained even in a passage which tries to cope with Tarwater's mind as seriously as the following:

> The boy did not intend to go to the schoolteacher's until daylight and when he went he intended to make it plain that he had not come to be beholden or to be studied for a schoolteacher magazine. He began trying to remember the schoolteacher's face so that he could stare him down in his mind before he actually faced him. He felt that the more he could recall about him, the less advantage the new uncle would have over him. The face had not been one that held together in his mind, though he remembered the sloping jaw and the black-rimmed glasses. What he could not picture were the eyes behind the glasses. He had no memory of them and there was every kind of contradiction in the rubble of his great-uncle's descriptions. Sometimes the old man had said the nephew's eyes were black and sometimes brown. The boy kept trying to find eyes that fit mouth, nose that fit chin, but every time he thought he had a face put together, it fell apart and he

had to begin on a new one. It was as if the schoolteacher, like the devil, could take on any look that suited him.

Tarwater, in an interesting bit of speculation, tries to fit together from memory the diverse parts of his Uncle Rayber's (the schoolteacher) face. We get a revealing glimpse into the boy's mind. We can only expect, however, that Faulkner would have handled the interior monologue differently.

Years after her death, Flannery O'Connor's reputation in this country is assured. It is fairly certain that she will continue to be free from such devastating judgments as that implied in Gore Vidal's exclamation of despair in his review of *Clock Without Hands*: "Southern writing—we have had such a lot of it in the last thirty years!" From the many testimonials following her death, which appeared in such diverse places as the *Sewanee Review, The Christian Century, The New York Review of Books,* and *Jubilee,* we can be sure that she has a permanent place in American literature—perhaps next to her good friend Katherine Anne Porter.

Her reputation abroad is considerably less certain. Walter Allen's estimate in the special issue of *Esprit* puts the case for Britain: ". . . in England my guess is that her work was almost unknown outside Catholic circles. That England will catch up with her eventually, as it did however belatedly with Nathanael West, I don't doubt." He might have added Faulkner who has only received serious attention in England in the last few years.

Both *Wise Blood* (*La Sagesse dans le sang*) and *A Good Man Is Hard to Find* (*Les braves gens ne courent pas les rues*) have appeared in French under the imprint of Gallimard. *La Sagesse dans le sang* is the work of Faulkner's gifted translator, M. E. Coindreau, and contains a revealing introduction by him. He realizes that the French reader is almost thoroughly ignorant of American revivalism so he offers a brief history of its main currents, including sketches of Billy Sunday and Aimee Semple

McPherson. He also manages a fine appreciation of *Wise Blood* by speaking of the "monde tragi-comique de ces évangélistes" and by placing the novel in its proper historical perspective. Coindreau insists that Flannery O'Connor was the first fiction writer who justly appraised the evangelists and offered them an *entrée* into American literature. Coindreau's translation offers the same sensitive appreciation as his preface. He succeeds with Flannery O'Connor's idiom as he succeeded so well with Faulkner's in his translations of *As I Lay Dying, The Sound and the Fury, Light in August,* and *The Wild Palms.*

*Les braves gens ne courent pas les rues* is the work of Henri Morisset; it has no preface. The arrangement of the ten stories is the same as in the original. The anonymous reviewer for the *Bulletin Critique du Livre Français* gave this collection of stories a short paragraph in which he used such strong terms as "de fantaisie cruelle, d'humeur noir, d'horreur burlesque."

The most sympathetic response to her work that I have seen in any of the French periodicals is Michel Gresset's "Le petit monde de Flannery O'Connor" in the January, 1964 *Mercure de France.* Gresset starts off by suggesting that Southern literature stands to American literature in much the same way that Irish literature stood to English literature. (In vitality there is certainly a relationship between Southern literature since the first World War and Irish literature of the Gaelic Revival.) He places Flannery O'Connor within the Southern tradition and suggests a kinship between her work and that of Bosch, Poe, and Beckett. He finally defines the unlikely shape of Flannery O'Connor's Catholicism as being "nu, tragique et douloureux."

Both *A Good Man Is Hard to Find* (*Ein Kreis im Feuer*) and *The Violent Bear It Away* (*Das brennende Wort*) have appeared in German. The German translation of the collection of stories is somewhat unusual because the translator chose to use "A Circle in the Fire" as the title story, generally rearranged the order of the original volume, and omitted "A Stroke of Good Fortune" and "A Temple of the Holy Ghost." The German translators, who are not mentioned on the title pages but condemned to unreadable fine print on the copyright pages, have offered no introductory or explanatory material of any kind. (Elisabeth Schnack might at least have offered some reason for the absence of the two stories from *Ein Kreis im Feuer*.)

All that we can hope is that Europe will soon catch up with us and that we will have a European Flannery O'Connor just as we now have a European Faulkner and Hemingway. She has joined Faulkner and Hemingway on our side of the ocean; she should soon complete what Harry Levin has aptly termed a "transatlantic refraction."

# The Search for Redemption

## Flannery O'Connor's Fiction

### FREDERICK J. HOFFMAN

### I

THE FIRST impression one has of Flannery O'Connor's work is of its extraordinary lucidity; given, that is, what she expects to communicate, she does communicate it with most remarkable clarity and ease. Of course, one needs to know just what it is; she is concerned with the problem of how a writer, "by indirections, find[s] directions out." She has a reputation for obscurity, for not giving the expected turn to the reader, for not rewarding him for his having taken the trouble to read her.

The best statement she has given of her purpose and method is a talk she gave at the College of Saint Teresa (Winona, Minnesota) in the fall of 1960. Responding to a critic's suggestion that she is probably not a "Catholic novelist" because she doesn't write on "Catholic subjects," she said:

> . . . The Catholic novelist in the South is forced to follow the spirit into strange places and to recognize it in many forms not totally congenial to him. But the fact that the South is the Bible Belt increases rather than decreases his sympathy for what he sees. His interest will in all likelihood go immediately to those aspects of Southern life where the religious feeling is most in-

tense and where its outward forms are farthest from the Catholic. . . .[1]

Her major subjects are the struggle for redemption, the search for Jesus, and the meaning of "prophecy": all of these in an intensely evangelical Protestant South, where the need for Christ is expressed without shyness and where "prophecy" is intimately related to the ways in which men are daily challenged to define themselves.[2] The literary problem raised by this peculiarity of "place" (though it may be located elsewhere as well, as a "need for ceremony," or a desperate desire to "ritualize" life) is neatly described by Miss O'Connor: she must, she says, define in unnaturally emphatic terms what would not otherwise be accepted, or what might be misunderstood. The sentiment (or some emotional reaction) will get in the way. "There is something in us," she said, in the same talk, "as story-tellers and as listeners to stories, that demands the redemptive act, that demands that what falls at least be offered the chance to be restored."[3] But the rituals of any church are not comprehended by a large enough majority of readers; therefore,

> . . . When I write a novel in which the central action is a baptism, I know that for the larger percentage of my readers, baptism is a meaningless rite: therefore I have to imbue this action with an awe and terror which will suggest its awful mystery. . . .[4]

Miss O'Connor writes about intensely religious acts and dilemmas in a time when people are much divided on the question of what actually determines a "religious act." Definitions are not easy, and, frequently, what is being done with the utmost seriousness seems terribly naive, or simple-minded, to the reader. She must, therefore, force the statement of it into a pattern of "grotesque" action, which reminds one somewhat of Franz Kafka,[5] at least in its violation of normal expectations.

We have the phenomenon of a Catholic writer describing a Protestant, an evangelical, world, to a group of readers who

need to be forced or shocked and/or amused into accepting the
validity of religious states. The spirit of evil abounds, and the
premonition of disaster is almost invariably confirmed. Partly,
this is because the scene is itself grotesquely exaggerated
(though eminently plausible at the same time); partly it is
because Christian sensibilities have been, not so much blunted
as rendered bland and over-simple. The contrast of the fum-
bling grandmother and The Misfit, in Miss O'Connor's most
famous story, "A Good Man Is Hard to Find," is a case in point.
The grandmother is fully aware of the expected terror, but she
cannot react "violently" to it. She must therefore use common-
places to meet a most uncommon situation:

> "If you would pray," the old lady said, "Jesus would help you."
> "That's right," The Misfit said.
> "Well then, why don't you pray?" she asked trembling with de-
> light suddenly.
> "I don't want no hep," he said.
> "I'm doing all right by myself" [141].

Another truth about Miss O'Connor's fiction is its preoccupation with the Christ figure, a use of Him that is scarcely
equalled by her contemporaries. The Misfit offers an apparently
strange but actually a not uncommon observation:

> "Jesus was the only One that ever raised the dead, . . . and
> He shouldn't have done it. He thown everything off balance. If
> He did what He said, then it's nothing for you to do but thow
> away everything and follow Him, and if He didn't, then it's noth-
> ing for you to do but enjoy the few minutes you got left the best
> you can—by killing somebody or burning down his house or do-
> ing some other meanness to him. No pleasure but meanness," he
> said and his voice became almost a snarl [142].

One of Paul Tillich's most effective statements has to do with
the relationship of man to Jesus Christ, in volume two of his
most impressive *Systematic Theology.* "Jesus Christ," he says,
"combines the individual name with the title, 'the Christ,'"

and "Jesus as the Christ is both a historical fact and a subject of believing reception. . . ." [6] Perhaps more important, and in line with his attempt to review theology in existentialist terms, Tillich says: "Son of God becomes the title of the one in whom the essential unity of God and man has appeared under the conditions of existence. The essentially universal becomes existentially unique. . . ." [7]

As all of us know, the crucifixion was historically a defeat for the messianic cause, whose followers wanted Jesus literally to triumph over the Romans and to restore the Jews to power. But it was also, and most importantly, the source of grace; or, as Tillich puts it, " 'Christ' became an individual with supernatural powers who, through a voluntary sacrifice, made it possible for God to save those who believe in him. . . ." [8] It is this latter figure whom Miss O'Connor's heroes spend so much energy and time denying; many of them also are on the way to accepting Him.

## II

In almost all of Miss O'Connor's fiction, the central crisis involves a confrontation with Jesus, "the Christ." In the manner of Southern Protestantism, these encounters are quite colloquial and intimate. The "Jesus" on the lips of her characters is someone who hovers very near; with Him, her personalities frequently carry on a personal dialogue. The belief, or the disbelief, in Him is almost immediate. He is "Jesus" made almost entirely human and often limited in theological function. Man often "takes over" from Him, or threatens to do so. The so-called "grotesques" of Flannery O'Connor's fiction are most frequently individual souls, imbued with religious sentiments of various kinds, functioning in the role of the surrogate Christ or challenging Him to prove Himself. Not only for literary strategy, but because such manifestations *are* surreal, Miss O'Connor makes these acts weird demonstrations of human conduct: "irrational" in the sense of their taking issue with a rational view of events.

In terms of this interpretation, much of the fiction becomes clear. Every conceivable change is rung upon the theme. The little boy, Bevel, in the story "The River," looks at a picture "of a man wearing a white sheet. He had long hair and a gold circle around his head and he was sawing on a board while some children stood watching him . . ." (147). Later, he is convinced by the Reverend Bevel Summers that the river is "the River of Life, made out of Jesus' Blood" (151). And, finally, alone, he travels the route to his salvation:

> . . . He plunged under once and this time, the waiting current caught him like a long gentle hand and pulled him swiftly forward and down. For an instant he was overcome with surprise; then since he was moving quickly and knew that he was getting somewhere, all his fury and his fear left him [159].

The association with water is simple enough. The rite of baptism is inevitably so associated; the extreme of the experience is drowning. In *The Violent Bear It Away* (1960), the young Tarwater, who is struggling against both his great-uncle (who had demanded that he baptize the idiot child, Bishop), and his uncle (who tries to dissuade him), ultimately both baptizes and drowns the child, yielding momentarily to one demand, then in anger (or confusion) reacting violently to it.

The sensory vividness of religious imagery is especially stressed in the story, "A Temple of the Holy Ghost," in which the young girl has heard about a carnival freak, then later, in the convent chapel, faces God.

> . . . Her mind began to get quiet and then empty but when the priest raised the monstrance with the Host shining ivory-colored in the center of it, she was thinking of the tent at the fair that had the freak in it. The freak was saying, "I don't dispute hit. This is the way He wanted me to be" [193].

For the child, as was the case in "The River," the evocation of Christ must be vivid indeed. The freak's acceptance of his freakishness is heightened by the quality of the last image of this story: "The sun was a huge red ball like an elevated Host drenched in blood and when it sank out of sight, it left a line in the sky like a red clay road hanging over the trees" (194).[9]

## III

The basic struggle is with "Adam's sin," or—to put it in less portentous terms—the natural tendency of man to sin, against his conscience, a disapproving society, or whatever metaphor he chooses to identify with his aberrant ways. The Christ-figure is liberally used, and there is little true identification with theological explanations of Him. He is a weight, a burden, a task, even an enemy. Miss O'Connor's first novel-length portrayal of His effects is *Wise Blood* (1952). Here, Jesus is the object of attack when He is not subject to exploitation along the lines of a "con man," collecting fees for salvation from easy victims.

The novel is charged with death and burial imagery. Hazel Motes, returned from the War, to a town that no longer exists, goes on to the city of Taulkinham, there to start a new Church, "without Christ." On the train, he lies in an upper berth, which reminds him of coffins in his past: "He was closed up in the thing except for a little space over the curtain" (14). He dreams, or half-dreams, of his grandfather, a circuit preacher, "a waspish old man who had ridden over three counties with Jesus hidden in his head like a stinger" (15). Then he thinks of his father's burial: "He saw him humped over on his hands and knees in the coffin, being carried that way to the grave-yard" (15).

Last things are with him, as he moves toward Taulkinham,

and "prophecy." Because his grandfather had always associated Jesus with sin, Motes decides that "the way to avoid Jesus was to avoid sin" (16). Hazel Motes is one of a series of religious rebels, whose rebellion and contrition are both deeply personal. He must convince his fellow men that there is no Jesus, or at least that Jesus is not necessary to the moral life. In accents similar to those in Nathanael West's *Miss Lonelyhearts*,[10] Motes fights the idea and the image of Christ; he also competes with a variety of other "prophets," including Asa Hawks, a fake blind man who insists that "you can't run away from Jesus. Jesus is a fact" (32). For Motes, this is tantamount to saying that sin is a fact, and that he has sinned. He strives to solve the problem of moral conscience entirely without the aid of the Christ-figure.

But he is so earnest, so frantic and stubborn about it, that it is obvious to anyone that he is obsessed by the challenge of Christ and will one day surrender to it. Meanwhile, he preaches ". . . the church of truth without Jesus Christ Crucified."

". . . Every one of you people are clean and let me tell you why if you think it's because of Jesus Christ Crucified you're wrong. I don't say he wasn't crucified but I say it wasn't for you . . ." [34].[11]

The challenge is to begin a Church which depends entirely on the defiant, soulless individual. Motes thinks that if he can control the theological circumstances, he will be able to set the terms of his morality. But things do not work that way. In a situation that resembles West's hero of *A Cool Million* (1934) and some of Samuel Beckett's, Hazel Motes deliberately, but slowly, destroys himself: first by blinding himself, then by exposing himself to the cold; finally he is discovered almost dead in a drainage ditch. "The outline of a skull was plain under his skin and the deep burned eye sockets seemed to lead into the dark tunnel where he had disappeared" (126).

One of the more interesting facts of *Wise Blood* is its literally taking into account the necessity of redemption. In fact, in its own way, the novel describes in detail three stages of the journey to death: 1) the recognition of death (images of coffins and of long dark corridors and the "dark tunnel" of the above passage are corroborating evidence); 2) the rebellion against grace, against the idea of *depending* upon some figure or ikon, or supernatural being (this is, of course, as much a rebellion against his grandfather as it is an act of violence against religion); and 3) self-immolation, or the individual move toward redemption. It is interesting that in the second stage, in "the big city," Motes goes "deep into" a "thin cardboard-smelling store that got darker as it got deeper," and emerges with a "glare-blue" suit (18). The color of the suit matches that of a cloudless sky, as if man's limits were nature's own. In stage three, the sheen of the suit wears off, and it takes on a greyish, darkish appearance as Motes himself changes halfway into the cadaver he will appear finally to his landlady.

*Wise Blood* presents a powerful, mad resistance to the familiar pathways to redemption. The intensity of Motes's personal reaction is a deliberate underscoring of the religious story. Motes must eventually give way, and he does so, but not before he has had several very shocking and absurd experiences. He is proved to be unequal to the task of controlling his own fate, and his death is a parody of the death of Jesus. The landlady, looking into the sockets where once his eyes were, sees eternity in the image of a dark tunnel with a pinpoint of light at the end of it. In his efforts to establish a new church, Motes has attracted the attention of Enoch Emery, a guard at the zoo, an almost perfect "grotesque" representation of the "man unknown." Like Motes, Emery is trying to fulfill a mission, but he has a far more imperfect sense of what it is.[12]

Emery has a "secret," which he must show only to Motes. It is a shrunken (three-foot) mummified man in the city's museum. "He was naked and a dried yellow color and his eyes were drawn almost shut as if a giant block of steel were falling down on top of him" (57). This figure, which Emery steals one day and brings to Motes as a present, is Emery's idea of the "new Jesus." Since it has never occurred to him that Motes wants to do without Jesus altogether, Emery feels that he must after all be looking for still another version of Him. In a sense, Motes does believe in *a* Jesus, "one that can't waste his blood redeeming people with it, because he's all man and ain't got any God in him" (68). But this kind of Jesus is beyond the power of his contemporaries to believe; Motes is, in any case, deeply engaged with his own inner struggles against his family and the fiery insistence his grandfather had put upon grace and redemption.

In this semi-comic ooze of what one of the shyster preachers calls "Soulsease" (86), only the absurd and the violent will have effect. Motes changes his course, from a defiant anti-preacher to a dedicated penitent, on the strength of a discovery, that Asa Hawks had faked blindness, and did not have the courage to go through with the act of blinding himself, to prove that Jesus had redeemed him. Motes substitutes a real blinding, and becomes, abruptly, the young penitent, the self-appointed saint. To his landlady, "the blind man had the look of seeing something. His face had a peculiar pushing look, as if it were going forward after something it could just distinguish in the distance . . ." (116-117).

## IV

This "something" is related to what the landlady calls "the eternal." It is also somehow akin to Motes's reversal (which is still self-centered, as the rebellion had originally been). He has gone the full route toward preaching the inutility of the Christ; now he will move back, to the point of self-inflicted immobility which enables him to join his relatives in the coffins he has remembered and dreamed about. There is so much of the extreme, the absurd, in *Wise Blood*, that it appears at least to be disjointed and all too simply plotted. Actually, every detail is part of a plan to portray the journey toward redemption in the setting of an extremely individualistic Protestant scene.

This journey is not only individualistic, but replete with suggestions of the Bible, particularly of the New Testament. Since Christ is a "prophet" in one sense, the messianic sense, in which He is actively sought out as a savior in a moral *and* a military attack upon worldly forces, the opposition to him must be portrayed as a self-motivated "anti-Christ" attack, which is eventually atoned for by a personally maneuvered journey toward redemption. The action taken, the gestures, the decisions, are all non-biblical, and they appear absurd in the sense that none of them seems divinely inspired. In fact, they have the aspect of the diabolic. John Hawkes, in one of a few genuine tributes to Flannery O'Connor, speaks of her use of "the devil's voice":

> I would propose that [Nathanael] West and Flannery O'Connor are very nearly alone today in their pure creation of "aesthetic authority," and would also propose, of course, that they are very nearly alone in their employment of the devil's voice as vehicle for their satire or for what we may call their tone (or accurate) vision of our godless actuality. . . .[13]

This is ingenious, and it is true at least insofar as it suggests the extreme remoteness Miss O'Connor's situations seem to have from anything verifiable in the Christian story. There *is* something "diabolic" in the scope of her heroes' opposition to orthodox Christianity but eventually, it can be seen as a struggle with the redeeming angels, so violent that it appears offered in a refracted light. For Miss O'Connor is for the most part describing two states of man: 1) the desperate need of redemption; and 2) the condition that exists in the absence (or the apparent absence) of redemption. These conditions have their own diabolic appearances, as in The Misfit's distorted version of the Pascalian "wager" (142).

We eventually "come down" to the meaning of her quotation from Saint Matthew, used as an epigraph of her brilliant work,

*The Violent Bear It Away*: "From the days of John the Baptist until now, the Kingdom of Heaven suffereth violence, and the violent bear it away." [14] Violence is, virtually, a quality of the religious act in Miss O'Connor's fiction; it is also a signature of her characters' own personality, to testify to their approaching Jesus on their own initiative, after much and vigorous resistance, and their finally making a personal symbolic act in accepting him. In all of her fiction the way to salvation is dangerous, thorny, rocky, and devious, but there is this distinction, that her heroes put their own barriers in the way of achieving it.

In the situation of her second novel, the central figure, a young man, called Tarwater after his great-uncle, Mason Tarwater, is placed in conflict with two very strong influences: that of the great-uncle's fiery demand, that he baptize the idiot son of his uncle Rayber; and that of Rayber himself, the "rationalist," who believes that we are born only once and that we achieve only "ourselves." The violence exists within the three characters: the towering "two-hundred pound mountain" hovers over his great-nephew both in life and in death; the young Tarwater is anxious to remain free both of him and of Rayber; and Rayber, rather pathetically but also comically, opposes the oldtime religion with the new rationalism.

As to the latter, it is obviously more an object of comedy than it is of serious representation. There is the matter of the hearing aid, made necessary because the elder Tarwater had once shot one of Rayber's ears full of buckshot. Tarwater the younger looks at the box outside him:

> He gazed briefly at the pained eyes behind his uncle's glasses, appearing to abandon a search for something that could not possibly be there. The glint in his eyes fell on the metal box half-sticking out of Rayber's shirt. "Do you think in the box," he asked, "or do you think in your head?" [367]

The box does indeed at least affect his thinking, by intensifying his sense experiences whenever he turns it up. It distorts reality, despite (or because of) its being a marvel of engineering, the rational mind contributing an artificial aid to itself. It has bizarre effects, such as when Rayber is talking to the young Tarwater: he "heard his own heart, magnified by the hearing aid, suddenly begin to pound like the works of a gigantic machine in his chest" (368).

Tarwater remains "free" of the persuasions of his uncle; he doesn't *need* his assertions of the rational "faith," nor does he intend to remember the irrational preachments of his great-uncle. He "wore his isolation like a mantle, wrapped it around himself as if it were a garment signifying the elect" (370). But he is not so free as he thinks. Memories of evangelical demands and warnings echo through his brain; and, while he remains coolly indifferent to his uncle ("I'm free," he says; "I'm outside your head. I ain't in it" [371]), in the end he too has an impact upon him. The impact is, ultimately, not rationalistic, but rather a communication of the quality and strength of conviction that have no respect of content. For Rayber is not himself wholly free of the contact with the irrational, despite his comical refutations of it. Ultimately, Tarwater's reactions to Rayber are violent (he baptizes the idiot child), and his feelings about both elders are stringent (he also drowns the child).[15]

Like Hazel Motes of *Wise Blood*, the young Tarwater must rebel against the act he is committed to sponsoring. Hence, he half agrees with his uncle, that "the great dignity of man . . . is his ability to say: I am born once and no more" (405). But Rayber is also aware that Tarwater's eyes "were the eyes of the crazy student father, the personality was the old man's, and somewhere between the two, Rayber's own image was struggling to survive and he was not able to reach it" (373).

In these extremely unorthodox circumstances, the acts of the young man must be violent, must appear to be "diabolic," though they are at most the consequence of two basic drives: his desire to remain free of "the box" (the hearing-aid, which he associates with Rayber's "enlightenment") "outside" his head, and his resistance to the late great-uncle's pressures. He is in a sense both doomed and free; for, though he says the baptismal words over the boy, he also drowns him: "The words just came out of themselves but it don't mean nothing. You can't be born again." This is a testimony to Rayber's influence, or to Tarwater's rebellion against the old man. "I only meant to drown him," the boy said. "You're only born once. They were just some words that run out of my mouth and spilled in the water" (428). There is something terribly confused in Tarwater's explanation. He is in the grip of these alien influences, yet he powerfully wishes to resist them. He is alternately under the eye of the old man and within the "box" (the mind) of Rayber. The acts committed are therefore both profane and solemnly virtuous. He is trying really to account for too much, and has somehow to act almost as if the three others (including the idiot boy, who is the victim) were acting for him. Miss O'Connor proves that the urge to religious action is present in all men: even in Rayber, who makes a fetish of proving his evangelically obsessed uncle mad; even in the idiot boy, who rides to his baptism on Tarwater's back.

In each case, the religious necessities take on a special image. They are madness to the old man's neighbors, "imprisonment in the irrational" for Rayber, "nonsense" to the truck driver who picks up Tarwater after the drowning. In the end, Tarwater is left with much to undo. He has sought to exorcise the spirit of his great-uncle through fire (as he had tried to eliminate his body by burning the house). The fact is that none of his acts has been clearly a triumph: the drowning *was* a baptism after all; the house-burning did not succeed in getting rid of the body. And, a murderer twice, once of his dead elder in an act of ritual monstrosity, another time of a small child, Tarwater must somehow return to the city, without true knowledge of the meaning of what he has done.

> His singed eyes, black in their deep sockets, seemed already to envision the fate that awaited him but he moved steadily on, his face set toward the dark city, where the children of God lay sleeping [447].

## V

He has, in short, just begun to walk the path to redemption. But, while Tarwater stands out as a person of strong character, it is not his particular trouble that is important, except in the sense that it is exemplary. Miss O'Connor is dramatizing, in *The Violent Bear It Away,* the intrinsic necessity for grace in the human personality. The figure of Jesus haunts almost all of her characters. They are, half the time, violently opposed to Him (or, in His image, opposed to some elder who has tried to force His necessity upon them), because they cannot see beyond themselves to a transcendent existence. Hazel Motes and Tarwater are both haunted by the rank and stinking corporeality of their elders, whom they have seen dead and—in dream or in reality—been obliged to bury.

These experiences serve to make them resist the compunctions of grace, and turn away from the prospects of redemption. But the alternative is singularly uninviting. Hazel Motes has no success preaching the new church "without Christ," and Tarwater finds his uncle either pathetic or farcical. They react violently at the turn of their journeys: Motes blinds himself in a mixture of the desire for penitence and the will to prove his courage; Tarwater has recourse both to water and fire, from mixed motives of defiance and fear.

This clarity of vision comes in part from Miss O'Connor's having herself had a satisfactory explanation of these religious drives, and therefore being in a position to portray the violent acts of those who possess the drives but are unable to define goals or direct energies toward them. The grotesqueries of her fiction are in effect a consequence of her seeing what she calls "the Manichaean spirit of the times," in which the religious metaphors retain their power but cannot be precisely delineated by persons driven by the necessities they see in them. Violence, in this setting, assumes a religious meaning; it is, in effect, the sparks caused by the clash of religious desire and disbelief.

> The novelist with Christian concerns will find in modern life distortions which are repugnant to him, and his problem will be to make these appear as distortions to an audience which is used to seeing them as natural; and he may well be forced to take ever more violent means to get his vision across to his hostile audience. . . .[16]

The matter becomes extremely delicate, in the light of her other observations: for example, that "Art requires a delicate adjustment of the outer and inner worlds in such a way that, without changing their nature, they can be seen through each other." [17] This remark suggests that the religious metaphors are, above all, psychological realities; that these are dramatized in the desperate struggles her characters have, at one time against but finally in the mood of accepting the Christian demands and rewards. When Miss O'Connor makes the following summary of her vision, therefore, she is simply defining the ultimate goals of her characters, whether they have been represented or not in the act of achieving them.

> . . . I see from the standpoint of Christian orthodoxy. This means that for me the meaning of life is centered in our Redemption by Christ and that what I see in the world I see in its relation to that. I don't think that this is a position that can be taken halfway or one that is particularly easy in these times to make transparent in fiction.[18]

## Notes

1. Flannery O'Connor, "The Role of the Catholic Novelist," *Greyfriar* [Siena Studies in Literature], VII (1964), 8.
2. See Sister M. Bernetta Quinn, "View from a Rock: The Fiction of Flannery O'Connor and J. F. Powers," *Critique*, II (Fall, 1958), 19-27: ". . . The center of all Catholic fiction is the Redemption. However mean or miserable or degraded human life may seem to the natural gaze, it must never be forgotten that God considered it valuable enough to send His only Son that He might reclaim it . . ." (21). See *A Handbook*

*of Christian Theology* (New York: Meridian Books, 1958), p. 296: "Thus the God who ransoms, redeems, and delivers Israel out of her bondage is the God who, in Christ, pays the price which restores sinful mankind to freedom and new life. In this act of redemption two interrelated theological emphases are dominant: God's *love* by which He takes the initiative, and man's sin which occasions the situation from which God redeems him."

3. "The Role of the Catholic Novelist," pp. 10-11.

4. *Ibid.*, p. 11.

5. See Melvin J. Friedman, in *Recent American Fiction*, edited by Joseph J. Waldmeir (Boston: Houghton Mifflin, 1963), p. 241. Friedman also cites Nathanael West, as does John Hawkes, "Flannery O'Connor's Devil," *Sewanee Review*, LXX (Summer, 1962), 396. Hawkes mentions an interesting conjunction of influences on himself: ". . . it was Melville's granddaughter [Eleanor Melville Metcalf], a lady I was privileged to know in Cambridge, Massachusetts, who first urged me to read the fiction of Flannery O'Connor, and—further— . . . this experience occurred just at the time I had discovered the short novels of Nathanael West."

6. *Systematic Theology* (Chicago: University of Chicago Press, 1951), vol. II, p. 98. It is interesting that many of Miss O'Connor's characters want to "see a sign": that is, they want Christ's divinity manifested directly. The Misfit is such a one; Hazel Motes of *Wise Blood* struggles against a Christian mission on the grounds that Christ as God has never revealed Himself; Mr. Head and his grandson have a remarkable experience of illumination, when they see the plaster statue of a Negro (in "The Artificial Nigger"); and the young Tarwater of *The Violent Bear It Away* has a "voice" (variously called "stranger," "friend," and "mentor") who tries to deny Jesus because there has been no "sign" of Him.

7. *Ibid.*, p. 110.

8. *Ibid.*, p. 111.

9. The imagery of fire in *The Violent Bear It Away* is especially ambiguous; perhaps it is a "resourceful ambiguity." At the beginning, the young Tarwater sets fire to the cabin which he thinks has the body of his great-uncle; this latter has urged him to bury him, but the boy's inner voice advises him to forget all that nonsense. When he is riding toward the city, Tarwater momentarily confuses the lights with the fire he has just set. But, in Part Three of the novel, fire seems to have become a source of illumination as well as a means of triumphing over the devil, to "burn him out."

10. See both Friedman and Hawkes, *op. cit.* By way of distinction from *Miss Lonelyhearts*, *Wise Blood* has its hero almost reach the Christ. After Hazel Motes begins his atonement by blinding himself, and shortly following his death, his landlady sees into his eyes and through them to that "dark tunnel" which is apparently the illumination of Christ. Motes ambiguously becomes the *way* to the light and the light itself: "She sat staring with her eyes shut, into his eyes, and felt as if she had

finally got to the beginning of something she couldn't begin, and she saw him moving farther and farther away, farther and farther into the darkness until he was the pin point of light" (126).

11. See also p. 60: "I'm going to preach there was no Fall because there was nothing to fall from and no Redemption because there was no Fall and no Judgment because there wasn't the first two. Nothing matters but that Jesus was a liar."

12. See p. 104: ". . . He wanted to be THE young man of the future, like the ones in the insurance ads. He wanted, some day, to see a line of people waiting to shake his hand."

13. "Flannery O'Connor's Devil," p. 396.

14. See Sumner J. Ferris, "The Outside and the Inside," *Critique*, III (Winter-Spring, 1960), 11-19. He suggests two interpretations: ". . . that of the believer and that of the unbeliever, the violent and the passive, the saved and the damned" (15). Miss O'Connor uses the Douai version of Matthew XI, 12. The sense in which she probably wishes to use the quotation is indicated at the very end of the novel: the young Tarwater "felt his hunger no longer as a pain but as a tide. He felt it rising in himself through time and darkness, rising through the centuries, and he knew that it rose in a line of men whose lives were chosen to sustain it, who would wander in the world, strangers from that violent country where the silence is never broken except to shout the truth" (446-47).

15. See Miss O'Connor's own remarks, at the College of Saint Teresa, quoted above. That Rayber is at times very close himself to the "madness" of "love" is suggested again and again. He thinks of an "affliction," a "madness," which affects the entire family: "It lay hidden in the line of blood that touched them, flowing from some ancient source. . . . Those it touched were condemned to fight it constantly or be ruled by it" (372). It is true that Rayber is more frequently than not the subject of comic treatment; also, he goes "the wrong way" and finally misunderstands his young nephew. But he is aware of himself as a more complex person than the abstract term "rationalist" would suggest. In fact, in certain respects, he suffers from "*un malaise rationaliste*," as when he is described as undergoing "what amounts to a rigid ascetic discipline" (373). This is a secularized version of the regimen of the saint; applied to Rayber, it tends to give him a comical and even a ludicrous aspect, but actually it indicates how close he is to the "madness" of the old Tarwater and how easy it might have been for him to become another version of the prophet. This fact his young nephew recognizes when he tells Rayber that "the seed" had fallen "deep" in him: "It ain't a thing you can do about it. It fell on bad ground but it fell in deep" (416).

16. "The Fiction Writer and His Country," in *The Living Novel, a Symposium*, edited by Granville Hicks (New York: Macmillan, 1957), pp. 162-63.

17. *Ibid.*, p. 163.

18. *Ibid.*, p. 162.

# Flannery O'Connor and the Bible Belt

LOUIS D. RUBIN, JR.

If I join a community where a tongue other than my own is the medium of intercourse, I simply must learn the language of the place to the best of my ability. Gustave Weigel, S.J.

THERE IS much to be said for the theory that what makes a writer is a built-in conflict of vision, together with the desire to resolve it. Let him be born into one set of values, and let him be instructed in another and opposed set of values in the life he confronts each day, and the result will be either schizophrenia or else a new perception whereby his experience will be thrown into the sharp illumination that comes of seeing things in stereoscopic distance.

This thesis has frequently been applied to the Southern writers of our time, who were moderns reared in a traditional kind of society that during their youth was in the process of breaking up. They saw the new through the eyes of the old and vice versa, and their stories and poems gave form and order to the human image in changing times.

Whatever else may be said of this notion, it does seem to be borne out in the instance of Flannery O'Connor. For this young

49

woman of genius, who in an all-too-brief literary career established herself as one of the finest writers of her time, was surely
exposed to several of the most revealing and dramatic contrasts of viewpoint and value possible to her time and place.
She was a Southerner, born in a city but reared in the rural
South, from which she journeyed forth for long stays in the
Midwest and Northeast. As if that were not enough, however,
she was also by birth and by faith a Roman Catholic, which in
the rural, Protestant South is an alien sect. Beyond the Southern cities the religious sentiment is evangelical all the way—
some low-Church Episcopalians and some Presbyterians, who
generally constitute the cultural and financial elite, but especially Methodists and Baptists, the last-named ranging from
the solid middle-class respectability of the large churches to all
manner of Hard-Shell, Fundamentalist, Revivalist, Pentecostal,
and other primitive offshoots of evangelical Protestantism. In
the little wooden churches of the back-country South and in the
unpainted tabernacles of the Southern urban slums, the Pope
of Rome is a minion of Satan, and a Catholic priest a mysterious
and dangerous man.

The ways of the fundamentalist South, especially in its more
primitive levels of religious experience, are not those of the
Roman Catholic Church. Primitive Protestantism in the South
is puritanical, much more so than the Presbyterian Church itself
is nowadays; the struggle against Satan is individual, continu-
ous and desperate, and salvation is a personal problem, which
comes not through ritual and sacrament, but in the gripping
fervor of immediate confrontation with eternity. The rural
South is not so much Christ-centered as Christ-haunted. PRE-
PARE TO MEET THY GOD, the signs along the highway
counsel the motorist, and WHERE WILL YOU SPEND
ETERNITY? "The people believe strongly in an anthropomorphic Satan," an Episcopal bishop has written. "One gets the
impression that they believe more in the reality of Satan than
in the reality of God." [1]

Miss O'Connor, one critic remarks, "has imposed her Catholic theology on the local image, and the marriage of Rome and South Georgia is odd to say the least." [2] It is that, and it is also highly revealing. The Catholic novelist in the South, as Miss O'Connor herself tells us, "is forced to follow the spirit into strange places and to recognize it in many forms not totally congenial to him. But the fact that the South is the Bible Belt increases rather than decreases his sympathy for what he sees. His interest will in all likelihood go immediately to those aspects of Southern life where the religious feeling is most intense and where its outward forms are farthest from the Catholic." [3] Both her novels and most of her short stories are directly concerned with religion. In the commentary that follows, I want to discuss this strange union of evangelical Protestantism and Roman Catholicism as it manifests itself in Flannery O'Connor's novels. I shall neglect the short stories both because I have on several previous occasions written about them,[4] and because it is especially in the two novels that she conducts an exploration of backwoods Southern primitive Protestantism. It is only fair, however, for me to point out that I think Miss O'Connor was primarily a short story writer, one of the very best of her century, rather than a novelist. I mean this in much the same sense that Malcolm Cowley means it when he declares that William Faulkner was likewise a short story writer rather than a novelist: "his stories do not occur to him in book-length units of 70,000 to 150,000 words" and "almost all his novels have some weakness in structure." [5] But if in these novels we sense some structural flaws, if especially some of the secondary characters seem insufficiently developed to fit the longer form of the novel, nevertheless, the two novels that Flannery O'Connor has left us are remarkable works of fiction, and not likely to be forgotten any time soon.

The behavior of Southern rural Christians of the primitivistic persuasion has of course long been a stock in trade of the Southern writer. For a novelist such as Erskine Caldwell, who exploited the Georgia countryside in books that have achieved record-breaking sales, the Southern preacher is a humorous figure, and a backwoods revival an exploration into sexual comedy. Miss O'Connor's depiction of Southern rural Protestantism, however, never stops at the comic surfaces. Underlying the often pathetically crude and naive exteriors of Southern fundamentalism she recognizes the presence of an intense spiritual life, which however grotesque its forms is authentic and very much worthy of respect.

Like Caldwell, and also another Georgia writer, Carson McCullers, Miss O'Connor has throughout her career showed an affinity for the strange, the grotesque, the deformed. In abnormality she has perceived the exaggeration, the outsized proportions whereby a commentary is made on the normal and conventional. Her characters are for the most part not "normal" or "sane"; neither, for that matter, are William Faulkner's and for the very good reason that in the exaggeration, the grotesque proportions of their people, a telling critique is thereby possible of the "normal and sane." Yet there is a considerable difference between the grotesque as handled by Miss O'Connor and Faulkner on the one hand, and by Caldwell and Miss McCullers on the other. Caldwell dotes on the physically grotesque; he gives us a Georgia freak show. Sister Bessie of *Tobacco Road,* with her nose so turned up that she is imperiled when it rains, serves the purposes of low comedy and little more. Miss McCullers likewise goes in for the physically deformed and maimed in her work; for her, however, grotesqueness is designed not to provoke amusement but to convey the sense of loneliness and isolation that comes with abnormality. Pain is the motif of her fiction; her characters move about in a haze of *angst* and misery. In her best work, the strange novella entitled *The Ballad of the Sad Café,* a tall, sexless, masculine woman and a hunchback dwarf convey through their very oddness and deformity the loneliness, the pain of thwarted and unfulfilled love that is Miss McCullers' picture of our experience.

Like Faulkner, however, Miss O'Connor's version of Southern Gothic emphasizes not so much physical as mental and spiritual deformity. She has, it is true, some physical grotesques among her characters, but even with these she makes no attempt to capitalize on the reader's curiosity about the morbid and unnatural. Rather, her true grotesques are those who are spiritually maimed and twisted, who cannot view the everyday life around them with the equanimity and complacency that ordinary, "well-adjusted" people manage. Asked once why it was that Southern writers tend to dwell so often on freaks and grotesques, she replied that the South was the only American region where a freak could still be recognized when seen. The roster of Miss O'Connor's freaks is brilliant and frightening. From Hazel Motes in *Wise Blood,* who preached the Church Without Christ and who ultimately blinded himself to shut out the vision of sin, to Francis Marion Tarwater of *The Violent Bear It Away,* struggling vainly to escape from the terrible burden of baptism and prophecy laid upon him by his fanatical old great-uncle, Miss O'Connor's people are afflicted with a savage inability and unwillingness to accept the normal conditions of everyday life, and are driven into violent deeds of protest and retribution.

It is in this light that Miss O'Connor views Southern fundamentalist Protestantism. The fanaticism and torment that characterize the emotion-torn, apocalyptic primitive Protestantism of the back-country South, with its revivals, evangelists, testimonies, visions, prophets and hallucinations, become in her fiction the unlettered, naive search for spiritual existence in a world grown complacent and materialistic. Her sympathies lie not with the prosperous, well-adjusted, comfortable middle-class churches, but with those who stand outside the respectable community, refuse to accept its accommodations and compromises, and preach the fire and the plague. They alone, she implies, are willing to confront evil; they alone believe in redemption; only for them is the Devil a real and tangible presence. "I see a damned soul before my eyes!" the child evangelist declares. "I see a dead man Jesus hasn't raised. His head is in the window but his ear is deaf to the Holy Word!" (385). And she points her finger at the educated, rationalistic school-teacher who has been watching her and telling himself how wretched is the kind of religion that would exploit a little child in this manner. The schoolteacher drops to the ground in terror and dismay, and fumbles for the switch that will turn off his artificial hearing apparatus and restore him to the blessed condition of silence. The easy tolerance, the complacent rationalism of the schoolteacher are for the moment quite helpless against the onslaught of religious fervor of the child.

I do not want to imply that Miss O'Connor, though a Roman Catholic, feels that the wild, hallucinatory emotionalism, the primitive and unlettered evangelicism of the Bible Belt is the true apprehension of God. It is rather that as a Roman Catholic in the modern South she considered fundamentalist Protestantism a manifestation, however grotesque and distorted, of a belief in the supremacy of the spirit over the materialistic ethics and bland rationalism of modern "respectable" theology, and an assertion of true religious identity in a society rapidly losing its sense of dependence on God. That Miss O'Connor's attitude is not an uncommon one for a Roman Catholic may be illustrated by a quotation from a recent work by a Catholic theologian, the late Fr. Gustave Weigel, S.J.:

> Even though the fundamentalist is traditionally opposed to the Scarlet Woman of Rome and her ways, yet he clings to certain positions which are as fundamental for him as for Catholics. He believes in the divinity of Jesus of Nazareth, the Virgin birth, the objectively atoning death of Jesus and His physical resurrection. The liberals vacillate ambiguously in their adherence to these dogmas. In consequence, the Catholic feels sympathy for the fundamentalist in spite of the latent antipathy felt by that group toward Catholicism. The liberals are far more friendly and cordial but the Catholic is appalled by their radical reconstructions of Christianity.[6]

Yet despite this agreement on certain theological essentials, the way of the primitive fundamentalists is not the way of the

Catholic, and it is a mistake, I feel, to read Miss O'Connor's novels without remembering this—for reasons that I shall discuss later in this essay. In the primitive fervor, and also the error, of fundamentalism she perceives the waste and the horror of that spiritual integrity. We must keep in mind that in their blind and confused zeal, the protagonists of both her novels commit crimes. Their warped but powerful consciousness of human sinfulness gives them purpose and integrity in a materialistic society, but it also leads them to do grievous harm. In part, of course, this is the fault of society: in a world in which God is ignored, those who cannot acquiesce in godlessness are forced to travel along strange paths, and in their ignorance to do evil deeds. A society which fails to instruct its members in righteousness drives them to hate. Such is Miss O'Connor's South, as depicted in her novels.

Hazel Motes, the protagonist of Miss O'Connor's first novel, *Wise Blood,* is just such a person. Imbued as a child with a fanatical sense of guilt for his sinfulness, he comes out of the army to find the hamlet where he had lived deserted. Naive, ignorant, confused, he sets out for the city of Taulkinham, obsessed with the need to deny the existence of Christ. He buys an old Essex automobile to serve as his temple, and he moves about the city preaching the Church Without Christ. He sins, blasphemes, degrades himself. Jesus did not die for you, he tells the townsfolk; there is no sin, no redemption of sin, no salvation. But the citizens of Taulkinham respond only with utter unconcern. He visits a prostitute, not out of desire but out of the compulsion to sin by fornication. "What I mean to have you know is: I'm no goddam preacher," he tells her. "That's okay, son," the woman responds. "Momma don't mind if you ain't a preacher" (23). He finds a blind revivalist and his daughter; the man has supposedly blinded himself to justify his belief in Christ's redemption. But the blind man proves to be not blind at all, and his daughter is a hard-bitten slut. A clever evangelist sees Haze preaching his Church Without Christ, breaks into the gathering, calls Haze the Prophet, and seeks to ally himself with him in order to extract money from the crowd. Haze refuses, whereupon the evangelist finds another man to serve as prophet for such a church. Haze runs over this false prophet with his automobile; as the man lies dying in the road, Haze denounces him for pretending not to believe in Christ when actually he does. Haze hears the false prophet's dying words, "Jesus hep me," (111) and from then on he is without rest. Ultimately he blinds himself, sleeps with barbed wire wrapped around his chest. His landlady asks him why he does these things. "It's natural" (122), he tells her. "Well, it's not normal," she declares. "It's like one of them gory stories, it's something that people have quit doing—like boiling in oil or being a saint or walling up cats. . . . There's no reason for it. People have quit doing it" (122). To which Haze replies, "They ain't quit doing it as long as I'm doing it" (122). Eventually he is found dying in the winter streets of the city, and the police, after hitting him over the head to keep him quiet, bring him back to the landlady, but he dies on the way.

There is also Enoch Emery, a loveless, unattractive youth who like Hazel Motes has come to the city from the backwoods, and who wants friendship. Haze will have none of him, but Enoch continues to tag along; Haze is his Prophet, and Enoch is overcome with the sense of having a mission, which consists finally of stealing the mummified body of a man from a museum and giving it to Motes. After that he steals a gorilla suit from a truck, and we last see him as, wearing the suit, he frightens away a man and a woman who are out in the country watching the view.

The theological ramifications of *Wise Blood* have been widely noted. As Jonathan Baumbach points out in an excellent essay on the novel,[7] both Hazel Motes and Enoch Emery come to the city of Taulkinham in search of help. Hazel blasphemes, sins, preaches the denial of Christ's redemptive power, seeking to provoke a response, to be struck down for his sinfulness, to come up against something greater than himself if only in negation. But the city merely ignores him. The citizenry of Taulkinham—modernity, civilized urban society—is so "well adjusted" to its comfortable complacency that a prophet stalking its streets to preach that there is no God is considered a freak, a harmless religious fanatic who is simply unnoticed. For the city dwellers the denial of Christ and His redemption is not important; they are not troubled by such matters. If at the end Haze, a blasphemer and a murderer, is saved, it is because alone of them all he has the integrity to know guilt, to feel that he is "not clean."

As for Enoch Emery, he comes to Taulkinham looking for love, for human affection, but nobody wishes remotely to know him or love him. When he steals the mummy from the museum and presents it to Haze, he is giving him the ultimate proof of what men are if there is no God and no redemption—shrunken figures of dust. And it is only when Enoch steals the gorilla costume and comes out to frighten the spooning couple that he is able to evoke any sort of human response to his existence.

Miss O'Connor's intentions in *Wise Blood* are stated squarely in the little prefatory note she wrote for the second edition of the novel when it was published in 1962:

> That belief in Christ is to some a matter of life and death has been a stumbling block for readers who would prefer to think it a matter of no great consequence. For them Hazel Motes' integrity lies in his trying with such vigor to get rid of the ragged figure who moves from tree to tree in the back of his mind. For the author Hazel's integrity lies in his not being able to [8].

Haze is indeed a freak, a grotesque figure, but is he not thereby "natural"? Rather, as Haze replies to his landlady when she tells him that civilized people no longer mortify their flesh to punish themselves for sinfulness, it is the complacent, secular society of the city that is "unnatural," if man is the religious creature that both Catholic and Protestant theology believes he is. And it is just such an "unnatural" society that forces the Hazel Moteses and Enoch Emerys to find meaning only in violence.

The violence of Hazel Motes is the warped and inarticulate protest of one for whom salvation is of crucial importance, against a society for whom God is dead. That Enoch Emery becomes in effect a wild animal is likewise to be expected in a society which will not offer him elementary love and compassion.

The same theme is present in Miss O'Connor's other and much later novel, *The Violent Bear It Away,* but the protagonist of that novel is both less bizarre and more sympathetic a character than Hazel Motes. Discussing the task of the Catholic novelist as she sees it, Miss O'Connor has written that "when I write a novel in which the central action is baptism, I know that for the larger percentage of my readers, baptism is a meaningless rite; therefore I have to imbue this action with an awe and terror which will suggest its awful mystery. I have to distort the look of the thing in order to represent as I see them both the mystery and the fact." [8] The reference is obviously to *The Violent Bear It Away.* In this novel a youth, Francis Marion Tarwater, has been charged by the fanatical old great-uncle who had reared him with the task of baptizing an idiot cousin and then taking on his burden of prophecy. With his great-uncle the youth had lived on a farm remote from the city. On one occasion an uncle, a schoolteacher named Rayber, had come out from town with a welfare worker to try to take the youth from the old man, but the great-uncle had driven Rayber away, wounding him twice with a rifle in the process. When the old man dies, young Tarwater, instead of burying the great-uncle as he had been enjoined to do, decides to burn down the farmhouse with the old man's body inside, and afterwards heads for town, where he joins Rayber and the schoolteacher's mentally defective son Bishop. There ensues a contest in which Rayber, who though he once exposed himself to the great-uncle's fanaticism has secured an education and become an expert in educational psychology, seeks to rid the youth of his compulsive attachment to the old man's fanaticism.

Tarwater does not want to baptize the idiot child Bishop, as his great-uncle had commanded, but so strong is the hold that the old man's memory has on him that the injunction is constantly in his thoughts. To save the boy from fanaticism, Rayber takes him on tours of the city, trying to win his confidence and to acquaint him with what the schoolteacher considers the attractions of the modern world. Tarwater, however, is not impressed. One night the youth steals out of Rayber's house and, with the barefooted and half-dressed schoolteacher in pursuit, goes to a revivalist meeting in which a little girl delivers a highly rhapsodic address on God's love. The schoolteacher, who is watching through the window, is at first disgusted with the way in which the girl's innocence is being exploited; then he begins to feel a growing emotional yearning for her, and imagines, when the child keeps glancing toward his face in the window, that some "miraculous communication" is taking place between them—only to have the girl point to him and denounce him for his unbelief. When Tarwater comes out of the meeting and joins the disconcerted Rayber, the youth seems finally on the verge of breaking through his distrust and suspicion and wanting to talk with his uncle. But the distraught, confused Rayber refuses to respond. The next day the opportunity is gone, and the youth is as hostile and closemouthed as ever.

By now Tarwater has come to feel that the only way he can throw off the yoke of his dead great-uncle's will is to drown the little boy Bishop, in whose features he sees the old man's. Rayber takes Tarwater and Bishop to a lake resort not too far from the site of the great-uncle's onetime farm, and after a time he lets Tarwater take Bishop out in a rowboat. When much later he hears a cry across the water, he knows what has happened.

Tarwater has drowned Bishop, but in so doing the youth realizes that he has not repudiated the old great-uncle's command but instead has obeyed it, since the drowning also constituted the act of baptism. Despairing and desperate, the youth makes his way back to the site of the farm; on the way he is picked up by a sex pervert, drugged, and attacked. Finally he gets to the farmhouse; he had left it after setting it afire, thinking that in so doing he had cremated the dead great-uncle's body. Now he finds that the old man's body had not been in the house at the time; a Negro neighbor had removed it, dug a grave, and buried it. The will of the old man has been fulfilled; he has been buried and Bishop has been baptized. So Tarwater, after setting fire to the woods, sets out for the city, confirmed now in the mission of prophecy bequeathed him by the dead old man, going forth to warn the children of God of the terrible speed of mercy.

When *The Violent Bear It Away* appeared, it was savagely attacked by several Roman Catholic critics, including the novelist Robert O. Bowen, who wrote that "beyond not being Catholic, the novel is distinctly anti-Catholic in being a thorough, point-by-point dramatic argument against Free Will, Redemption, and Divine Justice, among other aspects of Catholic thought." [9] To such onslaughts other Catholic critics replied, notably Rainulf A. Stelzmann in an excellent essay in *Xavier University Studies*.[10] (I am told that Stelzmann's interpretation of the novel received the enthusiastic approval of Miss O'Connor herself.) Stelzmann sees the struggle within Tarwater as being one between an unwillingness to accept the mission of prophecy to the ungodly, and loyalty to the spiritual conviction that the old man had sought to instill within him. The voice which throughout the novel argues with the youth, telling him that the old man's ideas were false and that he need not heed them, Stelzmann asserts was that of the Devil. The schoolteacher Rayber is seen as the weak-willed, spiritually impotent spokesman for modernity, seeking, in the name of rationality, to nullify the boy's spiritual consciousness. When the boy realizes that in drowning Bishop he has fulfilled the mission of baptism, and learns that he has not cremated the old great-uncle after all, his religious integrity reasserts itself, he defies the counsel of the Devil, and takes up the prophetic burden as his great-uncle had hoped.

Now if this is really the full meaning of *The Violent Bear It Away*, then it would seem to me that there is much to be said for the kind of criticism leveled against the novel by Bowen and others. I am no theologian, of course, and being neither Catholic nor Protestant may be said to be peculiarly ill-equipped to settle the question of the heresy, if any, in Miss O'Connor's novel; indeed, I note that Stelzmann himself has described a reading which I gave to Miss O'Connor's story "The Displaced Person" as being nihilistic and deterministic, which if true is certainly not what I had in mind.[11] But if the struggle within young Tarwater *is* between whether or not to take up the prophetic mission bequeathed him by the old man, and if in attempting to negate the mission he only succeeds in trapping himself into acquiescence, then it seems to me quite arguable that it is not his own free will that makes him do so. His struggle would appear to be to avoid his destined task, much as the characters in Greek tragedy do, and the moral would seem to be that it cannot be done. Miss O'Connor speaks of "man so free that with his last breath he can say No." [12] Yet it seems to me that the one thing that young Tarwater cannot do, if we accept the Stelzmann hypothesis, is to say No.

But is the struggle in young Tarwater precisely that proposed by Stelzmann? I think not. Rather, it seems to me that such a reading of *The Violent Bear It Away* overlooks several very important episodes, in particular the business of the revival that Tarwater attends and Rayber observes through the window. We recall that the little girl evangelist preached a sermon about God's love:

> "Do you know who Jesus is?" she cried. "Jesus is the word of God and Jesus is love. The Word of God is love and do you know what love is, you people? If you don't know what love is you won't know Jesus when He comes. You won't be ready. I want to

tell you people the story of the world, how it never known when love come, so when love comes again, you'll be ready" [382].

When Tarwater comes out of the revival meeting afterward, he is for the first time in the novel genuinely open to help, desirous of his uncle Rayber's companionship and guidance. But Rayber is at that moment completely unable and unwilling to respond to the youth's overture, so shaken up and resentful is he after the episode with the little girl at the window. Why is Rayber so distraught? Not simply from embarrassment; rather, it is because Rayber had done the one thing he fears most of all doing. Listening to the little girl, he had forgotten his sophisticated rationalism and had given way to an emotional response: "Come away with me! he silently implored, and I'll teach you the truth, I'll save you, beautiful child!" (384).

Rayber has long since learned to fear and distrust emotion. His own early exposure to the old man had so devastated him that in self-defense he has erected a wall of scientific detachment and objective rationality about himself. His reliance upon behavioral psychology is a device on his part to avoid emotional involvement in human relationships. Emotionalism, passion, violence; these are what Rayber most abhors, because he recognizes that within himself lies the latent capacity for all three. The seed of the old man's fanaticism "fell in us both alike," he tells Tarwater. "The difference is that I know it's in me and I keep it under control. I weed it out but you're too blind to know it's in you. You don't even know what makes you do the things you do" (416). For the schoolteacher, emotion is something to be avoided, because it negates reason. There is an important passage in which Rayber thinks about his idiot son Bishop:

> For the most part Rayber lived with him without being painfully aware of his presence but the moments would still come when, rushing from some inexplicable part of himself, he would experience a love for the child so outrageous that he would be left

shocked and depressed for days, and trembling for his sanity. It was only a touch of the curse that lay in his blood.

. . . . . . . . . . . . . .

He was not afraid of love in general. He knew the value of it and how it could be used. He had seen it transform in cases where nothing else had worked, such as with his poor sister. None of this had the least bearing on his situation. The love that would overcome him was of a different order entirely. It was not the kind that could be used for the child's improvement or his own. It was love without reason, love for something futureless, love that appeared to exist only to be itself, imperious and all demanding, the kind that would cause him to make a fool of himself in an instant. And it only began with Bishop. It began with Bishop and then like an avalanche covered everything his reason hated. He always felt with it a rush of longing to have the old man's eyes—insane, fish-colored, violent in their impossible vision of a world transfigured—turned on him once again. The longing was like an undertow in his blood dragging him backwards to what he knew to be madness [372].

It is the schoolteacher's fear of the emotion of love that prevents him from being able to help Tarwater. He will not give in to the irrational, the emotional; he is afraid of it. Yet it was precisely the little girl's message of a God of love that had almost broken the spell of the great-uncle's fanaticism over Tarwater; had Rayber been able to realize this, had he sought then to replace the mission of fanatical hate that the old man had instilled in Tarwater—"The Lord is preparing a prophet with fire in his hand and eye and the prophet is moving toward the city with his warning" (339)—with the joy of God's love and mercy, he could have saved the youth from his fate. But to Rayber overmastering love was as dangerous as hatred, and he chose instead to try to combat the boy's fixation by sterile logic and specious reason, only to bring about the death of his own son and the final violation of Tarwater. The rape of the youth by the sex pervert was only the last mockery of Tarwater's failure to find in human society the love and affection he needed if he was to be saved. The remedy for the fanatical terror and wrath that had gripped the youth, then, was not the denial of emotion in favor of cold behavioristic rationalism, but the equally emotional fanaticism of love. Without love the needs of the soul are capable of being met only by wrath and violence. The violent do indeed bear it away.

The struggle within Tarwater's mind therefore is not simply that between heeding or denying the burden of prophecy bequeathed him by the old man; it is between the creative, life-giving emotion of love and the destructive, death-bringing emotion of hatred and violence. He wants to love, but he has been taught only to hate. There is another scene which bears this out: that in which the youth Tarwater, as he meditates taking Bishop out in the boat to drown him, stands on the staircase of the resort before the little boy, and Bishop asks him to tie his shoes. Before this simple act of trust and dependence, "the country boy stopped still. He hung over him like someone bewitched, his long arms bent uncertainly." As the woman resort-keeper watches, Tarwater reaches over then and ties the shoes. "When the boy finished tying them, he straightened himself and said in a querulous voice, 'Now git on and quit bothering me with them laces,' and the child flipped over on his hands and feet and scrambled up the stairs, making a great din." The woman, "confused by this kindness," calls to him then, looks into Tarwater's eyes, "and for an instant she thought she saw something fleeing across the surface of them, a lost light that came from nowhere and vanished into nothing" (397). What is it she thinks she sees, if it is not that even at that late moment, Tarwater was almost swayed from his purpose by the simple need of the child, and the helpless affection implicit in the child's dependence upon him? But just as with Rayber at the revival, the woman will not speak gently and kindly to the youth. A few minutes previously she had admonished him:

"Mind how you talk to one of them there, you boy!" the woman hissed.

He looked at her as if it were the first time she had spoken to him. "Them there what?" he murmured.

"That there kind," she said, looking at him fiercely as if he had profaned the holy.

He looked back at the afflicted child and the woman was startled by the expression on his face. He seemed to see the little boy and nothing else, no air around him, no room, no nothing, as if his gaze had slipped and fallen into the center of the child's eyes and was still falling down and down and down [396].

Now, when Tarwater looks back at her after having tied the child's laces, the woman only says, "Whatever devil's work you mean to do, don't do it here" (397). And the youth's last, forlorn chance of being rescued by the reality of love is gone. Such is the meaning of the scene, I think, and such is the true conflict within young Tarwater. The youth's spiritual integrity, invulnerable to the schoolmaster's complacent scientific rationalism, could have been directed toward love instead of wrath, had such love been offered him. But in a world ignorant and disdainful of God's love—"Suffer little children to come unto me"—the only response possible is wrath: "His singed eyes, black in their deep sockets, seemed already to envision the fate that awaited him but he moved steadily on, his face set toward the dark city, where the children of God lay sleeping" (447).

In a world in which "faith supported by love" cannot survive the attack of secular materialism, only faith achieved through hatred is possible. Because there is no one in young Tarwater's world to instruct him in God's love, he can be won back to faith only through the passionate hatred involved in the effort to drown the boy Bishop. Extremes, Rayber tells Tarwater, "are for violent people" (390). But in the world they inhabit, it is only the primitive fundamentalism exemplified by the old great-uncle which is violent. We recall T. S.

Eliot's lines, "Remember us—if at all—not as lost / Violent souls, but only / As the hollow men / The stuffed men." For Eliot the collapse of faith in the western world has made us all hollow men, but Flannery O'Connor shows faith alive and glowing in the fanatical compulsions of the Bible Belt prophets. Yet the price that Tarwater must pay for the attainment of such faith is the denial and utter extinction of the possibility of love.

If this interpretation of the meaning of this novel is valid, then not only do the scenes at the revival and on the resort staircase make sense, but the attack on Tarwater by the sex pervert becomes something more than an act of gratuitous violence. Furthermore, it seems obvious that in such an interpretation there can be no question of Tarwater's not possessing the free will that a Catholic critic such as Robert O. Bowen declares is absent from the novel. Tarwater is not *fated* to take up the old man's burden of prophecy; he does so because the world, and not fate, compels him to do it. We can also say that he is redeemed—but at a hideous price in suffering. Nor is Divine Justice mocked, as Bowen claims; for what happens to Tarwater happens because of the refusal of those who ostensibly care for the youth to give him the love he requires if he is to be turned from his terrible purpose: "For I the Lord thy God am a jealous God, visiting the iniquities of the fathers upon the children unto the third and fourth generation of them that hate me."

But I desist from theology, and prefer to rest my case on the text of *The Violent Bear It Away*, which contains several scenes which, if the interpretation which I have offered is not admissible, seem oddly tangential to what the novel is then supposed to be about.

*The Violent Bear It Away* is, among other things, a critique of primitive Southern fundamentalism in action; not that Miss O'Connor set out with such a purpose in mind, for I doubt that she did. In such matters the author's conscious intention,

as Austin Warren remarks of Hawthorne and the meaning of
*The Scarlet Letter,* does not possess "any more authority than
that of another critic: it may even, conceivably, have less." [13]
My guess is that Miss O'Connor intended the voice speaking to
Tarwater to be that of the Devil himself, and I doubt that she
was attempting, consciously at any rate, to set up any such
schism as I have proposed between a God of Wrath and a God
of Love. I rather imagine she would have considered that my
emphasis on the scene at the revival and that on the staircase
of the resort was misplaced, and that my insistence upon their
importance was the result of my own unwillingness to believe
in the reality of the Devil—that is to say, of my modern rationalistic secularism. So be it; nevertheless I persist in seeing
this schism, and in believing that if there is confusion, it comes
about in part at least because of a confusion of attitude within
the novel itself. When Miss O'Connor is dealing with modern
secularism, she is scathing in her satire. The scene in which
Rayber attempts to administer intelligence and aptitude tests
to Tarwater is almost too crude to be believable, and the same
is true of the scene in which the schoolmaster tries to show
Tarwater the wonder of modern science by promising him a
ride in an airplane, "the greatest engineering achievement of
man," only to have the youth retort that "a buzzard can fly"
(406). Miss O'Connor even supplies a passage on the unattrac-
tiveness of modern packages of breakfast cereal in contrast to
healthy, nourishing country food. Whenever Rayber is portrayed as the modern rationalist attempting to reason Tarwater
away from his mission, the satire is ruthless and devastating.
But the difficulty is that this is only part of the characterization
of Rayber, and there is also the Rayber who recognizes within
himself the potentiality of emotional irrationality and tries *to
protect himself from it by being scientific and rational.* For this
aspect of Rayber, satire is obviously inappropriate, for the
satirical mode precludes any feeling of compassion, since it di-
minishes the stature of the satirical object. The outcome of
this is that we tend to undervalue the importance of the con-

flict within Rayber, who is too often made the object of contempt rather than pity. It is precisely this failure, I think, which has caused some critics to ignore the importance, for example, of the scene at the revival meeting, and thus to misunderstand where Rayber's real failure lies, which is not in his rationalism as such, but in his inability to counter the hold of the old man's fanaticism upon young Tarwater with the love that the boy craves and needs if he is to be dissuaded from carrying out his mission. The only alternative to a God of Wrath is a God of Love, but so savagely does Miss O'Connor satirize Rayber the rationalist that we have difficulty in seeing his rationalism as the barrier which, erected in defense against the Wrath, keeps out the God of Love as well.

Because Rayber's stature is diminished, Miss O'Connor's depiction of the struggle going on within Tarwater is weakened, and the suspense becomes mostly a matter of whether or not he is going to baptize Bishop. Tarwater also becomes a less complex character, and also a less sympathetic one. The result, I think, is a diminution of the potentialities for genuine tragedy; Tarwater tends to remain a freak. "No one, I think," Walter Sullivan has written, "ever identifies with Flannery O'Connor's people." [14] This is going too far, but it is difficult to sympathize with Tarwater, and for that matter with Rayber as well, when the pity and fear that make for the tragic resolution demand just such identification. In a somewhat different way the same difficulty arises with Hazel Motes in *Wise Blood*. Like Tarwater, Haze is trying to throw off the religious bondage, but cannot do so. The only alternative offered him is the materialism and godlessness of the city of Taulkinham, which he cannot accept however much he would like to do so. But the completely satirical, one-sided picture of the modern city that Miss O'Connor gives is such that we never seriously consider that Haze will succumb. The result is that because the element of choice is removed from Haze's characterization, he remains throughout a grotesque character.

Why is this? I am not so sure but that the reason lies in part at least with Miss O'Connor's attitude, as a Roman Catholic, to Southern Protestant fundamentalism. We have seen that when it comes to a choice between primitive Protestantism and urban secular materialism, Miss O'Connor will come down on the side of Protestantism every time. As noted both in her own statements and in that by Fr. Gustave Weigel, fundamentalist Protestantism and Roman Catholicism share a literal approach to religious dogma. A distinguished Southern historian, Francis B. Simkins, has remarked on this as well; "the strength of the Southern Baptist church," he declared in a discussion of the fundamentalism controversy of the 1920s, "stemmed from the same cause as that of the Roman Catholic church: its utter refusal to compromise with liberal tendencies of other churches." [15] Yet it is possible, I think, to overstress that affinity. It is true that there is agreement on the divinity of Christ, the Virgin Birth, the Redemptive Power, the physical resurrection. But there are also several important differences between Roman Catholicism and rural Southern fundamentalism. The Catholic Church emphatically does not believe in the direct and un-aided revelation of prophecy that is so typical of fundamental-ism; Catholicism is a liturgical faith, and the untutored and frenzied emotionalism, unchecked by dogma and unaided by reason, that characterizes primitive fundamentalism is foreign to the Catholic religious experience. Catholicism does not dis-pense with reason; far from it. For the Catholic, reason is a valuable tool to be used within the larger experience of faith. It is the reason of the secular mind, unaided by dogma and faith, that the Catholic Church opposes. Indeed, Miss O'Connor has been criticized by one Catholic writer for neglecting some-times "to place enough emphasis on reason as a corrective of too much heart." [16]

Whether this objection is valid or not, it is well to keep in mind that however much Miss O'Connor may admire certain aspects of Southern fundamentalism, she is not herself a Southern fundamentalist, and as a Roman Catholic is both ill at ease with the messianic fervor of the direct prophetic revelation, and profoundly suspicious of its consequences.

Therefore, while her fundamentalists may retain the religious spirit in an otherwise secularized society, they are nonetheless and inevitably portrayed as grotesques. Once again, we must not overlook the fact that both Hazel Motes and Francis Marion Tarwater, in the frenzy of their warped religious experience, are driven to commit murder. Nor is Tarwater's fanatical old great-uncle an attractive or sympathetic character, for all that Miss O'Connor may approve of his religious dedication. The violent bear it away in both novels, for they are primitive Southern fundamentalist characters in the fiction of a Southern Roman Catholic author.

The truth is that, in the words of the Episcopal bishop quoted earlier, primitive Southern Protestant fundamentalism is an often violent faith, in which Satan is seemingly more real than God. All too frequently it is the kind of orgiastic, hyper-emotional religion that anyone who has ever lived in the South has heard preached on the numerous little low-wattage radio stations, interspersed with the Hillbilly Hit Parade and the anti-communistic, anti-liberal, Texas-sponsored political harangues, the last-named often delivered by ministers themselves. It is fanatical, intolerant, anti-intellectual; the God of the Old Testament and of the Book of Revelation is there, but the God of the Sermon on the Mount is seldom invoked. And for what the Virgin Mary can mean to the Catholic, there is no room at all. Its prophets agitate and exhort, shout and shriek as they seek to stir up the lagging faithful. However similar some of its tenets may be to that of Roman Catholicism, in its approach, its attitude, its appeal it is profoundly alien and antithetical to the Catholic mind and heart. Or so it seems to me.

What I would suggest is that much of the dramatic tension that makes Flannery O'Connor's fiction so gripping and memorable lies in the insight into religious experience afforded her by her double heritage as both Catholic and Southerner. The two forms of orthodoxy—the primitive fundamentalism of her region, the Roman Catholicism of her faith—work sometimes with and sometimes against each other in a literary counter-point that has enabled her to create some of the most distinguished and exciting fiction of her time.

I keep using the present tense, not the past definite, as if Flannery O'Connor were still with us. And of course she is, for however much those who knew her may miss the friendly, attractive, engaging young woman we used to know, with her fine sense of humor, her superb courage in the face of terrible adversity, she remains with us in her novels and stories which, because they contain so much of Flannery O'Connor, possess the dignity and beauty of lasting art.

## Notes

1. Robert Raymond Brown, "Southern Religion: Mid-Century," in *The Lasting South*, edited by Louis D. Rubin, Jr., and James Jackson Kilpatrick (Chicago: H. Regnery, 1957), p. 138.

2. Walter Sullivan, "The Continuing Renascence: Southern Fiction in the Fifties," in *South: Modern Southern Literature in Its Cultural Setting*, edited by Louis D. Rubin, Jr., and Robert D. Jacobs (Garden City: Doubleday, 1961), p. 380.

3. Flannery O'Connor, "The Role of the Catholic Novelist," *Greyfriar* [Siena Studies in Literature], VII (1964), 8.

4. See Rubin, "Two Ladies of the South," *Sewanee Review*, LXIII (Autumn, 1955), 671-81; and "Flannery O'Connor: A Note on Literary Fashions," *Critique*, II (Fall, 1958), 11-18.

5. Malcolm Cowley, "Introduction" to *The Viking Portable Library Faulkner* (New York: Viking Press, 1946), p. 18.

6. Gustave Weigel, S.J., *Faith and Understanding in America* (New York: Macmillan, 1959), p. 69.

7. Jonathan Baumbach, "The Acid of God's Grace: *Wise Blood* by Flannery O'Connor," in *The Landscape of Nightmare: Studies in the Contemporary American Novel* (New York: New York University Press, 1965), pp. 87-100.

8. Flannery O'Connor, "The Role of the Catholic Novelist," p. 11.

9. Robert O. Bowen, "Hope vs. Despair in the New Gothic Novel" [rev. of *The Violent Bear It Away*], *Renascence*, XIII (Spring, 1961), 147-52.

10. Rainulf A. Stelzmann, "Shock and Orthodoxy: An Interpretation of Flannery O'Connor's Novels and Short Stories," *Xavier University Studies*, II (March, 1963), 4-21.

11. *Ibid.*, 5n.

12. Flannery O'Connor, "The Role of the Catholic Novelist," p. 8.

13. Austin Warren, "*The Scarlet Letter*: A Literary Exercise in Moral Theology," *Southern Review*, I, New Series (1965), 26.

14. Sullivan, in Rubin and Jacobs, eds., *South*, p. 379.

15. Francis Butler Simkins, *A History of the South*, third ed. (New York: Knopf, 1963), p. 599.

16. *Cf.* Warren Eugene Freeman, S.J., "The Social and Theological Implications in Flannery O'Connor's *A Good Man Is Hard to Find*," unpublished M.A. thesis (University of North Carolina, 1962), p. 42.

# Her Rue with a Difference

Flannery O'Connor and the Southern Literary Tradition

C. HUGH HOLMAN

NATHANIEL HAWTHORNE once stated his intention "to achieve a novel that should evolve some deep lesson and should possess physical substance enough to stand alone." [1] He was describing the ambition of many writers of fiction, but his remark is peculiarly appropriate to the work of Flannery O'Connor, a brilliantly gifted writer whose death at the age of thirty-nine silenced one of the finest voices of American fiction. Hawthorne's statement is particularly useful in looking at Miss O'Connor's work because of his separation—or at least his distinction—between meaning and matter, a distinction often overlooked by the numerous reviewers who have seen Flannery O'Connor as simply another writer of Southern Gothic and have easily grouped her with other Southern writers of the grotesque such as Erskine Caldwell, Carson McCullers, Truman Capote, and Tennessee Williams. Indeed, Caroline Gordon once derisively quoted the assertion of a critic that "if the name of the author were deleted it would be hard to tell a story by Miss O'Connor from a story by Truman Capote, Carson McCullers or Tennessee Williams." [2]

However wrong that critic was, there certainly can be little question that Miss O'Connor was a Southern writer. The South, particularly that of piedmont Georgia and eastern Tennessee, is what she called her "country." "The country that the writer is concerned with in the most objective way is," she said, ". . . the region that most immediately surrounds him, or simply the country, with its body of manners, that he knows well enough to employ." [3] Out of this South and its people she quarried the "physical substance" which gave her work the living elements of successful fiction.

But, as has been obvious to all but the most unperceptive of her critics, this "physical substance" for her was not an end in itself; she hungered passionately for meaning and worked hard to "evolve" from her country "some deep lesson." Here, too, she was a part of a "Southern literary tradition." For if she seemed in immediate subject matter to belong to the "school of the Southern Gothic," she seemed also to find in the Southern experience a lesson for the present, as did the Agrarians, or a cosmic truth, as did the apocalyptic mythologizers like Faulkner. Such association with any Southern "school," whether it be Agrarian or that preoccupied, as she said, "with everything deformed and grotesque," [4] irritated her. She declared, "The woods are full of regional writers, and it is the great horror of every serious Southern writer that he will become one of them." [5] I not only sympathize with her attitude; I also find her relation to the Southern literary tradition to be unusual and illuminating both about her and about the tradition itself. Indeed, in looking at her native Georgia, like many modern Southerners, Miss O'Connor's vision was touched with rue, but she wore her "rue with a difference"—a difference that helps to define her essential quality and to give us a deeper insight into her "country," both of soil and spirit.

Geographically, hers was a special South, remote from the moss-draped melancholy great oaks and the stable social order of the Atlantic seaboard and equally distant from the tropical lushness and fecundity of the gulf-coast Deep South. She knew and wrote of piedmont Georgia and eastern Tennessee—a rolling, sparsely wooded land where both the spring freshets and the ravishing plow pierce its surface to leave gaping wounds of dark red clay. It is cotton country, made up of small farms, small towns, and widely-spaced small cities—a country at the mercy of capricious weather and the vicissitudes of the cotton market, which has been in a fluctuating state but one that has always remained depressed since the 1920s. It is a land wracked by diseases peculiar to poverty, by a vicious sharecropper system, by little education, and a superstitious, intense, pietistic but non-theological religious passion. Hers is not the South of the Virginia Tidewater or the Carolina low-country, regions that are nominally Episcopal in religion, aristocratic in dream if not in fact, and tied to a past culture that reverenced learning, practiced law, and dreamed of a republican government of merit founded upon the doctrines of the eighteenth-century enlightenment.

Miss O'Connor's segment of the South was settled, in large measure, by the Scotch-Irish who came down the inland cattle trails from Pennsylvania. By 1790 the Scotch-Irish represented over a quarter of a million Americans. They had entered principally through the ports of Philadelphia, Chester, or New Castle, and had followed the Great Valley westward for about a hundred miles, until tall mountains blocked their trail. Then they had turned south into Virginia, the Carolinas, Tennessee, and Georgia. They were a poverty-stricken, harsh, impetuous people, with a deep sense of integrity, a tendency to make their own laws, and to worship God with individual and singular fervor. Once in the Southern piedmont, they fanned out to encompass the region, and to help define its qualities, among whose most noticeable characteristics was a widespread social crudity marked, as even the sympathetic historians of the Scotch-Irish point out, by brutal fights, animal cruelty, and folk hilarity.[6] The journal of the Anglican Reverend Charles Woodmason is a graphic account of the shocking effect which this primitive life made upon a Tidewater minister who visited it and saw its chief characteristics as lawlessness, vile manners, ignorance, slovenliness, and primitive emotionalism in religion.[7] These people's pragmatic frugality, their oversimplified

—almost folk-version—Calvinistic religion, and their intense individualism formed a distinct but not always attractive culture. Here, in the foothills near the early rises of the mountains, the Scotch-Irish were joined by the refugees and malcontents of the established seaboard society to form a harsh and unmannered world.

There has not been a time since the eighteenth century when this piedmont South has lacked chroniclers, and there has been a remarkable unanimity of opinion and attitude toward its inhabitants by its recorders. William Byrd in his *History of the Dividing Line* (1728) and *A Journey to the Land of Eden* (1733) portrayed back-country North Carolinians with a detached amusement and a sense of their comic grotesqueness. Augustus Baldwin Longstreet described these people in the sketches which he wrote for newspapers in the 1820s and 1830s and collected as *Georgia Scenes* in 1835. Here the detached view of a cultivated lawyer and judge established a vantage point which gave aesthetic distance to his portraits of the cruel, unlearned, but shrewd denizens of the piedmont, weighing these people against the implicit concept of the ordered seaboard society which Judge Longstreet revered. As a result the figures in *Georgia Scenes* are comic grotesques. The early novels of the Southern frontier describe these same kinds of people and similarly judge them against an aristocratic social order, a method common to William Gilmore Simms's "Border Romances"—notably *Guy Rivers* (1834), which is laid in Miss O'Connor's native Georgia.

In the local color movement of the latter part of the nineteenth century, three Souths existed—the plantation South of Thomas Nelson Page, the Deep South of George Washington Cable and Kate Chopin, and the Tennessee-Georgia South of writers like "Charles Egbert Craddock" (Mary Noallies Murphree). And three differing attitudes were presented: Page's was an apologia through the portrayal of a glorious past, Cable's a social concern through an impassioned attack on the social and racial evils of his world, and Miss Murphree's a whimsical interest through a summer visitor's condescension to the illiterate Tennessee mountaineer.

Faulkner's *Absalom, Absalom!* has a theme pertinent to these issues, and is in one sense at least almost an historical allegory of these three Souths. In it Thomas Sutpen, from the Virginia piedmont, encounters Tidewater aristocracy which he admires but to which he is refused entrance, and he goes to Mississippi, by way of the Caribbean, to attempt to create on Sutpen's Hundred by violence, greed, and lust, the outward signs of an inner grace which he can envy but cannot understand or truly possess.

It is with these piedmont people whose literary representation has always been as grotesques that Miss O'Connor deals; they constitute the "physical substance" out of which she fashioned her vision of reality. In our time much these same groups of Southerners have been the subject matter of Erskine Caldwell, Carson McCullers, and the Southern Gothic School in general.

The representation of the grotesque is a characteristic of much twentieth-century writing, Southern and otherwise. In a fruitful and provocative essay on "The Grotesque: An American Genre," William Van O'Connor, who includes Miss O'Connor among the writers he discusses, states that the representation of an inverted world in which "what most of us would take to be normal is presented as monstrous" results from the fact that "the old agricultural system depleted the land and poverty breeds abnormality; in many cases people were living with a code that was no longer applicable, and this meant a detachment from reality and loss of vitality." [8] Although he sees "clear antecedents" in Edgar Allan Poe and finds the genre practiced by Caldwell, Faulkner, Robert Penn Warren, Eudora Welty, Carson McCullers, and Tennessee Williams, all of whom certainly use Southern grotesques, his emphasis on a decayed order and lost wealth, an emphasis pertinent to many Southern writers, does not seem to apply very well to Miss O'Connor's works.

He comes much closer to her position when he quotes Thomas Mann on the grotesque as resulting from the fact that modern art "has ceased to recognize the categories of tragic and comic. . . . It sees life as tragi-comedy, with the result that the grotesque is its most genuine style . . . the only guise in which the sublime may appear." [9] Miss O'Connor seemed to have the same view of the grotesque. In a preface written in 1962 for a reprinting of *Wise Blood* she said, "It is a comic novel about a Christian *malgré lui,* and as such, very serious, for all comic novels that are any good must be about matters of life and death" (8). For, while there is no question that Flannery O'Connor deals with Southern characters who are grotesques, the grotesque element in her work has other sources than the heat of social anger which warms Erskine Caldwell's or the sense of the absurdity of human existence which shapes the grotesqueries of our young existentialists.

She is more nearly central to the Southern literary tradition in her persistent passion for order. Confronted with a modern, mechanized, scientifically-oriented world, the leading literary spokesmen for the South have usually shared the discomfort that most producers of humane art experience in the presence of the mechanical, and, like the twelve at Vanderbilt in 1930, they "tend to support a Southern way of life against what may be called the American or prevailing way." [10] Almost all artists feel a hunger for meaning, a need for structure, and rage for order in existence, and believe that the human spirit should never calmly surrender its endless search for order. Twentieth-century writers confronted by the spectacle of the mechanized culture of America have taken many different roads to many different regions of the spirit. Some have sought in art itself a kind of solipsistic answer to the need of order and thus have made a religion of art. Some have sought in activist movements bent on social change a way to establish meaning in the world. The Southerner, predisposed to look backward as a result of his concern with the past,[11] has tended to impose a desire for a social structure that reflects moral principles and he has tried to see in the past of his region at least the shadowy outlines of a viable and admirable moral-social world. Allen Tate, in 1952, in a retrospective glance at the Agrarian movement said:

> I never thought of Agrarianism as a *restoration* of anything in the Old South; I saw it as something to be created, as I think it will in the long run be created as the result of a profound change, not only in the South, but elsewhere, in the moral and religious outlook of western man. . . . What I had in mind twenty years ago . . . presupposes, with us, a prior order, the order of a unified Christendom. The Old South perpetuated many of the virtues of such an order; but to try to "revive" the Old South, and to build a wall around it, would be a kind of idolatry; it would prefer the accident to the substance. If there is a useful program that we might undertake in the South, would it not be towards the greater unity of the varieties of Southern Protestantism, with the ultimate aim the full unity of all Christians? We are told by our Northern friends that the greatest menace to the South is ignorance; but there is even greater ignorance of the delusion of progressive enlightenment.[12]

Miss O'Connor was generally in sympathy with such views of the Agrarians. When she makes statements such as this one from "The Fiction Writer and His Country" she seems almost to be echoing their beliefs: "The anguish that most of us have observed for some time now has been caused not by the fact that the South is alienated from the rest of the country, but by the fact that it is not alienated enough, that every day we are getting more and more like the rest of the country, that we are being forced out, not only of our many sins but of our few virtues."[13] And certainly one could hardly call a friend of science the creator of Hulga Hopewell, in "Good Country People," who has a Ph.D. in philosophy, a wooden leg, and a willingness to be seduced by a fake Bible salesman who steals the leg and leaves her betrayed and helpless in the hay loft. Hulga underlines this statement in one of the books that she endlessly reads and marks up:

Science, on the other hand, has to assert its soberness and seriousness afresh and declare that it is concerned solely with what-is.
Nothing—how can it be for science anything but a horror and a
phantasm? If science is right, then one thing stands firm: science
wishes to know nothing of nothing. Such is after all the strictly
scientific approach to Nothing. We know it by wishing to know
nothing of Nothing [248].

The girl, like others of Miss O'Connor's few intellectuals, declares to the Bible salesman, "We are all damned . . . but
some of us have taken off our blindfolds and see that there's
nothing to see. It's a kind of salvation" (258).[14] Similarly Rayber, in *The Violent Bear It Away*, with all his knowledge seems
to be rendered more helpless by all he learns, and falls the
semi-credulous victim of a lustful child who is not really a
spokesman for love but simply for the power of emotion.

"The Displaced Person," a short story that recounts the in-
trusion into a widow's farm of an efficient and effective displaced person, is typical of the way in which Miss O'Connor's
situations can be read in frames not unlike those of the Agrarians. Here the "displaced person" may be taken as symbolic
of the mechanical world intruding itself from the outside to
disrupt the "order" of a Southern farm.[15] Read this way the
story is not unlike Robert Penn Warren's "The Patented Gate
and the Mean Hamburger,"[16] and yet a careful examination of
Miss O'Connor's tone and action makes one, I think, suspicious
of such a reading, a suspicion confirmed for the reader by the
fact that Mrs. McIntyre, the widow who owns the farm, rejects its chance of salvation by Mr. Guizac, effectively destroys
him, and declares to Father Flynn, who has been his friend
and advocate, "As far as I'm concerned . . . Christ was just
another D.P." (294).

Flannery O'Connor's work is sufficiently similar to that of
her contemporaries in the South to justify our feeling that,
in one sense at least, she shares not only a common subject
but many common concerns. She has other characteristics in
common with her Southern contemporaries that are worth men-

tioning. For her, as for them—and, indeed, for any depicter of an agrarian culture—the social unit is the family. For her, as it seemingly did for Faulkner and Wolfe, concrete expressions of meaning seem to come in relatively small actions and limited scenes. Wolfe is most impressive as an artist in his short stories and short novels, and much of Faulkner's best work appeared in brief episodes which were later woven into novels. Miss O'Connor, too, is better as a writer of short stories than she is as a novelist. To examine, for example, *Wise Blood* as a novel after looking at the original appearance of some of its parts as short stories is to question to some degree her wisdom in attempting the larger organization.

She also has an awareness of the caste structures that a relatively fixed social order produces and which have fascinated many Southern writers, even though she does not often write of any except her "poor whites." For example, in her story "Revelation," she says:

> Sometimes Mrs. Turpin occupied herself at night naming the classes of people. On the bottom of the heap were most colored people, not the kind she would have been if she had been one, but most of them; then next to them—not above, just away from —were the white-trash; then above them were the home-owners, and above them the home-and-land owners, to which she and Claud belonged. Above she and Claud were people with a lot of money and much bigger houses and much more land. But here the complexity of it would begin to bear in on her, for some of the people with a lot of money were common and ought to be below she and Claud and some of the people who had good blood had lost their money and had to rent and then there were colored people who owned their homes and land as well. There was a colored dentist in town who had two red Lincolns and a swimming pool and a farm with registered white-face cattle on it.[17]

Miss O'Connor's sense that this kind of class distinction is meaningless is made plain here, and such things seem finally to be of much less interest to her than they are to most Southern writers.

But these, after all, are largely quibbles. The crucial similarities and differences lie elsewhere. They lie with the concern she has for a religious order, and her most significant differences with her Southern contemporaries are in the same area.

The crucial difference between Miss O'Connor and most of her fellow Southerners lies in a simple fact, which she seldom passed up an opportunity to emphasize. She was a Catholic novelist in the Protestant South.[18] Indeed, she speaks of the writing of fiction in terms of religious vocation, and she declares, "I see from the standpoint of Christian orthodoxy. This means that for me the meaning of life is centered in our Redemption by Christ and that what I see in the world I see in its relation to that." [19] Hence the order she sees in the world, the order which redeems it from chaos and gives it community, is fundamentally religious. And the tragedy she sees is the failure of the seeking soul to find rest in an adequate God.

The Agrarians who sought an ordered past had sought it in a social world and a political-economic system. Both John Crowe Ransom and Allen Tate, however, had perceived that such an order needed a religious basis but neither of them believed that such a basis had existed in the South. Ransom's *God Without Thunder* (1930) is an heretical (he assumes that God is an anthropomorphic myth created by man) defense of a certain kind of orthodoxy, the orthodoxy that makes the old Hebraic God of thunder and wrath—unpredictable, awesome, awful, unappeasable—the potent and controlling force in the world. The modern God, on the other hand, Ransom thought to be a product of our age which is incapable of the wonder, the awe, or the sense of mystery which can give meaning to the world.

Tate felt that the South should have been Catholic; his essay on religion in *I'll Take My Stand* is an argument with his fellow Southerners against establishing an ordered world that lacks a religious frame. A social order, he felt, must be undergirded and crowned by a firm and ritualistic religion if it is to be good. Tate himself later embraced the Catholic faith, but he knew that both the unified Christendom which he dreamed that the South had had in the past and that which his South knew in the present were not very far from the intense, individualistic, pietistic Protestantism of those like Stonewall Jackson, whose biography Tate had written. It found expression in the nontheological passion of Methodists, Baptists, and Holiness evangelists. The anguish of the soul, he felt, could not be assuaged by the introspective groping of the individual. Yet he was, with the exception of his wife, Caroline Gordon, and Ransom, unique in this persistent cry for a religious structure for his world.

Tate's view of the religion of the South was historically accurate. As James McBride Dabbs has recently noted, ". . . the formal religion of the South did not grow out of its complete life and therefore could not crown that life with meaning." [20] As I have argued elsewhere, the South knew and knows an intense, individualistic puritanism.[21] Even in the Deep South, where the religious culture of New Orleans might have made itself felt, Faulkner, attempting a representation of a theological view in *Light in August,* turns from the ranks of the prolific Baptists and Methodists and makes his religious figures members of the numerically minor sect of Presbyterians, who alone of Southern Protestants retained a discernible vestige of a dogma.[22] Thus the region lacked a religious orientation that could establish a meaningful community, while it was justly known as a "Bible Belt" of individual religious fanatics.

It is this aspect of the South—and pretty clearly by only slight extrapolation, of the modern world—which is, I believe, Miss O'Connor's obsessive theme. In what other modern writer is there a comparable pattern to Miss O'Connor's disturbed and desperate seekers? Where else do we find so many men and women for whom, as she expressed it, "belief in Christ is . . . a matter of life and death"? (8)

The fact of Jesus believed in as a continuing divine force is at the root of her world. For the fact of Jesus demands that

we do something about Him. In "A Good Man Is Hard to Find,"
the old lady asks the murdering Misfit why he doesn't pray,
and he gives the modern answer, "I don't want no hep. . . .
I'm doing all right by myself" (141). But he later declares of
Jesus,

> He thown everything off balance. If He did what He said, then
> it's nothing for you to do but thow away everything and follow
> Him, and if He didn't, then it's nothing for you to do but enjoy
> the few minutes you got left the best way you can—by killing
> somebody or burning down his house or doing some other mean-
> ness to him. No pleasure but meanness [142].

In "The Artificial Nigger," Mr. Head, Miss O'Connor wrote,

> stood appalled, judging himself with the thoroughness of God,
> while the action of mercy covered his pride like a flame and con-
> sumed it. He had never thought himself a great sinner before but
> he saw now that his true depravity had been hidden from him lest
> it cause him despair. He realized that he was forgiven for sins from
> the beginning of time, when he had conceived in his own heart
> the sin of Adam, until the present, when he had denied poor
> Nelson. He saw that no sin was too monstrous for him to claim as
> his own, and since God loved in proportion as He forgave, he felt
> ready at that instant to enter Paradise [213–14].

Mrs. Shortley, in "The Displaced Person," had

> never given much thought to the devil for she felt that religion
> was essentially for those people who didn't have the brains to
> avoid evil without it. For people like herself, for people of gump-
> tion, it was a social occasion providing the opportunity to sing;
> but if she had ever given it much thought, she would have con-
> sidered the devil the head of it and God the hanger-on [270].

"Christ in the conversation," Miss O'Connor says of Mrs. Mc-
Intyre, "embarrassed her the way sex had her mother" (291).
The mystic Hazel Motes, in *Wise Blood*, is an inverted saint,
preaching the "Church Without Christ," and willing to die

like a martyr to deny the power and reality of Jesus.

James McBride Dabbs says, ". . . at the deepest level the Southern white was an individualistic Protestant modern, who did not really believe in community, who did not bring the community before God or hold his membership in it under God, but who faced God in an awful, breathtaking aloneness." [23]

The representation of these lost and passionate seekers becomes naturally a representation of the grotesque. The folks of Miss O'Connor's country are distorted and disturbed because their deepest selves, she believes, seek with undeniable passion a meaning and order which the Protestant South cannot give. "My own feeling," she declared

> is that writers who see by the light of their Christian faith will have, in these times, the sharpest eyes for the grotesque, for the perverse, and for the unacceptable. In some cases, these writers may be unconsciously infected with the Manichaean spirit of the times and suffer the much discussed disjunction between sensibility and belief, but I think that more often the reason for this attention to the perverse is the difference between their beliefs and the beliefs of the audience. . . . The novelist with Christian concerns will find in modern life distortions which are repugnant to him, and his problem will be to make these appear as distortions to an audience which is used to seeing them as natural; and he may well be forced to take ever more violent means to get his vision across to this audience.[24]

A writer's country, she maintained, was both the inner and the outer reality. It seems to me that of her country we may declare its outer self plainly and unmistakably Southern, its rage for order common to the twentieth-century Southern literary concern, and the reality against which she ultimately judges it to be one which goes far to indict the South for its spiritual sterility, for the way it emasculates its saints and sentimentizes its poets.

"Our souls," St. Augustine said, "are restless till they find rest in Thee." Flannery O'Connor's restless souls belong to people primitive in mind and Protestant in religion, who with all their difference, share a common, deep, and personal awareness of the awful and awesome presence and power of God in the world. Like Francis Thompson in "The Hound of Heaven" no matter how much they flee "Him down the labyrinthine ways," they cannot deny either His reality or His intolerable demands. Living in a world not ordered to an adequate sense of the power and presence of God, they seek either to deny Him or to pervert Him, and thus they become grotesque and unnatural. The human hunger for love cannot be satisfied with hatred; the human passion for order cannot willingly accept disorder as the principle of its universe; the ultimate dignity of man does not lie in his own hands, and when he tries to take violent hold of it, he destroys himself. That, it seems to me, is the anti-existentialist message that a brave and thoughtful Catholic woman gave to a South hungry, as it has been for a century and a half, for a stable order and a sensible meaning. Because she was Southern, she used the South as matter and addressed it as audience. But what she said transcends her region and speaks with the authority of art to the great world outside.

## Notes

1. "The Old Manse," *Mosses from an Old Manse*, in *The Riverside Edition of the Complete Works of Nathaniel Hawthorne* (Boston: Houghton Mifflin Company, 1883), II, p. 13.

2. "Flannery O'Connor's *Wise Blood*," *Critique*, II (Fall, 1958), 3.

3. "The Fiction Writer and His Country," in *The Living Novel, a Symposium*, edited by Granville Hicks (New York: Macmillan, 1957), p. 159.

4. *Ibid.*

5. *Ibid.*, p. 160.

6. James G. Leyburn, in *The Scotch-Irish: A Social History* (Chapel Hill: University of North Carolina Press, 1962), describes in great detail the migration, settlement, and customs of this group, which is very important to the understanding of the South but which is seldom looked at. Of particular usefulness to me have been his treatments of Scotch-Irish settlements and frontier society, pp. 184-295.

7. The Reverend Mr. Woodmason's journal has been edited by Richard J. Hooker and published as *The Carolina Backcountry on the Eve of the Revolution* (Chapel Hill: University of North Carolina Press, 1953). This primary document emphasizes the almost unbelievable difference between the Low-Country and Up-Country Southerner.

8. *The Grotesque: An American Genre and Other Essays* (Carbondale: Southern Illinois University Press, 1962), pp. 13, 6.

9. *Ibid.*, p. 5.

10. Twelve Southerners, *I'll Take My Stand* (New York: Harper & Brothers, 1930), p. ix.

11. Louis D. Rubin, Jr., "Southern Literature: The Historical Image," in *South: Modern Southern Literature in Its Cultural Setting*, edited by Louis D. Rubin, Jr., and Robert D. Jacobs (Garden City: Doubleday, 1961), pp. 29-47.

12. Allen Tate, in "The Agrarians Today: A Symposium," *Shenandoah*, III (Summer, 1952), 28-29.

13. "The Fiction Writer and His Country, " p. 159.

14. Bartlett C. Jones, in "Depth Psychology and Literary Study," *Midcontinent American Studies Journal*, V (Fall, 1964), 50-56, gives an interesting and illuminating Freudian reading of this story, while never losing sight of Miss O'Connor's non-Freudian intention in writing the tale.

15. Louis D. Rubin, Jr., suggests, although he does not accept, such a reading. See Rubin's review, "Two Ladies of the South," *Sewanee Review*, LXIII (Autumn, 1955), 671-81; his article, "Flannery O'Connor: A Note on Literary Fashions," *Critique*, II (Fall, 1958), 11-18; and his volume *The Faraway Country* (Seattle: University of Washington Press, 1963), p. 238, where he says that The Displaced Person "has irretrievably disrupted the customary patterns of Southern rural society."

16. In Robert Penn Warren, *The Circus in the Attic and Other Stories* (New York: Harcourt, Brace, 1947).

17. "Revelation," *Sewanee Review*, LXXII (Spring, 1964), 181-82, and *Everything*, 195-196.

18. See, for example, her essay, "The Role of the Catholic Novelist," *Greyfriar* [Siena Studies in Literature], VII (1964), or her essay, "The Fiction Writer and His Country," in *The Living Novel*.

19. "The Fiction Writer and His Country," pp. 161-62.

20. *Who Speaks for the South?* (New York: Funk & Wagnalls, 1964), p. 113.

21. "The Southerner as American Writer," in *The Southerner as American*, edited by Charles G. Sellers, Jr. (Chapel Hill: University of North Carolina Press, 1960), p. 193.

22. C. Hugh Holman, "The Unity of Faulkner's *Light in August*," *PMLA*, LXXIII (March, 1958), 155-66.

23. *Who Speaks for the South?*, p. 258.

24. "The Fiction Writer and His Country," pp. 162-63.

# The Novelist as Prophet

## P. ALBERT DUHAMEL

IN 1930 twelve unreconstructed Southerners rallied together and published a collection of essays in defense of Southern, crotchety individualism against the encroachments of Northern, homogenizing industrialism. John Crowe Ransom's opening essay, "Reconstructed But Unregenerate," defined the defense perimeter of *I'll Take My Stand* with an eloquent plea for the recognition of the greater authenticity and promise of a Southern culture that was conservative, agrarian, and humanistic. He ventured the hope that "some prophet may even find it possible to expect that it will yet rise again." [1]

In her second novel, *The Violent Bear It Away,* published just thirty years after *I'll Take My Stand,* Flannery O'Connor dramatized the making of a prophet whose mission was the same as the function of her novel—to burn the South's eyes clean so that it could recognize its true heritage. In his contribution to *I'll Take My Stand,* Andrew Nelson Lytle had also been concerned with the possible coming of prophets. He had warned the South against the heresies that would "roll from the tongues of false prophets," and admonished them to remember that true "prophets do not come from cities, promising riches and store clothes. They have always come from the wilderness, stinking of goats and running with lice and telling of a different sort of treasure, one a corporation head would not understand." [2] This is just the way *The Violent Bear It Away* ends, with a picture of the true prophet: his clothes fouled, his eyes singed, his forehead smeared with dirt from his great-uncle's grave, moving toward "the dark city, where the children of God lay sleeping" to tell them of the only satisfaction of man's enduring hunger and to warn them "OF THE TERRIBLE SPEED OF MERCY" (447).

*The Violent Bear It Away* and *I'll Take My Stand* share a similar purpose, "to aid the South in its reorientation and in a return to its true philosophy," [3] as well as many common attitudes. The collection of essays brought together conveniently in one volume several of the Fugitives, especially Ransom, Tate, and Warren, who had a great influence in shaping the mind and art of Flannery O'Connor. But her art had a larger purpose and it is only the possibility of clarifying that purpose and increasing the realization of her achievement which can justify the juxtaposing of art and propaganda. Though the essays of the Fugitives may represent somewhat the matrix from which Flannery O'Connor's vision developed, she certainly intended much more than to update the concerns of a generation ago by substituting scientism for industrialism and she certainly addressed herself to problems larger than those of a challenged sectionalism. Her definition of the prophetic vision is at once methodological and substantive: a definition of how the novelist must "see" if he is to have something to say, and a definition of a system of values which alone can make our culture, both Northern and Southern, viable.

Flannery O'Connor was occasionally amused by articles in the Catholic press which presumed to define what she and other Catholic novelists should "see" and write about. As a Catholic and a novelist, she had her own theories about the novel but she talked and wrote about them very infrequently, always preferring doing to talking. One of the few times she did discuss her ideas about the novel publicly and at any length was in a talk delivered at the College of Saint Teresa in Winona, Minnesota in 1960 just after she had finished writing *The Violent Bear It Away*. In that talk, her sense of humor was apparent in the way she referred to one of these articles which suggested that some Catholic novelist ought to "explore the possibilities inherent in factors," or, failing that, at least attempt a *positive* novel on life in the seminary. In her comments on these suggestions, she seemed to reflect an opinion that the novel was not to be defined in terms of its proper subject matter nor the novelist in terms of his attitudes. The novel she characterized as an expression of "prophetic vision" and the novelist as a kind of prophet who was a "realist of distances." She expanded on these insights a bit and concluded by applying them specifically to a definition of a novelist's function: "In the novelist's case, it is a matter of seeing things with their extensions of meaning and thus of seeing far things close up." [4] The prophetic vision proper to the novelist, therefore, is a paradoxical double vision which can simultaneously keep in focus the universal implications of a present particular as well as the potential particularization of a universal eternal.

This conception of the novelist's vision is reminiscent of Allen Tate's definition of the nature of metaphor in his essay "Tension in Poetry," first published in the *Southern Review* in 1938 but since then frequently reprinted and widely discussed. It was here that Tate first explained how he had arrived at an insight into the nature of metaphor by means of another metaphor. By lopping off the prefix from two logical terms, "extension" and "intension," he had been left with the word "tension" which he thought was a good summary of the peculiar way in which the poetic vision found expression. The following three sentences seem to come as close as any in the essay to summarizing what he was attempting.

What I am saying, of course, is that the meaning of poetry is its "tension," the full organized body of all the extension and intension that we can find in it. The remotest figurative significance that we can derive does not invalidate the extensions of the literal statement. Or we may begin with the literal statement and by stages develop the complications of metaphor: at every stage we may pause to state the meaning so far apprehended, and at every stage the meaning will be coherent.[5]

Thus Allen Tate in defining poetry and Flannery O'Connor in defining the novel used the same principle, the manner of "seeing" and expressing, and also used interchangeable terms. Her "seeing of near things with their extensions of meaning" and seeing "of far things close up" is the simultaneous vision in "tension" of Tate's intension and extensibility of terms.

As a corollary to this common conception of the nature of true artistic vision, Flannery O'Connor and Allen Tate also shared a common attitude toward its opposite, half-vision, or partial vision which refuses to see things whole and entire. The central thesis of Allen Tate's contribution to I'll Take My Stand, an essay entitled "Remarks on the Southern Religion," is that religion is a holoscopic view of reality, and any attempt to claim that religion is interested only in certain aspects of reality is a false view of the nature of religion. The essay several times refers to a comparison between a false, partial view of a horse and a distorted conception of religion which would view it as prescinding from some aspects of reality.

> This modern mind sees only half of the horse—that half which may become a dynamo, or an automobile, or any other horse-powered machine. If this mind had much respect for the full-dimensioned, grass-eating horse, it would never have invented the engine which represents only half of him. The religious mind, on the other hand, has this respect; it wants the whole horse, and it will be satisfied with nothing less.[6]

The Violent Bear It Away can be read as the story of the making of a prophet who comes to realize, in Tate's words, that "abstraction is the death of religion no less than the death of anything else," and that the only true religion, again using Tate's words, "is quite simply supernaturalism or the naive religion of the entire horse."[7]

The dialect of total or prophetic vision is the dialogue of the metaphor, the systematic interplay of symbolic images wherein the specific contains under tension an analogous universal. As Tate repeatedly used images, concrete examples in his essays to suggest the larger implications of his position, so the novel, in a more sustained and "tense" way, employs a series of images to convey ultimate meanings through present sensibilities. It is this methodology which differentiates art from propaganda. As Tate put it, "Images are only to be contemplated, and perhaps the act of contemplation after long exercise initiates a habit of imitation, and the setting up of absolute standards which are less formulas for action than an interior discipline of the mind."[8] *The Violent Bear It Away* is at once a defense of the prophetic vision of the novelist and a demonstration of how it can set up the beginnings of an interior discipline which might enable its readers to face up to the totality of nature and abandon pusillanimity where principles are at stake.

The "tension" in the novel takes two dimensions: the vertical and the horizontal. The vertical "tension" is the result of the development of characters and images which constantly tend to polarize either as particulars or universals. The horizontal "tension" is generated by a plot which has all the qualities Aristotle argued were essential to a unified *mythos*: clearly marked conflict, a peripeteia, and a significant anagnoresis. This sustained "tension" in two dimensions is perhaps the novel's most distinctive artistic achievement.

The novel's protagonist, Francis Marion Tarwater, is first of all an interesting individual with his own detailed history. Born prematurely as the result of an accident which took his mother's life, he was reared in a Georgia clearing known as Powderhead by a great-uncle who "taught him Figures, Reading, Writing, and History beginning with Adam expelled from the Garden and going on down through the presidents to Herbert Hoover[9] and on in speculation toward the Second Coming and the Day of Judgment" (305). But Francis Marion Tarwater is always presented in a way which simultaneously suggests his more general significance like a character in a morality play. Like Everyman he responds only to his last name and the name suggests that he, like all men, was tarred by the brush of original sin and redeemed by the waters of baptism. Whatever happens to him in the novel happens in a way intended to suggest that he is at once retracing old routes and pioneering for those to come after. Tarwater stands for man, a creature neither wholly bad nor entirely good. In *I'll Take My Stand*, Lyle H. Lanier had summarized the Christian view of man as of "a personality endowed with freedom and convicted of sin; his earthly sojourn . . . a period in which he should purge himself of sin through faith, in order to return to heaven at the end of it." [10] This is the view of man the species which supervenes upon the picture of man the individual as he develops in the novel and it is an acceptable approximation of the gist of the teachings of Tarwater's great-uncle.

The great-uncle, Mason Tarwater, the builder, who had taught Francis Marion Tarwater universal history had also taught the boy his own personal, individual history beginning with the great-uncle's own sister, the boy's grandmother, who had borne two children: a girl, promiscuous at eighteen, who became the boy's mother, and a boy, Rayber, who grew up to become a schoolteacher. When Tarwater's mother died, the schoolteacher set out to rescue him from Powderhead so that he could teach him the true history of the human race and administer a corrective to the great-uncle's prophetic view of history. The schoolteacher hoped to "stretch the boy's mind by introducing him to his ancestor, the fish, and to all the great wastes of unexplored time" (387). These two characters, the great-uncle, Mason Tarwater, and the schoolteacher-uncle, Rayber, are also fully realized individuals within the terms of the novel, but about them also cluster a group of attitudes symbol-

izing, as do their two opposed views of history, opposed phi-
losophies and theologies. Between these two characters and
what they stand for, the young boy, like Everyman, must make
a choice.

Tarwater has to make his own choice because even with the
help of a sentimental social worker, whom Rayber later married
and who presented him with an idiot son, ironically called
Bishop, the schoolteacher failed to kidnap him from Powderhead. The schoolteacher failed in his attempt because at critical moments "he could never take action." The great-uncle,
crotchety, passionate, violent—in that order—carried the day
because he always preferred doing to talking. The great-uncle
seems like an attempt to realize the kind of character suggested
by John Crowe Ransom in the opening essay of *I'll Take My
Stand*. Mason Tarwater was, in Ransom's words, one of those
"unreconstructed Southerners who persist in their regard for
a certain terrain, a certain history, and a certain inherited way
of living." [11] The scene of the attempted rescue seems like an
expansion of the following vignette taken from the Ransom
essay.

> In the country districts great numbers of these broken-down
> Southerners are still to be seen in patched blue-jeans, sitting on
> ancestral fences, shotguns across their laps and hound-dogs at
> their feet, surveying their unkempt acres while they comment
> shrewdly on the ways of God.[12]

When the schoolteacher, accompanied by his fiancée, a social
worker, came to Powderhead to rescue Tarwater, the uncle is
described as watching them coming through the unkempt corn
patches, waiting until the schoolteacher put his foot on the
front step and then shooting and wounding him. Later the
great-uncle would frequently remind the boy: "I saved you
to be free, your own self" (312); it was because he acted and
shot the schoolteacher that Tarwater could remain in Powderhead "a rich man, knowing the Truth, in the freedom of the
Lord Jesus Christ" (349).

The action of the novel proper begins with the death of the great-uncle at the age of eighty-four. He had enjoined upon the boy only one obligation, to see to it that he was properly buried: "I taken you and raised you and saved you from that ass in town and now all I'm asking in return is when I die to get me in the ground where the dead belong and set up a cross over me to show I'm there" (311). Like Everyman, Tarwater dislikes facing up to unpleasant realities, and "he did all he could to avoid this threatened intimacy of creation" (316).

Tarwater finds his great-uncle's supply of bootleg moonshine, and, impelled by a madness whispering from within, gets drunk and ends by burning the house down on the old man's corpse. Having failed in his one obligation and with no place left to live, Tarwater decides to set out for the city to seek shelter with his uncle, the schoolteacher. At this point the central conflict of the novel becomes as clear as the opposition in a morality play—will Tarwater move in with the schoolteacher and adopt his view of history? Or will he, as his great-uncle suggested, baptize the schoolteacher's idiot son, Bishop, as a token of his acceptance of a prophetic mission? This presents the boy with a real conflict on the literal level, but it is also obviously symbolic of a choice Everyman must make between opposed, total views of reality.

As the novel develops, the conflict focuses more and more sharply on the single issue, the baptism of Bishop. In her lecture "The Role of the Catholic Novelist," Flannery O'Connor expressly admitted that she had labored to give to this central incident of the novel a special significance. She had realized that when she had decided to write a novel "in which the central action is baptism," for the larger percentage of her readers baptism would seem a meaningless rite, and therefore she would "have to imbue this action with an awe and terror which will suggest its awful mystery." [13] The awe and terror she infuses into the act are not those which would be already familiar to believers in baptism's sacramental significance. For believers and non-believers alike, she metamorphoses the act into a metaphoric discriminant between opposed views of history and reality. According to the prophetic view of history, the view wherein the great-uncle reared Tarwater, baptism is the only means whereby man can be born again to live a life of freedom until his hunger is finally satisfied by the true Bread of Life. According to the schoolteacher's view of history, the new "social-scientism," baptism is an act without significance. It is just another washing, for "the great dignity of man . . . is his ability to say: I am born once and no more" (405).

Once Tarwater has taken refuge in his uncle's house, the schoolteacher begins his educational program intended to win the boy over to the new view of history. His philosophy is a vague synthesis of attitudes derived from the social sciences, especially psychology, education, and anthropology, and it is made to seem entirely appropriate for a man who is test administrator for the city school system and a contributor to the education journals. Calling upon some rather obvious psychology, which is represented as characteristic of the depth of his understanding, the schoolteacher tries to make Tarwater understand that his desire to baptize Bishop is only a compulsion and that all he has to do to free himself from the kind of mania which drove his grandfather mad is "to understand what it is that blocks you" (417).

Though the schoolteacher has a name, Rayber, the great-uncle rarely used it because to name a thing was to give it reality, and to the great-uncle the schoolteacher was not quite real. Tarwater uses his uncle's name occasionally, but usually thinks of him as his great-uncle had, as something less than real, an abstraction standing for a partial, half-vision of things, the new scientism. The schoolteacher is deaf and entirely dependent on his hearing aid; reality, especially at night, comes to him through the courtesy of engineering. To Tarwater it seemed as if his uncle did his thinking in the box containing the battery for his hearing aid and that "his head ran by electricity" (355). At one point, the boy asks his uncle, "What you wired for? . . . Does your head light up?" (366). For the great-uncle the danger in the schoolteacher's view of reality was that it tried to quantify everything, to convert warm, living, transcendent reality into "a piece of information inside his head" (313). The schoolteacher would even attempt to "grind the Lord into [his] head and spit out a number" (323).

Sometimes it seems as if the novel's attitude toward social scientism is an updating of the Fugitives' attitudes of a generation ago toward industrialism. The critical attitude toward quantification is apparent, perhaps in cruder terms, in the essay which Andrew Nelson Lytle contributed to *I'll Take My Stand*. Pointing to some of the dangers besetting Southern agrarianism in the twenties, he singled out quantification, in the form of the numbering and bookkeeping of resources, as bound to destroy the South's way of living "when the first page is turned and the first mark crosses the ledger." [14] In his essay in the same volume, Allen Tate had also called attention to the latent dangers of scientism.

> Since there is, in the Western mind, a radical division between the religious, the contemplative, the qualitative, on the one hand, and the scientific, the natural, the practical on the other, the scientific mind always plays havoc with the spiritual life when it is not powerfully enlisted in its cause; it cannot be permitted to operate alone. [15]

The advantage of a generation's hindsight makes many of the Fugitive statements seem unduly alarmist, but the novel's attitudes toward science are equally unreserved and incautious.

Tarwater does not take his uncle as seriously as the novel seems to want the reader to take the forces he represents. To Tarwater the schoolteacher is a pitiable and inconsistent fellow. If his uncle really believes in an anthropology which teaches that man is descended from the fish and can never be born again, why couldn't he go through with his attempt to drown his idiot son who is a burden to everyone? Rayber is confused. At times he views his son with scientific detachment, "as an $x$ signifying the general hideousness of fate," while

at others he becomes sentimental and feels "himself over-
whelmed by the horrifying love" for the idiot (372). Tarwater,
like his great-uncle, is consistent and resolute. He pays no attention to the schoolteacher's psychological explanations of
his and the great-uncle's supposed compulsions. "I ain't worried
what my underhead is doing," he shouts at one point; "I know
what I think when I do it and when I get ready to do it, I
don't talk no words. I do it" (405). Always afraid that his uncle
will try to do the same thing with his problems as he did with
the great-uncle's—write them up for an educational journal,
thereby getting the boy "in his head" as he did the old man—
Tarwater is determined to stay clear. "I'm outside your head.
. . . I ain't in it and I ain't about to be" (371).

The peripeteia of the novel occurs when Tarwater does *it*,
what the schoolteacher couldn't do. He drowns Bishop but
baptizes him at the same time. By the one action he makes his
commitment to the prophetic view of history and demonstrates
his superiority to the schoolteacher. When the schoolteacher
hears his son's howls and cries coming off the darkened lake,
he realizes that Bishop is struggling against Tarwater's attempts to drown him and he collapses. The collapse results not
from his sense of pity and loss, not from the realization that
Tarwater could indeed do what he could not bring himself to
do, but from the sudden realization that he feels nothing.

> He stood waiting for the raging pain, the intolerable hurt that
> was his due, to begin, so that he could ignore it, but he continued
> to feel nothing. He stood light-headed at the window and it was
> not until he realized there would be no pain that he collapsed
> [423].

By Bishop's death Rayber is revealed as a man incapable of action or feeling, limited to a surface view of reality and, like
his half-vision, only half a man.

In an essay on "The Church and the Fiction Writer," published in *America*, March 30, 1957, Flannery O'Connor quoted
with great approbation a statement which she attributed to

Monsignor Romano Guardini to the effect that "the roots of the eye are in the heart." [16] In her works true vision is vouchsafed only to the violent like Tarwater and his great-uncle because they are people of feeling who come to recognize the inadequacy of the merely rationalistic. The schoolteacher and all like him are doomed because they reject every impulse to passion.

> Anything he looked at too long could bring it [love] on. . . . It could be a stick or stone, the line of a shadow, the absurd old man's walk of a starling crossing the sidewalk. If, without thinking, he lent himself to it, he would feel suddenly a morbid surge of the love that terrified him—powerful enough to throw him to the ground in an act of idiot praise. It was completely irrational and abnormal [372].

His scientism keeps him from recognizing all the dimensions of his nature. He tries to "anesthetize his life," repeatedly shakes his head "to clear it of these unpleasant thoughts" which would force him to recognize his passions and relatedness with creation. He feels "a sinister pull on his consciousness, the familiar undertow of expectation, as if he were still a child waiting on Christ" (410-411). The schoolteacher could have saved himself, but he continually rejected the grace which would have made him free of a creation which he could only pretend to understand.

The novel contains an even more explicit caricature of a distorted conception of love as something which can be measured and prostituted to the most practical of uses. On his way to his uncle's house in the city, Tarwater is picked up by a copper flue salesman who takes the opportunity of the long ride to tell the boy some of the things he ought to know if he is going to make his way in the world. He tells Tarwater that "it had been his personal experience that you couldn't sell a copper flue to a man you didn't love" and that "love was the only policy that worked 95% of the time" (333). Meeks, the salesman, keeps a book wherein he maintains a record of the illnesses in his customers' families. When he calls upon a man and discovers that his wife is ill from cancer, he writes "cancer" next to her name so that he can inquire about her on his next sales visit. When anyone of his customers or members of their families died, Meeks always scratched out the name of the disease from which they had died and wrote "dead" in its place, thanking God "that's one less to remember." The man who lectured Tarwater that it was impossible to do anything without love finally concludes with a summary of his philosophy: "that's the way it ought to be in this world—nobody owing nobody nothing" (333). Meeks' travesty of love into a kind of Dale-Carnegie device intended to win friends and influence people, and his incredible inconsistency, are humorous but they are also a reminder that the practical, commercial view distorts as badly as the scientific.

Tarwater hopes that he can divest himself of all responsibilities and simply enjoy life. After he has baptized Bishop, he thinks that he has fulfilled all his obligations and that he can now return to Powderhead where: "Now all I have to do is mind my own bidnis until I die. I don't have to baptize or prophesy" (428). Like Everyman he dreams of living with rights and privileges but without responsibilities.

But this can never be and Tarwater's hunger is a symbol of that insatiable element in human nature which finds here no lasting home. Tarwater constantly recalls how his great-uncle would frequently talk of his hunger for the Bread of Life. He occasionally frightened the lad when he said "that as soon as he died, he would hasten to the banks of the Lake of Galilee to eat the loaves and fishes that the Lord had multiplied . . . forever" (315). This theme of man's hunger for something which the world cannot provide is constantly before the reader.

> The boy sensed that this was the heart of the great-uncle's madness, this hunger, and what he was secretly afraid of was that it might be passed down, might be hidden in the blood and might strike some day in him and then he would be torn by hunger like the old man, the bottom split out of his stomach so that nothing would heal or fill it but the bread of life [315].

The hunger does not really strike Tarwater until he tries to flee his obligations after drowning Bishop. It had been there all along but until then he had tried to make himself believe "in the darkest and most private part of his soul," that he was not "hungry for the bread of life." From the time he went to his uncle's house, from "the first day in the city he had become conscious of the strangeness in his stomach, a peculiar hunger. The city food only weakened him" (399). Later, as the days passed, the food not only weakened him; it sickened him so that on his return to Powderhead he is constantly hungry. He accepts a sandwich from a truck driver who offers him a ride, but he cannot make himself eat it. "His stomach alone rejected it; his face looked violently hungry and disappointed" (434). Tarwater is nonplussed and impatient with himself. He cannot understand what is happening to him, because "he was intolerant of unspiritual evils and with those of the flesh he had never truckled" (438). The closer he comes to Powderhead, the more insistent his hunger becomes. Given another ride by a youth, whose sallow countenance and demeanor suggest the vice of the morality play, he is offered a drink. He accepts and immediately becomes dizzy. He insists, however: "It's better than the Bread of Life!" (440). Having committed the sin of pride, he passes out and the stranger violates him. When he comes to and realizes what has happened: "His scorched eyes no longer looked hollow or as if they were meant only to guide him forward. They looked as if, touched with a coal like the lips of the prophet, they would never be used for ordinary sights again" (442).

He does make it back to Powderhead, and the same inner evil genius which had taken hold of him and led him to burn the house down around his dead great-uncle, reappears to tempt him again. This time he is tempted in terms which recall the temptation of Christ after fasting in the desert.

Go down and take it [Powderhead], his friend whispered. It's ours. We've won it. Ever since you first begun to dig the grave, I've stood by you, never left your side, and now we can take it over together, just you and me. You're not ever going to be alone again [444].

But by now his hunger is so overpowering that he cannot listen to the Tempter. "His hunger constricted him anew. It appeared to be outside him, surrounding him, almost as if it were visible before him, something he could reach out for and not quite touch" (445). His hunger is for something the Tempter cannot provide, and Tarwater comes to realize that, like his great-uncle, "his hunger was so great that he could have eaten all the loaves and fishes after they were multiplied" (446). With this realization growing within him, he turns his back on Powderhead and the illusion of primeval irresponsibility, and the last sentence of the novel reads: "His singed eyes, black in their deep sockets, seemed already to envision the fate that awaited him but he moved steadily on, his face set toward the dark city, where the children of God lay sleeping" (447). The promised prophet has appeared and with full vision he goes to warn the world—not the South alone—of its true heritage.

No summary of the literal, external events of the plot, even when combined with an attempt to suggest some of the multiple thematic implications of word and metaphor, can ever succeed in paraphrasing the achievement of the art work. Flannery O'Connor has brought together a multiplicity of meanings under tension, where they exist as in a magma, never polarized, never still. Hers is a peculiar *mimesis,* in the sense in which Erich Auerbach has used the word, for she does not imitate the universal as in a traditional allegory, nor the particular as in a contemporary novel, nor the typical alone as in a morality play, but a combination of these three.

She has succeeded because she has been able to anchor the universal-typical to the concrete-particular. Her metaphors are constantly of a kind wherein the vehicle sustains the interest in the particular whereas the tenor suggests the universal. Ordinary detail would not be strong enough to serve as an anchor for all the upward thrust toward universality it must sustain under tension, and consequently many of her details are extraordinary, unusual, or, like the act of baptism, made to seem so. Because the juxtaposition of unusual detail with traditional universal meanings frequently produces violent contrasts, her style can seem "garish" or "bizarre."

*The Violent Bear It Away* develops through a series of images, each with its own literal function, but each also intended to awaken the reader to a recognition of other levels of significance. Flannery O'Connor is attempting to do for her readers what the prophets did for their chosen people, enlarge their vision of reality. In her lecture, "The Role of the Catholic Novelist," she declared that for a Catholic writer "belief, since it simply includes more reality for him to deal with, does nothing but enlarge his problems." [17] This greater reality is that for which Tarwater hungers and which she has tried to suggest throughout the novel. Belief in this greater reality implies a sincere commitment, and commitment implies a willingness to take a stand. It is the importance of coming to see that vision implies commitment, getting out of the excluded middle, of acting out of passionate conviction which is suggested by the title of the novel, *The Violent Bear It Away*. With the Fugitive essayists, she believed that the whole man was a passionate man. Where there was no passion, there was no vision; where there was vision, there was passion.

In "The Role of the Catholic Novelist," she refers to *I'll Take My Stand* as a pamphlet published in the twenties. Actually it is a book of some 300 pages, published in 1930 when she was but a young girl of five. The book, like the song "Dixie" whose second line provided the title, is a rallying call. In his essay on the means of saving the Southern agrarian tradition, Andrew Lytle urges all Southerners "to turn away from the liberal capons who fill the pulpits as preachers" and to "seek a priesthood that may manifest the will and intelligence to renounce science and search out the Word in the authorities." [18] If any congregation of the twenties were heedful of this injunction, there must have been preachers in their pulpits who resembled Tarwater's great-uncle. The call for leaders like the great-uncle runs through the essays of *I'll Take My Stand,* appearing even in a restrained essay such as that of Lyle Lanier on the philosophy of progress which calls for "heroes," "geniuses," and "divine leaders." [19] These leaders were to be the kind of dedicated passionate men who would act, violently, if necessary. In his essay on Southern religion, Allen Tate raised the question of means: "How may the Southerner take hold of his Tradition?" To quote his answer precisely: "The answer is, by violence." [20]

On this issue, the novel and the collection of essays of a generation before are remarkably close. The full import of the novel's title, and consequently its significance, is perhaps most apparent in the speech Tarwater makes to the woman clerk in the resort hotel where they are staying when he drowns Bishop. The speech directly precedes the peripeteia of the novel. What precedes and what follows provide the assumptions and the consequences of this attitude.

> You can't just say NO, . . . . You got to do NO. You got to show it. You got to show you mean it by doing it. You got to show you're not going to do one thing by doing another. You got to make an end of it. One way or another [397].

The Fugitive essayists were calling upon the South to say NO to an all-engulfing Northern industrialism; Flannery O'Connor wrote to discipline her readers to a willingness to say NO to the forces denying God's place in reality.

Donald Davidson's essay "A Mirror for Artists " [21] also urged the artist to enter the political arena and to fight against the encroachments of industrialism. Just how an artist was to keep his distance from a mass society to avoid the destruction of his art and still become actively involved in the deliberations of that society as a citizen was not made clear. Perhaps Flannery O'Connor was prevented by her illness from taking part as much as she would have liked in the public deliberations which ultimately affect the life of the arts. Perhaps, however, she saw more clearly how a novelist might contribute to the preservation and improvement of the state of the arts. In her lecture on "The Role of the Catholic Novelist," she explained how a novelist can work for the improvement of his society.

> We should realize that if the novelist is a healer at all, it will only be through his being a poet. The poet is traditionally a blind man, but the Christian poet is like the blind man cured in the gospels, who looked then and saw men as if they were trees, but walking. This is the beginning of vision, and I think it is the kind of vision that we shall have to learn to accept if, in the coming years, we want to recognize the Christian literature we hope for.[22]

*The Violent Bear It Away* is a demonstration of that kind of vision, a Christian vision, intended to discipline others to an awareness of the richness of their heritage and to encourage them to witness, violently, for that heritage. Active participation in public deliberation could achieve no more.

In the same lecture reflecting on the functions of the Catholic novelist, Flannery O'Connor summarized the attitudes of many articles one can frequently find in the Catholic press when she said: "Frequently in reading articles about the failures of the Catholic novelist, you will get the idea that he is to raise himself from the stuff of his own imagination by beginning with Christian principles and finding the life that will illustrate them."[23] It is true that too often these articles make it seem that the Catholic novelist is, or should be, little more than an intermediary for the dramatization of dogma, a kind of deductive instrument which takes ideas from the theoretical level and reduces them to the imaginative. She then went on: "He forgets that the writer does not write about general beliefs but about men with free will and that there is nothing in our Faith that implies a foregone optimism for man so free that with his last breath he can say No."[24] The suspense in her novel is based on the quality of her central character, Tarwater, who could at any time say and do No.

The novelist does not work deductively, but inductively starting from a particular. The novelist's imagination is not so much free as bound. It is "bound through the senses to a particular society and a particular history, to particular sounds and a particular idiom." [25] For Flannery O'Connor that particular culture was the South in which she grew up and lived and whose heritage she saw in much the same terms as the Fugitive essayists of *I'll Take My Stand*. But her conception of the function of a novel was distinctively hers, and like her characters she could not only talk eloquently about what should be done, she could do it. In the doing she not only demonstrated her conceptions but enabled her readers to see with the kind of vision they must develop if they are to avoid the tragic errors of a pitiable schoolmaster, the prophetic vision.

## Notes

1. John Crowe Ransom, "Reconstructed But Unregenerate," *I'll Take My Stand* (New York: Harper & Brothers, 1930), p. 3.
2. Andrew Nelson Lytle, "The Hind Tit," *I'll Take My Stand*, p. 206.
3. Frank Lawrence Owsley, "The Irrepressible Conflict," *I'll Take My Stand*, p. 67.
4. Flannery O'Connor, "The Role of the Catholic Novelist," *Greyfriar* [Siena Studies in Literature], VII (1964), 9.
5. Allen Tate, "Tension in Poetry," perhaps most widely accessible in *Critiques and Essays in Criticism,* edited by Robert W. Stallman (New York: Ronald, 1949), p. 60.
6. Allen Tate, "Remarks on the Southern Religion," *I'll Take My Stand*, p. 157.
7. *Ibid.*, pp. 156, 163.
8. *Ibid.*, p. 169.
9. The Hoover administration also marked the end of recorded history for the Fugitive essayists in *I'll Take My Stand*.
10. Lyle H. Lanier, "A Critique of the Philosophy of Progress," *I'll Take My Stand*, pp. 125-26.
11. John Crowe Ransom, "Reconstructed But Unregenerate," p. 1.
12. *Ibid.*, p. 16.
13. Flannery O'Connor, "The Role of the Catholic Novelist," p. 11.
14. Andrew Nelson Lytle, "The Hind Tit," p. 234.
15. Allen Tate, "Remarks on the Southern Religion," p. 173.
16. Flannery O'Connor, "The Church and the Fiction Writer," *America*, XCVI (March 30, 1957), 733.
17. Flannery O'Connor, "The Role of the Catholic Novelist," p. 6.
18. Andrew Nelson Lytle, "The Hind Tit," p. 244.

19. Lyle H. Lanier, "A Critique of the Philosophy of Progress," p. 145.
20. Allen Tate, "Remarks on the Southern Religion," p. 174.
21. Donald Davidson, "A Mirror for Artists," *I'll Take My Stand*, p. 60.
22. Flannery O'Connor, "The Role of the Catholic Novelist," p. 12.
23. *Ibid.*, p. 8.
24. *Ibid.*, p. 8.
25. *Ibid.*, p. 7.

# Flannery O'Connor and the Grotesque

## IRVING MALIN

IN "The Fiction Writer and His Country" Flannery O'Connor states: "My own feeling is that writers who see by the light of their Christian faith will have, in these times, the sharpest eyes for the grotesque, for the perverse, and for the unacceptable." [1] Although she believes that Christian faith can help her recognize the grotesque, she does not completely explain the reasons for this belief. It would be risky to rebel against her formulation—to imply that it is *not* responsible for her startling fiction —but I think we can say that her grotesquerie is related to that of Capote, Hawkes, Carson McCullers, and Purdy. It is, in many ways, "pre-Christian."

The grotesque is the "poetry of disorder"—to use Richard Chase's term. It arises when traditional categories disintegrate. The Christian writer believes that sin and the grotesque are joined because sin violates cosmic order. When a sinner is "proud," he disturbs "the great chain of being"; he steps out of his spiritual domain and in the attempt to rise—to God's loftiness?—falls into animalistic depths. He becomes freakish. Although the four writers I have mentioned do not believe in orthodox concepts of sin, they also see the horrible failings of self-love. My point is simply this: although Miss O'Connor associates sin and distortion, she is remarkably modern—and pre-Christian?—in giving us the poetry of disorder—poetry which is dreamlike and unconscious.

In this essay I will explore the grotesque as theme and image in her fiction, emphasizing her psychological awareness, not her Christian faith which, I think, often conflicts with this awareness.

## I

The very title of *Wise Blood* introduces us to a strange world in which blood and wisdom, instinct and reason, are dangerously married. They are not in their "proper" places; they are unbalanced. When we first see Hazel Motes—even his name suggests dark uncertainty—we realize that he does not act in conventional ways. He battles the other passengers on the train. He sits "at a forward angle on the green plush train seat, looking one minute at the window as if he might want to jump out of it" (9). Hazel Motes listens to his wise blood—his compulsive narcissism—which forces him to shout at others: "Nothing matters but that Jesus don't exist" (33). Because he has yielded to this one "truth," he has lost his complete, risk-filled humanity. He is automatic, sharp, and "non-human."

Miss O'Connor does not really care about Hazel's background—his reasons for submitting to this religious fanaticism. She informs us that his mother, a firm believer in Jesus, used her belief as the shield against humanity: she did not carry over her love to her family. She constantly punished Hazel: "Jesus died to redeem you," she reminded him. To which he answered: "I never ast him" (39). Hazel is desperately rebelling against Jesus because He is linked with the Evil Mother. It is fitting that he sleeps with Mrs. Leora Watts, almost immediately after he leaves the train. She "mothers" him and, of course, he hates her.

Miss O'Connor is so concerned with Hazel's present actions that she introduces other grotesques who also live by one truth: Enoch Emery, Asa Hawks, and Sabbath Lily Hawks. Enoch claims that he has "wise blood"; he waits for its commands: "His blood all morning had been saying the person would come today" (47). By stealing the mummy from the museum, Enoch can supply a "new jesus" to the Church Without Christ, and become the true disciple of Hazel. Asa Hawks and his "daughter" hate each other because they cannot get out of their self-centered designs; they both want to escape from their commitments. They kill Jesus for their own profit.

There are few normal observers to offset the effects of these "lovers." When Hazel buys a car, he bargains with two men who care only about money. The salesman demonstrating his potato-peeling machine is also non-human. The landlady at the end of the novel is snoopy and selfish. It is easy to condemn Miss O'Connor's fictional country—we would not want to live there!—by asserting that it is "unfair." But her bias affirms that the world has been "sold" to non-believers; it is totally "unacceptable" and claustrophobic.

Not only does Miss O'Connor fill the world with severely limited characters—it is hard to call them human beings—she reinforces their plight, which they themselves do not understand, with many grotesque images. When we consider the objects around us—rooms, grass, animals, and cars—we accept them as *part* of our lives; they do not *dominate* us. But in *Wise Blood* these objects have won; they are more "alive" than the flat characters who, by adopting one truth, have become "objective." Miss O'Connor's images capture the spiritual condition of Hazel and his followers.

There are many "prisons of the spirit." The title itself, which suggests a closed, unnatural system, prepares us for Hazel's entrapment: "He looked as if he were held by a rope caught in the middle of his back and attached to the train ceiling" (11).

He has no free space in which to breathe; he bumps into other passengers. When he sleeps, he dreams of his grandfather's coffin, of his young brother's coffin, and of his father "flattened out like anybody else" (15). The outside world is also a tomb—before getting on this train he visited his old "skeleton of [a] house" and was covered by a falling piece of timber (18). Hazel remembers and yells: "I can't be closed up . . ." (19). He has no choice. Later he locks himself in the men's room; he gazes at the potato-peeling machine (another box!), and sees the man trapped in blindness. The images overwhelm him and he thinks of a childhood incident. Once he went to a carnival where he saw "something white . . . lying, squirming a little, in a box lined with red cloth. For a second he thought it was a skinned animal and then he saw it was a woman" (38). The trapped woman is not only associated in his mind with death but with his own fears. The ambivalence—wanting to join her, afraid to—never leaves him. Because he is attacked by these images, he resembles Enoch's mummy, who is "naked and a dried yellow color and his eyes [are] drawn almost shut as if a giant block of steel were falling down on top of him" (57). Thus these imprisonments—metallic, violent, and inhuman—choke Hazel and us.

In this closed novel the grotesque is "beautiful." By underlining the false vision of her characters, Miss O'Connor makes their spiritual plight more horrifying. Just as Hazel Motes, the man of clouded vision, continually sees a distorted Jesus before him, so do the other characters *stare* at the world, misunderstanding it. On the train a passenger leans forward to look at Hazel's eyes: his "eyes were what held her attention longest. Their settings were so deep that they seemed, to her, almost like passages leading somewhere and she leaned halfway across the space that separated the two seats, trying to see into them" (10). Hazel thinks he knows the Negro porter; the other passengers regard *him* as a preacher. Although he carries his mother's glasses—"if his vision should ever become dim"—he cannot really see through her Christian eyes—except "inversely." After he gets off the train, he confronts more ambiguities, doubles, and odd reflections. First he spends a night with Mrs. Watts (or "Momma" as she would like to be called)—the inverse reflection of his self-righteous mother. Then he meets Asa Hawks and his "child." Hawks has on dark glasses—he also has dim perception—because he is supposed to be blind. This false preacher, like the potato-peeling salesman, stares at profits and nothing else. And Hazel resembles him, caring more about the way he "looks" than about Jesus' message. These reflections continue throughout the novel—I do not have the space to list more of them—and they shape reality into a fun-house mirror.

*Wise Blood* is more than a mere exercise because of Miss O'Connor's irony. She can laugh bitterly at Enoch and the mummy-jesus, the battered car, the madness of Hazel, and her laughter, paradoxically enough, creates our occasional sympathy. We sense mysteriously the traditional beliefs—the Grand Design—by which Hazel and his disciples fall short. Irony, in other words, asserts the light of faith.

Unfortunately, Miss O'Connor does not stop here. She is unsure about her ability to "convert" us by means of black humor—in the way Nathanael West does—and she begins to preach. Hazel sees the light—no longer does he have distorted vision—after he kills Solace Layfield and hears his last words. Suddenly he becomes human—the "pin point of light" (119). We are not prepared for this transformation, unless we take it ironically as another act of grotesque narcissism. Perhaps the conflict we feel arises from the fact that Miss O'Connor herself is torn by the "needs" of the grotesque *and* Christian faith. *She gives up one for the other, unable to hold both at the end of her novel.* I think this is what John Hawkes means when he writes:

Certainly Flannery O'Connor reveals what can only be called brilliant creative perversity when she brings to life a denuded *actuality* and writes about a "cat-faced baby" or a confidence man with "an honest look that fitted into his face like a set of false teeth" or an automobile horn that makes "a sound like a goat's laugh cut off with a buzz saw." This much, I should think, is happily on the side of the devil.[2]

Miss O'Connor's ability to render the grotesque—her worship of the pre-Christian?—is greater than her ability to capture Hazel's conversion. *Wise Blood* runs erratically.

## II

The stories in *A Good Man Is Hard to Find* are set in the same unbalanced world of *Wise Blood*. The villains are "flat" narcissists who love themselves more than Jesus. Their displacement is again represented by dominating images of entrapment, "falling," and odd vision. I can explore closely only three stories: "A Good Man Is Hard to Find," "The Artificial Nigger," and "The Displaced Person."

In "A Good Man Is Hard to Find" The Misfit is the same kind of fanatic as Hazel Motes. He also believes that things would be different if Jesus had really done what He said:

[He] thown everything off balance. If He did what He said, then it's nothing for you to do but thow away everything and follow Him, and if He didn't, then it's nothing for you to do but enjoy the few minutes you got left the best way you can—by killing somebody or burning down his house or doing some other meanness to him. No pleasure but meanness [142].

Although The Misfit claims that everything is Jesus' fault—if He ever lived!—he does not plan to let things stand. He will right the balance. *He will be the new Jesus of self-love.* But his Church of meanness gives him no pleasure or salvation. He continues to be anxious, empty, and metallic.

Miss O'Connor introduces a foil to The Misfit: the grandmother is a good person on the surface—at least the community thinks so—but she is also "mean." She forces her family to obey her; she sees them as an extension of herself; and she seizes "every chance to change" reality. Because she convinces her son to turn the car toward the house with the "secret panel," causing the family to meet The Misfit, she seals everyone's death. She tries to adopt The Misfit, giving him well-meaning advice and false love. He responds by shooting her three times.

Throughout the story Miss O'Connor uses images to reinforce the horror of self-love. The Tower, a restaurant owned by Red Sammy, is a "broken-down place"—"a long dark room" with tables, counter, and little dancing space. Once people went here to find pleasure; now Red Sammy is afraid to leave the door unlatched: he has succumbed to the "meanness" of the world. The plantation house which the Grandmother remembers is apparently peaceful—a sanctuary contrasted to the hellish Tower—and it holds glorious treasure. But Miss O'Connor shows us that this house—does it even exist?—is never reached; indeed, the Grandmother's self-centered wish to see it causes The Misfit to discover and murder the family. Both houses are, in effect, wrecks of the spirit.

Although Miss O'Connor wants her people to search for Truth, she realizes that they carry their self-love with them; their voyages are frenetic, unbalanced, or destructive. "A Good Man Is Hard to Find" begins with the Grandmother not wanting to go to Florida—The Misfit is headed there: "I wouldn't take my children in any direction with a criminal like that aloose in it." The child, John Wesley, answers, "Why dontcha stay at home?" (129). The new voyage to East Tennessee helps them to meet trouble; throughout the trip we see horrifying hints of their ultimate end: accidents, dumping grounds, the nervous driver, the dangerous embankment, and the monkey who devours fleas. Moving is as unsettling as imprisonment. By juxtaposing these various shelters and voyages, Miss O'Connor establishes the impossible task of redemption, especially when she ironically relates The Misfit to the Grandmother—the criminal to the good citizen. Claustrophobia, violence, and crooked sight—these are emblems of the grotesque.

In "The Artificial Nigger" Mr. Head, like the Grandmother, believes that he is a "suitable guide"; he will teach his grandson, Nelson, the way to live. But his "moral mission," as good as it appears on the surface, is full of grotesque delusion. Because he cares only about his self-image—which Miss O'Connor ironically relates to that of Vergil and Raphael—he joins Hazel Motes and The Misfit. In the city—always the test site —Mr. Head and Nelson cannot cope with their new surroundings. The spiritual guide loses his way: Nelson realizes that he must assume command—that he must become more than a ghost—but his transformation is incomplete. He continues to blunder, trying to find the way back to the train station. Suddenly he runs into an old woman who shouts to Mr. Head: "Your boy has broken my ankle! . . . Police!" The grandfather declares, "This is not my boy," when the policeman arrives, "I never seen him before" (209). Therefore the family tie—like the ones in "A Good Man Is Hard to Find" and *Wise Blood*—is violated by self-love.

It is at this point in the story that the grotesque *apparently* disappears and Christian faith enters. We find conversion. When Mr. Head begins "to feel the depth of his denial," he "[knows] now what time would be like without seasons . . . and what man would be like without salvation" (212). Nelson finds that although he sees his grandfather's severe limitations, he sympathizes with his human plight. Both share the "amazing" vision of the artificial nigger: they accept the statue as "some monument to another's victory that brought them together in their common defeat" (213). Their differences are "dissolved like an action of mercy," and they board the train, admitting that they will never leave their sanctuary. It is possible to read the conversion of Mr. Head and Nelson in an ironic way. They are still tinged by self-love; they cannot accept the intrusions of others—even if the others are "artificial." They have learned only to complete their entrapment. But if we accept this ironic reading of the conversion, we must establish the fact that Miss O'Connor denies the possibility of sudden love—of grace. Would it not be more ironic, and ultimately Christian, if Jesus were to use "artificial niggers"—the trivial, the commonplace, and the unreal—to transform sinners? I am not *sure* that Miss O'Connor is *sure*: she stands on the line between the grotesque and Christian epiphany, not fully committing herself. Her irony *saves* her as a writer, perhaps not as a believer.

"The Artificial Nigger" is full of imprisonments and reflections. These make me feel—but do not convince me—that Miss O'Connor denies the final transformation. The room in which Mr. Head wakes is "full of moonlight"; it is dignified by illusion. The only dark spot is Nelson's cot—he is a "simple" shadow who must see the light. After Mr. Head and Nelson undertake their voyage, they find no peaceful shelter: they walk by mistake into the kitchen of the train; they are lost in the "hollow tunnels" of the city streets; they see the "endless pitchblack tunnels" of sin everywhere; and when they finally confront the "monument," they are so stupefied that they retreat to their past shelter, where they will presumably be safe in their now-binding narcissism.

At first the reflections suggest the usual oddity of Gothic. Mr. Head thinks the chair awaits an order; his pants have "an almost noble air." Because Nelson has lived with him for such a long time, he also is spellbound. They reflect each other: "They were grandfather and grandson but they looked enough alike to be brothers and brothers not too far apart in age" (197). The Negro, for Mr. Head, is the freak who does not mirror white folks; throughout the story he holds Great Destiny—the Meaning. When Nelson and Mr. Head see the "artificial nigger," they interpret the object as a divinely-sent sign—recognizing that all people are miserable and "chipped"—and they lose their old ways of looking at the world. Now they are "spellbound" in a Christian way as the moon returns; "gigantic white clouds" illuminate the sky. Again the imagery mysteriously

moves from "doubleness" and inversion to true illumination—
remember *Wise Blood*. Because Miss O'Connor has emphasized
the oddity of their views—their pride which made them see
reality in quirky ways—it is difficult to accept the "epiphany"
as extraordinary.

In "The Displaced Person" Mrs. Shortley is so narcissistic
that she considers herself the ruler of the community. (She and
her family are tenant farmers.) Despite her name—another
wonderfully chosen one—she is "the giant wife of the countryside." Her granite nature, which has displaced her from humanity, does not allow her to see the D.P., Mr. Guizac, and
his family as more than demoniacal intruders or "rats with ty-
phoid fleas." Mrs. Shortley attempts to inform Mrs. McIntyre
(entire?) that she must get rid of these intruders. But the landlady does not obey. Pleased by the D.P.'s efficiency, she gets
rid of the Shortleys.

If the story were to end here, we would have faith in humanity. Miss O'Connor refuses to give us this happy ending.
She makes us realize that Mrs. McIntyre, left alone without
Mrs. Shortley, is unable to love others. She retreats inward,
loving herself so much that she turns upon the D.P., and she is,
finally, an accomplice in his murder. Then she swoons: "She
felt she was in some foreign country" (299). She begins to take
instructions from the foreign priest.

Again the imagery reinforces the grotesque, making us doubt
the validity of Mrs. McIntyre's conversion. The opening paragraph introduces the "private domain" of Mrs. Shortley. (Even
the sun seems to be an "intruder" here.) She refuses to allow
others to find sanctuary in her "Church of Self-Love." Because
she feels that her rule is being usurped, she has visions of entrapment. (Of course, she buried herself many years ago in one
truth.) She sees Polish words "all piled up in a room"—piled up
like the people in Europe, "the devil's experiment station." She
dislikes her husband's trick of swallowing a cigarette and she
fears billions of D.P.s "pushing their way into new places."
Her claustrophobia is reflected by Mrs. McIntyre. *She* remem-

bers her husband's room "left unchanged since his death" and the pressed grass near his "desecrated monument." The world "swells up" for her. Thus when Mr. Guizac is run over by the tractor, the accident serves as the "objective correlative" of all the entrapments—and meaningless voyages—in the story.

I have discussed only three stories from *A Good Man Is Hard to Find,* but I think that these illustrate most forcefully Miss O'Connor's preoccupation with self-love. She symbolizes this self-love—which destroys all "communities"—in terms of cold imprisonment, violent movement, and odd vision. It is ironic that her art compels us to fear that *we* cannot escape from the grotesque. Her instruction unbalances us; it does not convert us to Christian faith.

## III

In *The Violent Bear It Away* Miss O'Connor magnifies the family ties so much that one critic, Algene Ballif, has viewed the novel as an "elaborate fantasy of what one can only call homosexual incest." [3] The father-son relationships in her earlier fiction—in "The Artificial Nigger" and *Wise Blood*—are suffocating, but here they become completely destructive.

The great-uncle is a self-appointed preacher who undertakes the religious instruction of orphaned Tarwater. He thinks that he has learned by fire; anxious to perpetuate his "seed," he teaches him "in the evils that befall prophets; in those that come from the world, which are trifling, and those that come from the Lord and burn the prophet clean" (306). Does he not resemble Hazel Motes and The Misfit? His Church is one of self-love, despite his apparent orthodoxy; it contains narcissistic icons.

Although Tarwater is "innocent"—he lashes out verbally at this Church—he is unconsciously adopting the old man's

Truth: he is his *own* prophet and disciple, god and believer. But he is torn by these ambivalences. They are given body as a "stranger" who talks to him. At first the stranger is viewed as the "wise voice"—the true father? Be yourself! he whispers. But Tarwater is not certain whether he should be himself— whoever he is!—or his great-uncle. The stranger becomes fiendish.

The screw is turned once more. Tarwater clashes with a third "father," Rayber, who has another grotesque mission (disguised as humanitarianism). This uncle teaches rationalism; if he can convert Tarwater, if he can turn him from the false prophecy of the old man, he will exult in his own power. The boy's ambivalence is paralleled in Rayber. Rayber also has been "converted"—to self-love, not altruism—by the old man who kidnapped and baptized him at the age of seven. Never having come to terms with this event, he sees his own problems in the rebellious orphan. By winning Tarwater away from the old man, he will save *himself*.

The "sins" of these believers destroy Bishop. Bishop is worshipped by Rayber, his father, and Tarwater because he is *empty*: he can be used by both to exploit their narcissism. Tarwater has been instructed to baptize him—to save him from atheistic Rayber—and if he performs this ritual, he will be loved by the great-uncle (even after death). Rayber loves and hates his son for his anti-rationalism—his idiocy. Both "prophets" converge on the child and kill him, thereby demonstrating their own power. As Rayber gazes out the window at the lake where Tarwater has baptized and drowned the idiot, he "stood there waiting for the raging pain, the intolerable hurt that was his due, to begin, so that he could ignore it, but he continued to feel nothing" (423). *The violent narcissists bear humanity away; in Bishop's murder they confirm their own death.*

*The Violent Bear It Away* is, therefore, a "divine comedy." The new jesus—whether it be Tarwater or Rayber—achieves his salvation by killing. He loves himself so much that he sacrifices *others*. The irony involved is so bitter that we are prone to flee from it. We begin to have doubts; we partially "sympathize" with these believers. But I think that our sympathy is *not* wanted by Miss O'Connor. She wants us, instead, to have the "sacred rage"—Henry James's phrase—that rage which is close to cruel laughter. It is when we laugh at Rayber and Tarwater that we assert that we are *not grotesque*. Laughter, not sympathy, burns us clean.

Miss O'Connor's images horrify and delight us. On the first page she introduces the tomb-like atmosphere by mentioning the great-uncle's grave with "enough dirt on top to keep the dogs from digging it up" (305). From this "private place" we enter the old man's mind. Versed in the prophets (seeing his distorted image in them), he teaches Tarwater at home because school is a "prison." But the home—the backwoods—is the domain of false prophecy; he defends it from such intruders as Rayber and the city officials. The old man screams that he does not want to sit "inside anybody's head," unaware that he himself is trapped in the Church of Self-Love.

After Tarwater flees from his duty by neglecting to bury his great-uncle, he heads toward the city, which is viewed as a "larger part of the same pile, not yet buried so deep" (335-336). The entrance to this new grave is a "gaping concrete hole"—a gas station. He talks on the phone for the first time and hears the kind of "bubbling noise" someone would make under water. Finally he enters Rayber's house—another deceptive church—and he soon learns that here also his mind will be filled with rot. At one point Tarwater looks at his uncle's hearing aid and asks: " 'Do you think in the box . . . or do you think in your head?' " (367). Rayber is so enraged that his heart pounds "like the works of a gigantic machine in his chest" (368). He decides on other appeals, but Tarwater continues to wrap himself in hostile isolation: the "steely gleam in his eye was like the glint of a metal door sealed against an intruder" (387).

These images continue throughout the novel; they would be horrifying enough if they stood alone. Miss O'Connor, however, makes them more claustrophobic (and narcissistic) by her use of reflections: the trapped believers cannot see "the way out." *Reality is wavy.* On the first page we read that Tarwater and his great-uncle live together—the relationship of Mr. Head and Nelson comes to mind. "Tarwater" suggests a muddy view of reality—remember Hazel Motes!—and the fact that he is soon drunk reinforces this assumption. Miss O'Connor, telling us about the past, mentions the "rage of vision" of the great-uncle. This rage is accompanied by the fire which falls in his brain, purifying but also obscuring it. Along with the fire are the "wheels of light and strange beasts with giant wings of fire and four heads turned to the four points of the universe" (307-08). The great-uncle believes that he mirrors Ezekiel and the other prophets. After he dies, his eyes are "dead silver." Tarwater knows that he has to bury him, but he hears the voice of a stranger, his rebellious double: he now questions the meaning of his likeness to his great-uncle. His problem is clear: he has to choose between two reflections. He tries to "keep his vision located on an even level, to . . . let his eye stop at the surface of that" (315-16). He cannot. We could spend more time on these images—almost every page contains one—but the total effect is strong: Tarwater cannot choose correctly because his vision is odd.

Now ambiguity enters. Does Miss O'Connor claim that these characters are grotesque because they *choose* to be flat, self-haunted, and mechanical? Or does she affirm that reality *itself* is grotesque? She must believe *as a Christian* in free will and spiritual design. But *as a writer* she reinforces the grotesquerie of existence. The conflict is very powerful; it burns this novel clean.

## IV

The tension between the grotesque and Christian faith exists in Miss O'Connor's best work. She sees the world as upside-down and flat; if she can master the madness around her—if she can capture it in striking images and characters—she can then declare her sanity. I sense this great victory in the fiction which I have discussed.

I am horrified by her use of the grotesque, but it also delights me. How can the grotesque be pleasurable? Is horror fun? Tarwater wonders about Rayber's hearing aid; Sabbath Lily Hawks cuddles the mummy; The Misfit does not enjoy his meanness—these scenes are admirable because they assert that if we can understand the horror involved, and the comic inversions, we have not yielded to narcissism. We see truths *and* lies. We thus affirm our humanity.

When Miss O'Connor shakes us in this paradoxical way— working out her artistic salvation?—she affirms that she understands the Meaning of things. Her vision is crooked and violent; but this very fact demonstrates her kinship to us—even if we are not Catholics. We recognize our "fear and trembling"—and our sense that it is divinely inspired—in her enduring, chilly fiction.

## Notes

1. In *The Living Novel, a Symposium,* edited by Granville Hicks (New York: Macmillan, 1957), p. 162.
2. "Flannery O'Connor's Devil," *Sewanee Review,* LXX (Summer, 1962), 406.
3. "A Southern Allegory," *Commentary,* XXX (October, 1960), 360.

# An American Girl

### CAROLINE GORDON

SOME YEARS ago Witter Bynner sent Henry James a copy of one
of Willa Cather's novels. James thanked him for the gift and
deplored his inability to read "promiscuous novels"—"particularly when written by young ladies." I think we may assume
that when James used the adjective "promiscuous" in his letter
to the poet–editor he was using it in a technical sense. In
other words, that it is charged with meaning in the way so
many words in his notebooks are charged with meaning. James
was certainly what Percy Lubbock dubbed him: "the scholar
of the novel." But the novelist has little or no technical vocabulary at his command. James so felt the need of one that he
invented his own terminology and used it boldly both in his
self-communings in his notebooks and in his public discussions
of the mysteries of his art. He has told us that a novel "should
consist of 'a single impression.'" I take it that when he refers to
a "promiscuous novel," he means a novel which may be
original and highly readable but which is, nevertheless, not
constructed so that every incident in it contributes to this
"single impression." Confronted with such a novel, James is
likely to react the way a veteran architect might react at the

sight of a building erected on shifting sands and already ex-
hibiting—to his practiced eye, at least—a slight list. One can
almost hear him suavely declining the invitation: "No, thank
you, I never enter buildings designed by young ladies!"

The student of James's novels, his criticisms and his notebooks, experiences a recurring pleasure in observing the analo-
gies between his life and his work. Everything which he, himself, wrote, it seems to me, if viewed in large enough perspective, contributes toward that "single impression" which he
found the chief requisite for the novel. I believe, indeed, that
statements which, on the surface, appear contradictory, will
reconcile themselves if contemplated long enough. For instance, his refusal to read "promiscuous novels by young ladies"
may, at first glance, appear to negate what he has to say about
the American girl in *The American Scene,* the book he wrote
as the result of a visit to his native land after many years'
absence. James was impressed by the social dominance of
women in both Washington and other cities. He came to the
conclusion that largely as the result of this dominance, the
cultural future of this country was in the hands of the American girl, American men being too busy trying to make money
to concern themselves with culture.

He expresses his fear that the American girl will not be equal
to the task and even dramatizes her own fear that she will not
be able to live up to her awesome responsibilities in a fictional
apostrophe which is half baby talk and half the gibberish of
a mind on the verge of dissolution.

I gather that James never read any of Miss Cather's novels
and so never discovered that although she was still then a
comparatively young lady, she was, nevertheless, a master of
the architectonics of illusion. It is a matter of regret for Miss
Cather's many admirers that he never knew her work. I find
myself regretting, too, that he never had an opportunity to
read Flannery O'Connor's short stories and novels. I think that
he would have felt a kinship with her that might have tran-

scended his innate conviction that the writing of novels—a difficult and dangerous task, to begin with—is a task for which men are by nature better fitted than women.

If he had lived to read Miss O'Connor's stories, I suspect that he would also have derived from them the pleasure which any of us feels when he finds his own words coming true. For this young woman, who died in 1964 at the age of thirty-nine, comes nearer than anyone I can think of to enacting the role of "the American girl" whom James foresaw as charged with such great responsibilities.

If Miss O'Connor was James's "American girl" she wasted little time in baby talk or in bewailing her fate! She seems to have early envisioned the task that lay before her and during her short life all her energies were concentrated on its performance.

Her task, I think, resembled James's own task in many particulars. I believe, however, that the chief resemblance between the two writers consists in the fact that each was faced with an obstacle which, for a fiction writer, is almost always insuperable in his own lifetime. In order to create the world of illusion— which for him embodied fictional truth—both writers had to use a technique which was revolutionary.

The world contrived by the novelist or short story writer is, of course, an illusory world. Nevertheless, the analogy between fiction and real life holds—and must of necessity hold—if the novelist is to attain the verisimilitude which is his goal. The analogy holds, chiefly, I believe, because of the attitude which the reader shares with the natural man. The readers of novels are as firmly opposed to the use of any revolutionary technique in any novel as any one of us is naturally opposed to any invention which may change our way of life. We accept the inventions in the end, usually, but, as a rule, a great deal of energy has to be expended by somebody or many somebodies before we do accept it. The descendants of these people who used to shout "get a horse!" when the first automobile rolled past are doubtless crying out as shrilly as their grandfathers did at this moment, and in the same spirit. It is only the words of the slogan that have changed.

The history of literature provides a succession of examples of the reader's natural antipathy to revolutionary techniques; the reading public is consistent in its abhorrence of any innovation which enables a fiction writer to attain artistic effects which have not been attained before. Many a young novelist, however, has been astonished, dismayed, and profoundly depressed when he found that this attitude has been shared by the literary critics. As far as I can gather, there is no instance of a revolutionary talent—or technique—being recognized by any literary critic, who was not himself an artist. The first instance that comes to mind is Baudelaire's review of *Madame Bovary,* which, according to Flaubert, was the only review of the book which made sense to him. It was written by a fellow artist who happened to have a fine critical intelligence. James, himself, acknowledged the existence of this particular form of incomprehension in a review he wrote of one of Emil Faguet's books on Flaubert. He recognized M. Faguet's biography as definitive but he pointed out that the scholar's grasp is too "lax" to apprehend certain fictional effects.

Most literary critics, however, do not err through a kind of laxity of grasp but through misplaced belligerence. Ordinarily, the literary critic, when confronted with a revolutionary technique, not only refuses to accept it but hastens to fill the void of his incomprehension with brickbats, as it were. Witness the criticism which the contemporary literary critics accorded the early works of T. S. Eliot and James Joyce. Henry James, himself, contended with this lack of comprehension for a great part—the most important part—of his working life. So much so that he once wrote in his journal immediately after speaking of "the reader"—"Oh, if there only *were* a reader!"

Flaubert, whose works were long on the *Index,* chiefly, I have been told, because nobody had attempted to have them taken off, wrote Mme. Maurice Schlesinger that "*Madame Bovary* is a page out of the liturgy" but, he added, "the good folk who have the liturgy in their keeping cannot read very well." If Flaubert were alive today, I think that he might be inclined to revise his statement. I can even conceive his pointing out that some of "the good folk" are not only reading very well but writing very well! Certainly, anyone who surveys the contemporary literary scene cannot fail to be impressed by the fact that so many of our most talented young fiction writers not only write from a Catholic background (as Flaubert did, for all his personal skepticism), but are themselves practicing Catholics.

Of these young fiction writers Flannery O'Connor seems to me the most talented—and the most professional. My admiration for her work was first evoked when, in the line of duty, I contemplated the structure of "A Good Man Is Hard to Find" and found it written "in the one way that is mathematically right"—to borrow a phrase from James's notebooks.

Any expert performance is always more or less interesting to an audience. The spectacle of a young fiction writer achieving popular triumphs by the use of a technique which is not only revolutionary but universally derided is, for a fellow novelist, as exciting an experience as—a bullfight, say, can be for one who is *aficionado*. Indeed, I think we can profitably reflect upon one of those metaphors from the bullring in which Ernest Hemingway embodied his most profound conclusions about the art of fiction. He tells us in *The Sun Also Rises* that in a bullfight "there is the *terrain* of the man and the *terrain* of the bull." In a bullfight the unforgettable moments are those in which the matador sustains the invasion by the bull of his territory or, himself, invades the territory of the bull. During her short life, Miss O'Connor worked always "within the terrain of the bull." Perhaps that is one reason why she did not live longer.

Evelyn Waugh, when he first read one of her books, expressed a doubt that it had been written "by a young lady." Certainly, James's adjective "promiscuous" does not apply to her work. She, herself, felt that she was primarily a short story writer although she wrote two novels, *Wise Blood* and *The Violent Bear It Away*. Her best work, however, whether in the novel or the short story, has an outstanding characteristic. It is never "promiscuous." Her story is never "jerry-built"—if I understand James's use of that term. Indeed, it seems to me that she has a firmer grasp of the architectonics of fiction than any of her contemporaries. She has written four short stories, "A Good Man Is Hard to Find," "Good Country People," "The Displaced Person," and "The River," which seem to me nearly to approach perfection. "The Enduring Chill," "A Circle in the Fire" and "A Temple of the Holy Ghost" do not seem to me as successful.

But when Miss O'Connor falls short of her best work, the flaw is always in the *execution* of the story, not in its *structure*. In her architectural creations a turret may loom indistinctly or a roof line will slant so steeply that the eye follows it with difficulty but turret and roof and even battlements indistinctly limned are nevertheless recognized as integral parts of the structure. All her work is based upon the same architectural principle. This principle, fundamental but in our own times so fallen into disrepute that it has actually come to be thought of as an innovation, is, I think, the fact that any good story, no matter when it was written or in what language, or what its ostensible subject matter, shows both natural and supernatural grace operating in the lives of human beings. Her firm grasp of this great architectural principle is, I believe, in large part, responsible for Miss O'Connor's successes. A variety of causes may account for her failures or near-failures. Chief of them, of course, is the immense difficulty inherent in her subject matter. The chasm between natural and supernatural grace is sometimes an abyss, so deep that only the heroes—in fiction as in real life—can bear to contemplate it. "Look at the abyss long enough and it will look back at you," said Nietzsche, who was to experience at firsthand what he was talking about. In all her stories Miss O'Connor sets out to bridge this chasm, or, to speak more precisely, to do away with it. It is a task to appall the hardiest. No wonder her hand sometimes falters when the moment comes for the joining of the two terrains, as in "A Circle in the Fire" when "the Child" who figures frequently in Miss O'Connor's stories, sees in her mother's face "the new misery" she, herself, has just felt and sees also "[an old misery that] looked as if it might have belonged to anybody, a Negro or a European or to Powell himself" (232). Powell, the adolescent boy, finding that he can no longer even in memory possess the farm on which he spent the happiest days of his life, has just set the woods on fire.

> The child turned her head quickly, and past the Negroes' ambling figures she could see the column of smoke rising and widening unchecked inside the granite line of trees. She stood taut, listening, and could just catch in the distance a few wild high shrieks of joy as if the prophets were dancing in the fiery furnace, in the circle the angel had cleared for them [232].

The transition from the natural world to the supernatural seems to me too abrupt. Powell's response to the natural world is sensitive and passionate—"It was a horse named Gene . . . and a horse named George"—but so far he has excited only our compassion. We are not agile enough to visualize him as either Meshach, Shadrach or Abednego or even as enjoying the protection of an angel.

Sister Mariella Gable, O.S.B., speaks of Miss O'Connor as "the first great writer of ecumenical fiction anywhere in the world." [1] Catholic literary critics are not noted for their moderation or their interest in professional techniques. Time will doubtless tell us whether Miss O'Connor is one of our great fiction writers or whether she belongs in the ranks of the fine minor writers (where, after all, she would have quite distinguished company). But anyone who has followed the news of the world even casually may find himself agreeing with a part of Sister Mariella's encomium. It is an easily verifiable fact that Miss O'Connor was writing fiction in which men and women were involved in some of the same predicaments which were the subjects of discussion at the first ecumenical council—a good many years before John XXIII became Pope. She may not have considered her writing "ecumenical" but she was aware of its profound implications and their significance. This is evidenced by a letter she wrote Sister Mariella in 1963:

> Ideal Christianity doesn't exist, because anything the human being touches, even Christian truth, he deforms slightly to his own image. . . . To a lot of Protestants I know monks and nuns are fanatics, none greater. And to a lot of monks and nuns I know my Protestant prophets are fanatics. For my part, I think that the only difference between them is that if you are a Catholic and have this intensity of belief you join a convent and are heard of no more; whereas if you are Protestant and have it, there is no convent for you to join and you go about the world getting into all sorts of trouble and drawing the wrath of people who don't believe much of anything at all down on your head. . . .[2]

Philip Scharper has pointed out that "Flannery O'Connor was one of those artists—rare in any age—who saw life *sub specie aeternitatis.*" [3] It is certainly true that in her stories every incident is seen in the light of eternity, one of the marks of a creative imagination of the first rank. But she has another distinction, one which is unique in our day. She was a pioneer in a field which is not only considered dangerous for the fiction writer but is commonly regarded as forbidden ground. She was the first fiction writer to view her own region—it happened to be the rural South—through the eyes of Roman Catholic orthodoxy. In doing this she ran counter to the belief held by most novel readers and nearly all reviewers that religious conversion or, indeed, any of the operations of supernatural grace are not subjects for fictional rendition.

James, who in his notebooks referred to the writing of fiction as "the sacred calling," would not have hesitated, I suspect, to brand this conviction as a "heresy." It may be a sign of the degeneracy of letters in our times—where would Dante or Shakespeare have been if confronted with such a taboo? But no one can deny that it is firmly rooted in the contemporary mind. The literary magazines publish endless discussions of the "handicaps" which the novelist who is a practicing Catholic supposedly works under. The reviewers, if confronted, as one is inevitably confronted in any fictional masterpiece, with the workings of supernatural grace, are as prudish (theologically) as the Victorian lady is supposed to have been when apprised of some of the grosser manifestations of sex.

This taboo has had a constrictive effect on some of the best fictional talents of our times. The novelist who is a Catholic (and in some cases is a novelist because he is a Catholic) cannot fail to take the workings of supernatural grace into account in his novels but his rendition of its workings is frequently *sub rosa* and so oblique that the reader is not quite sure what has happened. In many cases the creative imagination suffers another kind of constriction. The novelist is so bewildered by the clamor from the marketplace that he cannot allow his imagination free play; the incident in which supernatural grace figures is not allowed to attain the proportions which are necessary if it is to have its desired effect. The result is a fictional structure which is "jerry-built." At any rate, such a novel does not create "the single impression" which James found requisite.

Miss O'Connor, almost alone among her contemporaries, adheres strictly to the great architectural principle (upon which James's three great later novels are based) that in the life of certain human beings supernatural grace operates as freely as natural grace—if only when being resisted.

Her work owed its first popularity to the fact that her stage is peopled by so many freaks. We like—everybody has always liked—to contemplate monsters—from a distance. One of Miss O'Connor's early critics wrote that one could not tell the difference between the characters in one of her stories and the characters in one of Truman Capote's stories.[4] There is all the difference in the world—both in the natural and the supernatural world! When we finish reading one of Mr. Capote's stories we are not in any doubt as to the fate of the chief character but weeks or months later we may find ourselves speculating as to how he "got that way." Such speculations do not arise in connection with Miss O'Connor's characters. If they are freaks, they are freaks for one reason only: they have been deprived of the sacraments. Of the Blood of Christ, as Enoch Emery and Haze Motes are deprived in *Wise Blood*, as the boy, Harry, is deprived in "The River," as the one-legged female doctor of philosophy and her seducer, the false Bible salesman, are deprived in "Good Country People."

The serious student of Miss O'Connor's stories will find it profitable, I think, to compare her life's work with that of Henry James. The novels of his "later" period deal with the imposition of supernatural grace upon natural grace. Lambert Strether's last meeting with Mme. de Vionnet is in a room in which the candles flicker as if upon "an altar." The "voice of Paris," which spoke to him so compellingly on the day of his first arrival in the city, comes in through the open windows but the vague, murmurous voices speak to him now of the tumult which accompanied the fall of the Bastille. They cry out for "*Blood!*" Mme. de Vionnet is dressed this evening in a way which reminds him of the way Mme. Roland must have looked as she rode in the tumbril to the guillotine. Mme. de Vionnet, who is clearly cast in the role of sacrificial victim, shows us that she understands her role when, in her conversation with Strether, she paraphrases one of the Beatitudes: "The thing is to give . . . never to take. That is the only thing that never plays you false." *The Wings of the Dove* rests similarly on a Christian foundation. Kate Croy and her fiancé, Merton Densher, are happy enough in their love for each other but Kate feels that they would be happier if they were not so poor. She persuades Densher to pay court to the ailing heiress, Milly Theale, in the hope that if he marries her she will leave them her money at her death. The woman tempted him and he fell. Milly Theale does leave her money to Densher when she dies, sooner than she would have died in the ordinary course of events. Densher is so overcome by the realization of his guilt that the Angel of the Flaming Sword speaks through his lips when he says to Kate: "We shall never again be as we were!"

Through his genius James apprehended the archetypal Christian patterns. He tells us, however, in *Notes of a Son and Brother* that neither he nor any of his brothers or his sister were "allowed to divine an item of devotional practice" in their childhood. Instead, they were sent to churches of first one denomination then another in order that they might choose the religion that suited them best. He records that he wondered, even as a small child, why "we were so religious" and yet practiced no religion. One of those great metaphors which illuminate his writings may have arisen first in his infant imagination. He visualized his household as a temple dedicated to what his mother called "Father's ideas." His mother, he tells us, seemed to enact the role of priestess. At least, she was nearly always to be found on the steps of the temple where "beakers of the divine fluid" were also always to be found, "though," he says, "I cannot remember that any of us ever quaffed from them."

That percipient critic, Austin Warren, has included the elder Henry James in his roster of *New England Saints*. The novelist's father was certainly a saintly figure. Henry James, Jr. paints a moving picture of his father seated every morning at his desk, pausing sometimes to sigh and pass his hand eerily over his forehead, then returning to his task: "the one book he was all his life writing."

The elder James, like many thoughtful men of his day, was influenced by the writings of Emanuel Swedenborg, but he was not wholly in agreement with him. Indeed, he was not wholly in agreement with anybody. His "New Church," whose tenets he spent his life setting forth, contained only one member, himself, or so one of his friends wittily averred.

His son William James said that editing his father's literary remains was the hardest task he ever faced. But both he and his brother, Henry James, Jr., felt that he did his father's memory full justice. A paragraph from a book called *Society the Redeemed Form of Man: An Earnest of God's Providence* shows us that William's task was, indeed, no easy one:

> It is in fact the venomous tradition of a natural as well as a personal disproportion between man and his maker—speciously cloaked as it is under the ascription of a supernatural being and existence to God,—that alone gives its intolerable odium and poignancy to men's otherwise healthful and restorative conscience of sin. That man's personality should utterly alienate him from God,—that is to say make him infinitely other and opposite to God,—this I grant you with all my heart; since if God were the least like me personally, all my hope in him would perish. . . . But that God should be also an infinitely *foreign* substance to me, —an infinitely other or foreign *nature*,—this wounds my spontaneous faith in him to its core, or leaves it a mere mercenary and servile homage. . . .

I do not know that Miss O'Connor was consciously influenced by the novelist Henry James's work. I am inclined to think that the affinity between the two writers is instinctive and unconscious. One of Miss O'Connor's "prophets," Hazel Motes, who preaches the "Church Without Christ," strongly resembles the elder Henry James. Both men have one lifelong preoccupation: theology. In the case of both men it is coupled with an inability to believe in the divinity of Christ. Both men are indifferent to worldly goods. The elder James never envisaged for any of his children a career which took into account the making of money. Hazel lives on the pension he receives for a disability incurred in the war. When his landlady calls his attention to four one dollar bills she has found in his wastebasket, he tells her that he threw them there because "they were left over." In addition to his practice of an almost Franciscan poverty, he practices mortifications of the flesh, putting pebbles and bits of broken glass in the bottoms of his shoes while he wears a strand of barbed wire coiled about his waist. In the end, he blinds him-

self with quicklime in his frenzied effort to see more clearly—
that which is invisible to mortal eyes.

James left us, along with the prodigious body of his work,
a complete, detailed record of his life as an artist. Those of us
who still cannot read his novels, cannot plead in self-defense
that he has not given us any clue how to go about reading them,
for he has given us explicit directions.

Miss O'Connor is almost as well documented as to her
artistic intentions. Dialogues, panels, discussions of the nature
of the creative process are much in vogue these days. Almost
every novelist has had to take part in such discussions on some
occasion. Miss O'Connor has been subjected to as many ques-
tionnaires as any writer I can think of. She has submitted with
an unusually good grace. Over and over she has explained, as
best she could, what she has been trying to do. I find her intentions admirably summed up in a colloquy which took place
between her and Gerard Sherry, editor of the *Georgia Bulletin*:

MR. SHERRY: What do you think is stifling the Catholic writer
of today . . .?
MISS O'CONNOR: I think it's the lack of a large intelligent reading
audience which believes Christ is God.[5]

I believe that a personal reminiscence may not be out of place
here. I had the privilege of visiting Flannery O'Connor in a
hospital a few weeks before her death. She told me that the
doctor had forbidden her to do any work. He said that it was
all right to write a little fiction, though, she added with a grin
and drew a notebook out from under her pillow. She kept it
there, she told me, and was trying to finish a story which she
hoped to include in the volume which we both knew would be
published posthumously. The story, "Parker's Back,"[6] does not
have the perfection of phrasing which characterizes "Good
Country People" or "A Good Man Is Hard to Find" but it is as
sound architecturally as either of them. Parker, a Georgia
hillbilly, becomes a collector of tattoos during his service in

the Navy. Only his back is unornamented. Finally, in an effort
to impress his wife, a religious fanatic, who tells him that the
tiger and panther which adorn his shoulders, the cobra coiled
about a torch on his chest, the hawks on his thighs are all "Vanity of vanities," he approaches an unusually high-priced "artist"
and tells him that he wants a picture of God tattooed on his
back. The artist asks:

> "Father, Son or Spirit?"
> "Just God," Parker said impatiently. "Christ. I don't care. Just
> so it's God" [*Everything*, 234].

He selects from the catalogue which the artist places before
him a representation of a "stern Christ with all-demanding
eyes," which the reader recognizes as Byzantine. After he has
made his choice he "sat there trembling; his heart began slowly
to beat again as if it were being brought to life by a subtle
power" (*Everything*, 235).

Parker tells the artist that his new tattoo is to be a surprise
for his wife. "You think she'll like it and lay off you for a while?"
the artist asks shrewdly. "She can't hep herself," Parker said.
"She can't say she don't like the looks of God" (*Everything*,
238).

Parker's wife wastes no words, however, when she sees the
image of Christ tattooed on his back. She seizes a broom and
belabors him until he is nearly senseless and the face of the
Christ is covered with bleeding welts. The American girl has
succeeded where the great Flaubert failed! In this story in
which there are no theological references other than those
which might be found on the lips of "good country people," the
author has embodied that particular heresy which denies Our
Lord corporeal substance. During his lifetime, Henry James
never found the reader he so ardently desired but I think that
in Flannery O'Connor there was a disciple of whom he could
have been proud.

## Notes

1. "The Ecumenic Core in the Fiction of Flannery O'Connor," *American Benedictine Review*, XV (June, 1964), 127-43.

2. *Ibid.*

3. "Flannery O'Connor—a tribute," *Esprit*, VIII (Winter, 1964), 45.

4. William Esty, "In America, Intellectual Bomb Shelters," *Commonweal*, LXVII (March 7, 1958), 586-88.

5. "An Interview with Flannery O'Connor," *Critic*, XXI (June-July, 1963), 29.

6. *Everything That Rises Must Converge*, pp. 219-44.

# Flannery O'Connor's Testimony

## The Pressure of Glory

NATHAN A. SCOTT, JR.

IN MANY of his books of recent years, the historian of religion, Mircea Eliade has been contending (as he says at one point in *Birth and Rebirth*[1]) that "modern man's originality, his newness in comparison with traditional societies, lies precisely . . . in his wish to live in a basically desacralized cosmos." And, for Professor Eliade, the *désacralisé* represents that style which human life takes on, when a decision is made to situate all value and aspiration within the dimension of the *profane* and when Transcendence is conceived to be a chimerical superstition of the pre-scientific imagination. Desacralization, in other words, as a kind of mutation in cultural history, entails something vastly more profound than the mere collapse of formal theistic religion. For the *désacralisé* cuts deeper than anything that might be said to be an affair of "ideology," and it involves that total secularization of consciousness which is distinguished by an inability to descry any reality in the world that evokes a sense of ultimacy or of radical significance.

The man whose sense of reality has been formed by the "advanced" culture of a profane society has lost, or is by way of losing, God; but, more basically, he is a man whose life is lived at a great distance from the Sacred. Indeed, like the hero of Hemingway's *A Farewell to Arms*, his first impulse is to be even a little embarrassed "by the [very] words sacred, glorious. . . ." For his experience is without any numinous "thresholds": he does not live on "the borderland of a something more." [2] His time is not intersected by any dimension of Eternity. Nature is untouched by Supernature; the threshold of the Holy is gone—and maybe (if we are to believe the sociology of what is called "depersonalization") even the "thresholds" that we are given by our relations with other persons, maybe even these are lost.

The English philosopher Ernest Gellner, in a brilliantly crotchety critique of Linguistic Analysis, says that, though this is a philosophic movement which "often considers the pursuit of world-views to be *the* cardinal sin of thought," [3] it yet does itself in fact have a view of the world—a view of the world which is statable in such a proposition as "The world is what it is" or "Things are as they are," or, as it was put in the proposition by Bishop Butler which G. E. Moore took over as a kind of motto of his own philosophy: "Everything is what it is and not another thing." And it is precisely such a banalization of reality as this that is the end-result of radical profanization: the world is experienced as silent and is conceived to be merely what it is, and not another thing. *All* the numinous thresholds of experience are lost: everything is *levelled* and (as a consequence) "platitudinized," so that man himself loses his substantial reality and becomes a creature filled with the kind of porousness that characterizes so many of the images of contemporary sculpture—"full of holes and gaps, faceless, riddled with doubts and negations, starkly finite." [4]

Nor should it be supposed that reflection upon the peculiar kind of spiritual tragedy involved in "desacralization" entails merely a shuffling and reshuffling of fictive counters invented by the Christian apologist for the sake of bullying into submission his secular brethren. This would, of course, be a misapprehension that has long since been undermined by the psychologists who deal in "the crisis of identity" and the sociologists who specialize in "alienation" and the "Mass-man." But, to say nothing of these dreary reports, we have only to recall

some of the representative heroes and anti-heroes in the literature of the last forty or fifty years—Eliot's Prufrock, Kafka's
Gregor Samsa (*Metamorphosis*), Graham Greene's Minty
(*England Made Me*), Sartre's Roquentin (*Nausea*), Arthur
Miller's Willy Loman (*Death of a Salesman*), Camus' Meur-
sault (*The Stranger*)—we have only to recall such modern
personages as these to be put in mind of a certain denudation
and a certain death that the human spirit itself seems to have
suffered as a result of having ousted itself from the precincts of
sacral reality.

But however much the desacralized universe of modern
secularity may be a universe without thresholds, the world
that is at man's disposal is not in truth merely

> A heap of broken images, where the sun beats
> And the dead tree gives no shelter, the cricket no relief,
> And the dry stone no sound of water. . . .[5]

It is, rather, a universe that asks us to be "radically amazed" at
"the silent allusion of [all] things to a meaning greater than
themselves." [6] For the world is not simply *what it is*; on the
contrary, it is filled with "the miracles which are daily with us,"
and these are not matters of the sensational and the magnificent
—like volcanic eruptions or uncommon psychic phenomena—
but of the ordinary and the commonplace, in that dimension of
their depth which forever eludes all our categories and *with-
stands* exhaustive analysis. A modern philosopher may smugly
say, in effect, "The world is what it is," but the more truly
human attitude is surely that of astonishment that there is a
world at all and that its processes and functioning are governed
by the regularities which science studies. Indeed, scientific
research itself, as Abraham Heschel reminds us, is only "an
entry into the endless, not a blind alley. . . . One answer
breeds a multitude of new questions. . . . Everything hints
at something that transcends it. . . . What appears to be a
center is but a point on the periphery of another center." [7]

And the ineffable dwells not merely in the grandiose and the remarkable but in every nook and cranny of our experience— in the rain's satisfying the desolation of the earth and the mysteries of vegetation, in the beauty of holiness and the radiance of true sagacity, in all the bounties of nature and civilization and in all the blessings and defeats of life.

Nor is the essential dignity of the world fully honored apart from the attitude of "radical amazement" before its amplitude and mystery and sublimity. Indeed, perhaps the surest sign of what Professor Eliade calls "desacralization" is the habit of *taking things for granted,* the habit of indifference to what is most primitively marvelous in man himself and in the world which constitutes the theatre of his living. And true wonder is not an indolent complacency or state of content with ignorance: it is not an indifference toward creative research and rational analysis, nor is it a reverencing of *the unknown.* For *mystery* is not the unknown but, rather, that surplusage of meaning in what is known, that inexhaustible Ground of reality by which we are moved when we perform an act of true attention before the creatures of the earth. And thus it is not something that arises out of the perceptual process itself; *mystery* is not, in other words, a name for a merely subjective reality. It is, rather, an ontological category, for it speaks not of anything foisted upon the world by the human imagination but of "a most powerful presence beyond the mind" which makes for "a fundamental norm of human consciousness." [8] It is not something which we infer from a psychological reaction but rather that to which the *sense* of mystery, of wonder, of amazement, is a response. "We do not come upon it only at the climax of thinking or in observing strange, extraordinary facts but in the startling fact that there are facts at all. . . . We may face it at every turn, in a grain of seed, in an atom, as well as in the stellar space. Everything holds the great secret. For it is the inescapable situation of all being to be involved in the infinite mystery. We may continue to disregard the mystery, but we can neither deny nor escape it. The world is something *we apprehend but cannot comprehend.*" [9] As Paul Tillich said in one of his finest sermons, ". . . you cannot think or say: Life has no depth! Life is shallow. Being itself is surface only." [10] And the human reality cannot legitimately be either thought or said to be merely an affair of surface and without depth, because it is never anything, if profoundly experienced, that can, as it were, be "seen through." The deep things of self-knowledge and love, of suffering and joy and holiness do always, finally, resist exhaustive analysis, and thus they offer a kind of attestation to the environing Mystery which is ineradicably a part of our human life-world.

So, insofar as it is the distinctive privilege and vocation of humankind to retain a sense of wonder before the "miracles which are daily with us"—insofar is man indeed a creature "trailing clouds of glory," for he is "isled" in an atmosphere effulgent of mystery and wonder, and glory. And for him to have lost any lively awareness of this fact is for him to have "fallen" into the profane: for this is what "desacralization" most deeply entails—not merely the deadening ossification of the creedal formularies of the great received traditions of religious orthodoxy but the death of all awareness of any animating power or *presence* amidst and within the familiar realities of nature and history, the loss of any radical amazement before the rich complexity and plenitude of the world. Thus it is that perhaps the extremest heresy which the human spirit can embrace is that which has, as it were, been codified by modern positivism, of supposing that man's only transaction is with those things which can be weighed and measured and handled in a calculating and deliberate way.

Indeed, it is just the inclination of the men and women of our age toward this most impertinent of all heresies that has sometimes awakened in the modern writer a kind of rage and led him to make his writing itself an act of violence. And, in Léon Bloy and Charles Péguy and the early T. S. Eliot and Georges Bernanos and Graham Greene (to mention only a few), we encounter a line of artists who confront the profanization of life in the modern world by saying in one way or another, and with a violent kind of urgency and harshness, *"J'accuse!"*

Now it is as a part of this tradition that we ought, I believe, to understand the legacy of that remarkably valiant and gifted young American, Flannery O'Connor, who departed this life at her home in Milledgeville, Georgia, in the summer of 1964, after a long and painful illness. The cruel fate which struck her down before her fortieth birthday kept her, unfortunately, from producing a large body of work. But in her two novels— *Wise Blood* (1952) and *The Violent Bear It Away* (1960)— and her two collections of stories, *A Good Man Is Hard to Find* (1955) and *Everything That Rises Must Converge* (1965), she leaves a body of work which is to be counted amongst the finest fiction produced anywhere by her literary generation. And what makes it in part so notable are the radical kinds of moral judgment into the service of which she was so intent on putting her art. It was indeed always an art that very much wanted to wake the spirit's sleep, to break that somnolence into which we flee from the exactions of the moral life; and it consistently expresses a fierce kind of rage at the feckless, lacklustre slum to which the human world is reduced when, through indolence of spirit or failure of imagination, men have lost all sense of the pressure of glory upon the mundane realities of experience and have thus "fallen" into the profane. It was, one feels, in just such a velleity as this that Flannery O'Connor found what she took to be most characteristically defective in the life of our time: for her, the major sickness of the age was something like what medieval doctors of the soul called *acedia*, and it is to this condition that her art is principally responding.

This is a response, however, which is not merely negative in its thrust. It has, of course, its negative side, and a part of what is most vivacious and cogent in Miss O'Connor's fiction is an affair of her genius for polemical engagement and for a stinging critique of the sterile banality of life-style that is bred by modern secularity. But there is also another side of her response to the modern scene, and one which I am helped to identify by a remark of the late C. S. Lewis about the Scottish fantasist, George MacDonald. Recalling the impact that Mac-Donald's *Phantastes* had upon him, when he first chanced to read it in his youth, he says: "It did nothing to my intellect nor (at that time) to my conscience. Their turn came far later and with the help of many other books and men. . . . What it actually did to me was to convert, even to baptize . . . my imagination."[11] And something like this may also be what Miss O'Connor was aiming at in part. She had, in other words, a constructive purpose as well as a negative purpose: she wanted not only to exhibit what is banal and trivializing in the desacralized world of modern unbelief but also to portray its vacuity in such a way as to stir the imagination into some fresh awareness of what has been lost—and thus to "baptize" it, to render it open and responsive once more to the dimension of the Sacred and the pressure of glory.

The negative and critical side of this stratagem is everywhere a part of Miss O'Connor's writing, but perhaps at no point can it be felt with such force as in her novel of 1960, *The Violent Bear It Away*. Francis Marion Tarwater is a fourteen-year-old boy who has been reared in the backwoods of Georgia by a great-uncle, Mason Tarwater, whose violent bibliolatry has determined him to raise up the boy "to justify his Redemption" (306). And the two lessons which the old man has year-in and year-out enjoined upon his nephew are the necessity of giving him a decent burial when he dies and his obligation somehow to do what he himself has never been able to manage, the baptizing of the idiot child of young Tarwater's uncle, Rayber, who lives in a neighboring city where he practices his profession of psychologist as a school official. At last, one morning the old man does die: as he sits down to his breakfast, "red ropes appear in his face" (309), a tremor passes over him, his mouth twists down sharply on one side, and he is dead, but remaining "perfectly balanced, his back a good six inches from the chair back and his stomach caught just under the edge of the table, . . . [h]is eyes, dead silver, . . . focussed on the boy across from him" (309).

But young Tarwater does not now proceed properly to inter the body: the morning heat is oppressive, and, after taking a few too many swigs of the old man's liquor, instead of digging a grave, he simply sets fire to the shack, with the body still inside. Then he leaves the little isolated strip of corn patch where they have lived together for so long and goes off to the city to look up Rayber. But the old man cannot so easily be gotten away from, and the central *agon* of the novel grows out of the fierce competition between Old Tarwater (or his spiritual legacy) and Rayber for the boy's suffrage to their respective views of reality.

The boy himself had at first been a ward of Rayber's, but had been kidnapped by Old Tarwater, lest the child become simply "a piece of information inside . . . [Rayber's] head" (313). For at a still earlier time, many years before, the old man, while living with Rayber, had discovered that the schoolteacher's apparent interest in his vocation as a prophet of the Lord was something all faked and dishonest. At first Rayber had asked the old man "numerous questions, the answers to which he had sometimes scratched down on a pad, his little eyes lighting every now and then as if in some discovery" (314). And Old Tarwater was by way of thinking that he was on the verge of converting his nephew—until he discovered that Rayber was making him the subject of magazine articles in which it was asserted that "[h]is fixation of being called by the Lord had its origin in insecurity" (314). Then it was that the old man realized that "every living thing that passed through . . . [Rayber's] eyes into his head was turned by his brain into a book or a paper or a chart" (314). "Where he wanted me was inside that schoolteacher magazine. He thought once he got me in there, I'd be as good as inside his head and done for and that would be that, that would be the end of it" (315). It was, he felt, a blasphemy that was being committed against his person, and so he left Rayber's house. And when, some years later, after young Tarwater's orphanage had necessitated his being taken over by his uncle, his great-uncle kidnapped him, bringing him to his little corn patch out in the country and thus rescuing him from what had very nearly been his own fate, of being simply a piece of information inside Rayber's head. "I saved you to be free, your own self!" he likes to shout at the boy—". . . not a piece of information inside his head!" (312-313). *And* Old Tarwater saves the boy in order that he might know that "Jesus is the bread of life" (315).

The old man, having been "schooled in the evils that befall prophets"—"in those that come from the world, which are trifling, and those that come from the Lord and burn the prophet clean" (306)—having been "schooled" in calamity and having been "called in his early youth," the old man is possessed by "a rage of vision," and his nerves have been made taut by his sense of the pressure of Glory: he is a man consecrated by his overpowering conviction that the true country of the soul is the Sacred. So, for all of his grotesque fantastications—his belief that the sun will one day "burst in blood and fire" and that "a finger of fire" will destroy the sinful human city—he has in himself the dignity of an absolute spiritual heroism.

But on Rayber the novel is merciless in venting a spleen whose malice is reserved for those who inhabit a world that is utterly desacralized. With all the heartless inhumanity of his psychological gadgetry—his charts and graphs and I.Q. tests —his is a "headpiece filled with straw." "He's full of nothing," says Old Tarwater—"taking secret tests on me . . . crawling into my soul through the back door and then . . . [saying] to me, 'Uncle, you're a type that's almost extinct!' " (320). He is a hollow man, a man full of nothing because, as Old Tarwater says, "He don't know it's anything he can't know, . . . That's his trouble. He thinks if it's something he can't know then somebody smarter than him can tell him about it and he can know it just the same. And if you were to go there, the first thing he would do would be to test your head and tell you what you were thinking and howcome you were thinking it and what you ought to be thinking instead. And before long you wouldn't belong to your self no more, you would belong to him." A man full of nothing—who cannot look intently at anything, not even at "a stick or a stone, the line of a shadow, the absurd old man's walk of a starling crossing the sidewalk," for to permit himself fully to encounter any aspect of the world is for him to run the risk of being cross-questioned out of the unreality in which he lives. So he is frightened of love—not of "love in general," for he "knew the value of it and how it could be used," but of the kind that was "without reason, love for something futureless, love that appeared to exist only to be itself, imperious and all demanding, the kind that would cause him to make a fool of himself in an instant" (336-337).

Old Tarwater had regarded Rayber's idiot son as "precious in the sight of the Lord," despite his incompetence—but, to the child's father, he is simply "a mistake of nature." And, suspecting what is true, that, despite young Tarwater's asserted unbelief, the old man's "seed" has fallen into him and that he intends to try to baptize the child (as Old Tarwater himself had tried on several occasions to do, till finally he was run away from Rayber's house by the police), Rayber says to him, "You want to avoid extremes. They are for violent people . . ." (390).

But Rayber's intuition about his nephew does indeed in the end prove to be right. For the old man's seed has fallen into young Tarwater, and he is quick to seize the first real chance that comes along to perform the duty laid upon him by his fanatical great-uncle. Rayber has taken the two, his little son and young Tarwater, out of the city to a lodge, a kind of motel, for a brief holiday, hoping that it will afford him some way of reaching his nephew and winning his confidence. But there it is that young Tarwater, after rowing the little boy out onto the bordering lake one afternoon, baptizes the child—and, in doing so, drowns him. From this point on, of course, he is a

criminal and an outlaw, hunted and pursued; but it is in this
extremity that he comes to realize that he does in truth belong
to "that violent country where the silence is never broken
except to shout the truth." He realizes, in other words, that the
fire which encircles him is that which "had encircled Daniel,
that had raised Elijah from the earth, that had spoken to
Moses." He knows himself to bear an inescapable vocation to
"WARN THE CHILDREN OF GOD OF THE TERRIBLE
SPEED OF MERCY": so he moves "steadily on, his face set
toward the dark city, where the children of God lay sleeping"
(447).

And thus it is that we are put in mind of what St. Matthew's
Gospel tells us, that "from the days of John the Baptist, the
kingdom of heaven suffereth violence and the violent bear it
away" (11:12). They, of course, by reason of their very violence, represent deformity and are misshapen: yet it is a hu-
manly comprehensible deformity, and its passionateness in the
things of the spirit can be, even if obliquely, a means of grace.
But, as Dante says, those "paltry, who never were alive," who
spend their substance "without infamy and without praise,"
are "of a truth . . . odious to God and to his enemies"; these
are they who, having forsaken all the numinous "thresholds" of
experience, are simply "full of nothing."

Of these *isolés* Rayber is an extreme instance in Flannery
O'Connor's fiction. But there are many other acidulous portraits—particularly in the stories collected in *A Good Man Is
Hard to Find*—of the reduction in human stature, of the sterility and desiccation, that are brought by the disease of positivism, of supposing that life can simply be brought to heel and
made to submit to management. And this sterile rationalism is
often, by some stroke of irony, doubled back upon its own essential incompetence (as in the Mrs. McIntyre of "The Displaced Person," or the Hulga Hopewell of "Good Country
People," or the Sheppard of "The Lame Shall Enter First").
Indeed, wherever the poison of secularity attacks the mind, a
terrible neutrality of spirit and dreariness of life sets in—as in

the Ruby Hill of "A Stroke of Good Fortune," disgustedly
fighting off knowledge of her own pregnancy with disgusted
recollections from childhood of her mother's various pregnan-
cies; or the drunken and neglectful parents of the hapless little
boy of "The River" (in A Good Man Is Hard to Find) who live
in a dreary little subway of the world and who provide an environment for their child's nurture in which there is the very
stench of the profane, the very odor of damnation itself.

But, then, Miss O'Connor's art finds its poise not merely in
horrified rejection of the dehumanizing wilderness that is
created by radical secularity. For it is also a part of its purpose
to "baptize" the modern imagination, to render the human
story in such a way as to stretch the secular memory to the
extremest possible limits, so that some awareness will be re-
awakened of how deep the deep places of human life really
are, and of how insistently a transcendent dimension presses
in upon the horizontal plane of existential reality. Her proce-
dure here, however, does not involve any sort of direct presen-
tation of the Christian evangel; it is, rather, something very
subtly circuitous and dialectical. As she herself said, "When
you can assume that your audience holds the same beliefs you
do, you can relax a little and use more normal ways of talking
to it; when you have to assume that it does not, then you have
to make your vision apparent by shock—to the hard of hearing
you shout, and for the almost blind you draw large and startling
figures." [12]

But her "figures" are never of faith and sanctity, or at least
they are so only rarely. For she felt that "writers who see by
the light of their Christian faith will have, in these times," to
run the risk of working with "the grotesque, . . . the perverse,
and . . . the unacceptable": they "will find in modern life
distortions which are repugnant to [them], and [their] problem
will be to make these appear as distortions to an audience
which is used to seeing them as natural; and [they] may well be
forced to take ever more violent means to get [their] vision
across to this hostile audience." [13]

This was in fact frequently the course that Miss O'Connor did herself take, and thus the figures that her fiction draws are not only large and startling, but, very often, they are figures of murderers and mountebanks, of rapists and gangsters and neurotic religious zealots, of the hopeless young and the desperate old. It might even be said that cheating and callousness and violence and the harming of the innocent and moral squalor are the bone and marrow of her art. Yet such a characterization of it would be acceptable, or partially so, only if it were also informed by the recognition that the ultimate law governing Flannery O'Connor's fiction is that of the *coincidentia oppositorum*. For what she seems to have felt is that, since the great pieties of Christian belief are not normally characteristic of our culture, they cannot therefore become the subject matter of an authentic contemporary art. But, if the human material of a truly contemporary literature has to be secular, then let it be radically secular, since negation, if it be profound enough, may itself, by reason of its very radicalism, begin to evoke sensibilities capable of a religious perception of reality—and thus the opposites will coincide, at the heart of darkness.

So it was, one suspects, the hope of achieving something like a *coincidentia oppositorum* that led Miss O'Connor to people her books with so many monsters of nihilism and blasphemy: it is by such a dialectical route as this, she seems to have felt, that the Christian writer stands his best chance of baptizing the secular imagination of our time.

Of this whole stratagem, it is undoubtedly her first novel, *Wise Blood* (1952), that affords the finest example. Its protagonist, Hazel Motes, is a young self-ordained evangelist of an hysterical nihilism, who comes out of the backwoods of Tennessee, proclaiming the gospel of "no truth behind all truths," that "nothing matters but that Jesus was a liar": his church is the "Church Without Christ" (60). Hazel's home, originally, was a little Tennessee hamlet called Eastrod, and there it was, as a boy of twelve (the age at which Jesus announced that he had to be about his Father's business), that he first felt a vocation to preach, partly no doubt as a result of the impact upon him of his grandfather who was an itinerant evangelist—"a waspish old man who had ridden over three counties with Jesus hidden in his head like a stinger" (15). But then came the Second World War and the requirement for Haze of military service, which he took to be simply a "trick to lead him into temptation"; and so, in a way, it was, for it was amidst the dislocations of army life that "he had all the time he could want to study his soul in"—and, studying it, he found "it was not there," that fornication and blasphemy and sin "ain't nothing but words," that "Jesus is a trick on niggers," and that "there was no Fall because there was nothing to fall from and no Redemption because there was no Fall and no Judgment because there wasn't the first two" (60).

After he is mustered out of the army, Haze returns to Eastrod, but there had originally been no more than about twenty-five inhabitants of the place, and, now, all are gone, his family house deserted, with weeds growing through the porch floor. He decides not to stay, but to go on to the city of Taulkinham, which is to be the scene and site of his curiously inverted evangelism in behalf of what is now for him the great truth, that there is no truth behind all truths. There, in the downtown streets, he mounts his old rat-colored Essex car to preach the Church Without Christ: "I'm member and preacher to that church where the blind don't see and the lame don't walk and what's dead stays that way. . . . it's the church that the blood of Jesus don't foul with redemption." But, despite its passionateness, his preaching elicits little more than a hunch of the shoulder from his bemused and perfunctory auditors: "He's a preacher," says a woman one night to her companions. "Let's go" (60).

Nor is the response that comes from the one person in whom he does strike a spark the sort that brings him any satisfaction. Little Enoch Emery encounters Haze soon after the young preacher comes to Taulkinham. He once attended, as he says, "thisyer Rodemill Boys' Bible Academy that a woman sent me to. If it's anything you want to know about Jesus, just ast me." But, formed as he has been by the fossilized banalities of a bankrupt fundamentalism, he is really unprepared to reckon with what is genuinely radical in Haze's testimony. So when he hears Haze inviting his streetcorner congregation one night to show him a "new jesus" (79), in order that this "jesus" might be set up in the Church Without Christ and that they might thereby be given proof that they haven't been redeemed —when Enoch hears this, his wise blood "confers with itself," and he decides to steal (and does steal) from the municipal museum a little shrunken mummy that has long fascinated him, offering it to Haze as a "new jesus." But Haze had been speaking ironically that night, and his nihilism does not in literal truth have any use at all for a "new jesus," for he wants nothing to shield him, or others, from the blank emptiness that he has seen beyond the world's horizon. As he says, "There's no such thing as any new jesus. That ain't anything but a way to say something" (87).

Indeed, Haze wants nothing that will adjust him "O.K. to the modern world," neither any orthodoxy of belief nor any new codification of heterodoxy. Nor does he allow himself to be distracted by the claims of sensuality. He has, it is true, affairs with two women, first with the blowzy prostitute, Mrs. Leora Watts, and then with Sabbath Lily Hawks, the serpentine daughter of a street-preacher. But, in each case, he makes us feel that he takes the woman "not for the sake of the pleasure in her, but to prove that he didn't believe in sin since he practiced what was called it" (63).

Sensuality, in other words, were it to be enjoyed and revelled in for its own sake, would mock the truth—the truth that there is no truth behind all truths, that there is nothing in reality that can be depended upon either to sanction or to comfort the human spirit. And just as surely would that truth be mocked, Haze feels, were its proclamation in any way to be commercialized. So he is infuriated when Hoover Shoats, an

oily confidence man who calls himself Onnie Jay Holy, pro-
poses that they form a business alliance. Shoats used to be on
the radio, with a program of "Mood, Melody, and Mentality"
called "Soulsease" that gave "real religious experiences to the
whole family" (86). He has a great gift for salesmanship and
knows a good racket when he finds one: so when he happens on
Haze preaching one night and hears the talk about a "new
jesus," he is immediately thrilled by his sense of the possibilities: "I never heard a idear before that had more in it than
that one. All it would need," he tells Haze, "is a little promo-
tion" (87). But Haze is repelled by the sliminess of the little
grafter and will have nothing to do with him—whereupon
Shoats promises to run him "out of business." And the next
night he appears on Haze's corner, with a man strikingly like
Haze in appearance who wears the same "glare-blue" suit and
white hat, a consumptive named Solace Layfield. Shoats gathers
the crowd around and takes up a collection after Layfield concludes the same sort of harangue Haze has been nightly de-
livering, from atop a high rat-colored car identical with Haze's
old machine. Haze watches the whole episode, and, afterwards, follows Layfield on his way home and runs him down
with his automobile (which is in truth, as Caroline Gordon
reminds us, his pulpit).[14] And the judgment he flings at the
dying man is short and blunt—"You ain't true" (110).

But Layfield's untruth is of a piece with what Haze everywhere encounters, whether it be that of Enoch or Hoover
Shoats or Asa Hawks (who, though an unbeliever, preaches
Christ, simply as a small business operation), or the indifferent
strangers who glare at him atop his Essex and dismiss him with
the epithet "wise guy" or "rabble rouser." And all these may
be instanced finally in the policeman who, in an act of gratuitous malevolence, pushes his Essex over an embankment and
thereby destroys his "pulpit."

Once his car is gone, Haze is, it seems, utterly undone, and,
having faced the agnosticism and unconcern and mendacity
of the world, there is nothing left for him to do but to destroy

his capacity to see anything more. So he does what Asa Hawks had years before only pretended to do: he blinds himself with quicklime. And thereafter—to the bafflement of his landlady, Mrs. Flood, who, carefully remarking his harmless oddity and his government pension, had decided to marry him—he submits himself to the sternest mortifications, lining his shoes with rocks and broken glass, wearing barbed wire underneath his shirt, eating only enough just barely to prevent starvation. And at last, after wandering one night for hours in a driving icy rain, he is discovered two days later by two young policemen cruising in a squad car who find him "lying in a drainage ditch near an abandoned construction project." "I want to go on where I'm going," he tells them in a hoarse whisper. And one of the officers—saying, "We don't want to have no trouble with him" (126)—hits him over the head with his new billy. Haze dies a few minutes later in the squad car.

So, first his automobile—or his pulpit—being destroyed and then his very life being taken by deputies of the World, the last state of the Enemy of God, in being itself a kind of crucifixion, puts us in mind of what we may all along have neglected to notice, namely, of how much the forms of his denial have had to be precisely those whose unreality he has wanted so strongly to assert. And thus there begins to come into view what may be the possibility of an ultimate *coincidentia oppositorum*. (In this connection, it is significant that, at the very last, as Mrs. Flood looks down upon Haze's dead body, it occurs to her, in a moment of sudden clarity, that this man who had moved so far and so deep into darkness had himself become a "pin point of light" [126].)

"It is all very neatly worked out," says Jonathan Baumbach in his essay on the novel, and he finds "this very neatness . . . [to be] the besetting limitation of Miss O'Connor's fictional world." [15] But neatness is surely a most shockingly incongruous term to use for the description of these brilliantly outrageous fables. For their special sort of bounce and rhythm is in large part an affair of the remarkable autonomy which Miss O'Connor allowed the creatures of her imagination and which is always by way of enabling these freaks and grotesques very nearly to get out of hand altogether and to slip outside the framing structures of the fictions. But the stability of the structures *is* finally maintained, and it is just the resistance that her characters offer to these structures which provides something of a measure of how superbly gifted was Flannery O'Connor's controlling hand. Her stories are often *almost* at the point of becoming a ghastly kind of comic strip, but they never quite become so, and the audacious funambulism with which this tightrope is negotiated is a fascinating thing to watch.

Hers was, to be sure, an art that found its chief materials in the eccentric and the deformed, and in the remote backwaters of the Southern Bible Belt. But, like the Hardy of the Wessex novels and the Faulkner of the Yoknapatawpha country, she knew how to turn the very remoteness of her scene to advantage: and, however *outré* may be the crankiness of her *dramatis personae*, if we look hard enough, we can find in the very crookedness of their aberrancy what she called "the lines that create spiritual motion."

And, finally, I cannot resist remarking, however irrelevantly, the charming bit of testimony which comes from one of her friends, that it was her habit invariably to end her letters with the word "Cheers"—which may just remind us that what is not least remarkable, in this late and difficult time, is that hers is a body of fiction made rich and radiant by a Christian presence whose wit and brilliance and (notwithstanding all the Gothic furniture) whose cheerfulness we are only now at last beginning to discern.

## Notes

1. Mircea Eliade, *Birth and Rebirth*, tr. by Willard R. Trask (New York: Harper & Row, 1958), p. 9.
2. Philip Wheelwright, *The Burning Fountain: A Study in the Lan-*

*guage of Symbolism* (Bloomington: Indiana University Press, 1954), p. 8.

3. Ernest Gellner, *Words and Things: A Critical Account of Linguistic Philosophy* (London: Victor Gollancz, 1959), p. 99.

4. William Barrett, *Irrational Man: A Study in Existential Philosophy* (Garden City: Doubleday, Anchor Books, 1958), p. 57.

5. T. S. Eliot, *The Waste Land*, in *Collected Poems of T. S. Eliot: 1909-1935* (New York: Harcourt, Brace, 1936), pp. 69-70.

6. Abraham J. Heschel, *Between God and Man*, edited by Fritz A. Rothschild (New York: Harper & Row, 1959), p. 38.

7. *Ibid.*, p. 46.

8. *Ibid.*, p. 54.

9. *Ibid.*, p. 45.

10. Paul Tillich, *The Shaking of the Foundations* (New York: Charles Scribner's Sons, 1948), p. 57.

11. C. S. Lewis, *George MacDonald: An Anthology* (New York: Macmillan, 1947), p. 21. My attention has been called to this passage by my student, Gunnar Urang, who, in his Ph.D. dissertation at the University of Chicago, finds C. S. Lewis's fiction to represent an attempt to "baptize" the modern imagination.

12. Flannery O'Connor, "The Fiction Writer and His Country," in *The Living Novel, a Symposium*, edited by Granville Hicks (New York: Collier Books, 1962—originally published by Macmillan in 1957), p. 163.

13. *Ibid.*, pp. 162-63.

14. Caroline Gordon, "Flannery O'Connor's *Wise Blood*," *Critique*, II (Fall, 1958), 6.

15. Jonathan Baumbach, *The Landscape of Nightmare: Studies in the Contemporary American Novel* (New York: New York University Press, 1965), p. 99.

# Flannery O'Connor, a Realist of Distances

### M . BERNETTA QUINN, O.S.F.

BRAINARD CHENEY, in a *Sewanee Review* tribute, has called
Flannery O'Connor the most significant fiction writer in our
time despite the slender volume she left to American letters.[1]
Miss O'Connor's stock, like that of John Fitzgerald Kennedy,
has tremendously increased in value since her death. Her importance in contemporary criticism can be ascribed to her prophetic vision as expressed in highly individualized invention.
She herself saw vividly the relationship between prophecy and
fiction. Once she told a college audience: "The prophet is a
realist of distances, and it is this kind of realism which goes
into great novels. It is a realism which does not hesitate to distort appearances in order to show a hidden truth." [2]

Although *prophet* comes from the Greek *prophetes*, "to speak
before," prophets are first of all forthtellers, not foretellers.
They understand the present, enunciating their inspired insights before the ordinary man sees more than the surface
level. They are men who deliver divine messages or interpret
the divine will.[3] Miss O'Connor identifies with her special
talent two very closely related words: *vision* and *revelation.*
*Vision,* from the past participle *visus,* refers to a mental representation of external objects as in a religious revelation or
dream. Such might be any transfiguration of the material world
as found in Miss O'Connor's work. *Revelation,* a key term in
her fiction, is the title of a short story published the spring

before she died.[4] Considered as an *unveiling* (*re* [back] & *velum* [veil]), it means to make visible, to show. To return to *prophet,* a synonym is *seer,* linking all four words.

One article on Flannery O'Connor makes the above identification explicit in its title, "Prophet in the Wilderness."[5] Silenced by death in August, 1964, the voice crying in the wilderness is at last getting its hearing. The Archbishop of Atlanta, the Most Reverend Paul Hallinan, in giving her funeral sermon, expressed the idea that to the artist as well as to the mother, nurse, social worker, and other equally obvious examples belongs the reward promised in St. Matthew, XXV: "Whatever you did for the least of these you did for Me." Miss O'Connor was fully aware of the God-given nature of her mission. As she told one journalist: "There is the prophetic sense of 'seeing through' reality and there is also the prophetic function of recalling people to known but ignored truths."[6]

Flannery O'Connor's faith enlarged her universe, gave it an added dimension, enabled her through Scripture study to penetrate reality. It is best to state this truth in her own words: "In the novelist's case, it is a matter of seeing near things with their extensions of meaning and thus of seeing far things close up."[7] What this meant, practically, for her craft, was that she, herself a prophet, had to create prophets. These characters are to do for reality what the Biblical prophets did: impart a fuller significance to what everyone experiences. They are not among those whom Eliot mentions in the *Four Quartets*: "We have had the experience but missed the meaning."

To recall people to ignored truths, Miss O'Connor, writing in a materialistic age, sometimes had to shout, that is, to exaggerate. Perhaps this is why certain readers tend to think of her fiction as gloomy and morbid, whereas actually her optimism decidedly outweighs her pessimism: more often than not, her distorted figures respond to prophecy and amend their lives. The same fruitful outcome of the prophet's warning in the Old Testament times is stressed by Father Carroll Stuhlmueller in *The Prophets and the Word of God*: "God's word, heard through the voice of the prophets, not only shattered rocks of stubbornness and prejudice, but it also pulled down mountains of pride and turned the rugged terrain of persecution into the broad valley of peace." [8] This quotation is a perfect summary of the effect in Flannery O'Connor's own favorite among her short stories, "The Artificial Nigger."

En route to show his grandson Nelson the city, Mr. Head reveals himself as smugly proud. Although he himself does not realize this pride, the prophetic author does as she constructs her symbolic parable. Once in the city, he puts a penny in a public weight machine and believes the description on the card to be quite accurate ("You are upright and brave and all your friends admire you"), while disregarding the fact that the weight figure, 120 pounds, is entirely wrong. After he denies knowing his grandson when the latter gets into an embarrassing scrape, he feels all the pangs of Judas until he obtains the boy's forgiveness when they encounter an object both are ignorant of: an artificial nigger decorating someone's yard.

That night, when the train slows down to let them off at their home town, Mr. Head undergoes an epiphany which links him to what Albert Schweitzer has called "the brotherhood of pain":

> Mr. Head stood very still and felt the action of mercy touch him again but this time he knew that there were no words in the world that could name it. He understood that it grew out of agony, which is not denied to any man and which is given in strange ways to children. He understood it was all a man could carry into death to give his Maker and he suddenly burned with shame that he had so little of it to take with him [213].

Mr. Head, a surname reminiscent of Hawthorne's dichotomy, has discovered what it means to be human.

The grandson also has seen deeply into reality: in this symbolic story Miss O'Connor does for Nelson what Sherwood Anderson does for his sixteen-year-old hero in "I Want to Know Why." Both boys are initiated into evil. During his day in the city Nelson has looked into a sewer hole "and understood for the first time how the world was put together in its lower parts" (204). But the experience climaxing in the "vision" of the artificial nigger has left both him and his betrayer (perhaps more fittingly compared to Peter as Head of the Church than to Judas) advanced in wisdom and rooted in charity.

Miss O'Connor's fiction, as one looks back at it now in its entirety, was steadily growing in affirmation during her last years. The early stories are less triumphant. "The Capture," a *Mademoiselle* piece, centers upon a symbolic wild turkey which apparently produces cynicism rather than hope or faith, but even here she plants seeds of recovery which will germinate with adulthood. The capture of the wild turkey by the boy-hero Ruller is taken by him to be a sign of Divine Providence. When some "country kids" rob him of the bird he has run after all the afternoon, the capture turns out to have quite a different implication for him. Working from within his point of view and in line with his imaginative if negative interpretation, Miss O'Connor midway through the story has described the turkey in terms of astonishing beauty. One thinks of how she loved her own peacocks or of how a peacock symbolizes Christ to the priest in "The Displaced Person." What the albatross is to the mariner the turkey is to the boy, even if at the end only author and reader recognize this fact.

Ruller, like many other persons in Flannery O'Connor's tales, feels no need for salvation; rather, as he returns home rejoicing in his superiority he keeps looking for a beggar: "He wanted to do something for God." Accepting reality—the loss of the turkey—was too humiliating, too high a price to pay for the maturity that this clear-sightedness would bring. Of course his youthful thoughts do not present the meaning of the incident in these terms. On the contrary, his belief in God is endangered by what has happened, by this unexpected blow which seems to him to obliterate Divine Mercy. Almost everyone can remember a similar disappointment, perhaps even a similar subjective reaction. "But time runs on," and with the years comes an absorption into one's life even of unmerited failure; though Ruller is left on the other side of this threshold, Miss O'Connor leaves us expectant that he will cross it.

Typical of the greater sympathy for human frailty evident in her later stories (each characterized more by "a Damascus Road experience, perhaps, rather than a consuming vision of judgment")[9] are "The Comforts of Home" and "The Partridge Festival." Thomas, nicknamed Tomsee, in the first and Calhoun in the second are instances of persons who through grace, especially when this takes a violent form, see the consequences of their actions and undergo conversion, or *metanoia*. The vision in both cases results in light, not darkness.

In "The Comforts of Home" Thomas, an apostle of mediocrity, does not believe in the devil. If he has any religion, his credo centers upon his personal *status quo*. From a cruel, corrupt father, Thomas has inherited a dearth of compassion. When his mother rescues from prison and brings home a nymphomaniac, Thomas keeps insulting the girl, among other ways by calling her Sarah rather than Star, as she has renamed herself from a motive just the reverse of Joy Hopewell's in calling herself Hulga ("Good Country People"). His rejection of the Biblical practice of name-changing is indicative of his secularism. Irony glitters in the fact that *Star* recalls the Epiphany, with its radiance drawing others to Christ, whereas Star herself (to Thomas, at least) has the appearance of the blind who don't know they are blind. Her pet name for him, Tomsee, is also ironic, when there is so much that he definitely does not see. In the story he is compared to non-human creatures: a bull, a turtle. His lack of faith, except in the "virtue" of moderation, contrasts with Star's belief in God, the devil, and hell, even though she despairs of salvation.

As is frequent in Miss O'Connor's fiction, when the characters are forced to realize through an epiphany the vile results of their actions, they undergo a reformation. In "The Comforts of Home" (as wonderfully satiric a title as most in the two collections), this change as it is occurring is seen through the eyes of the sheriff, comically named Farebrother though he is anything but fair or brotherly:

> As he scrutinized the scene, further insights were flashed to him. Over her body, the killer and the slut were about to collapse into each other's arms. The sheriff knew a nasty bit when he saw it. He was accustomed to enter upon scenes that were not as bad as he had hoped to find them, but this one met his expectations [*Everything*, 141–42].

Whatever the sheriff or others may think, Thomas's mother has not died in vain. Thomas has put his hand into the Lord's wounded side.

"The Partridge Festival," which appeared in 1961, was Miss O'Connor's first story published in a Catholic periodical.[10] In it, Calhoun, ambitious to be a writer but successful only in salesmanship, encounters evil and finds it transformed from a "notion," in the Newman sense, to a reality. He should have been prepared for this, since as he scornfully tells his partner in adventure, a bluestocking named Mary Elizabeth, he believes that: "Life does not abide in abstractions."[11] Though both Calhoun and Mary Elizabeth dread the revelation they know will come when they actually see the murderer, Singleton, confined in an asylum after killing several townspeople over his protest to the partridge festival, the two drive out to find him and nervously sit in the waiting room until he is brought in, wriggling like a spider, by the asylum attendants. Upon leaving the grounds, Calhoun sees the image of this criminal mirrored in Mary Elizabeth's spectacled eyes: "Round, innocent, undistinguished as an iron link, it was the face whose gift of life had pushed straight forward to the future to raise festival after festival. Like a master salesman, it seemed to have been waiting there from all time to claim him."[12] Prominent among different interpretations is Calhoun's embracement, finally, of his true vocation. Mary Elizabeth, an incomplete human being, remains in her state of sterility.

Probably the best example of grace in action, of prophecy

falling like good seed on good ground, is "A Temple of the Holy Ghost." It comes to us as a series of happenings perceived by a very human little girl. Her mind wanders, as ours all do, and she combines fervor with indifference: mischievous, yet at the same time devout. What Hemingway effects so well in *The Sun Also Rises* is also present here: Nature with its "gathering greenness," "dark woods," and the red ball of the sun is contrasted with the triviality and even the evil of humanity (the girl's silly cousins). Since the whole pattern of images, taken out of the thought-processes of the child, is Catholic, the sun as Host does not strike one as so out of place as it does in the famous passage from Crane's *The Red Badge of Courage*. When asked by student reviewers during her 1960 stay in Winona, Minnesota, why the sun is a common image in her stories, Miss O'Connor answered: "It's there. It's so obvious. And from time immemorial it's been a god." [13]

One gets the impression that "A Temple of the Holy Ghost" is another initiation story, such as "I Want to Know Why." The child knows that she is in the presence of evil but cannot understand it. However, her experience, unlike the incidents in the Sherwood Anderson story, is related to an eternal dimension. With genuine humility the child recognizes her faults, to her as serious as the sins of her elders, but makes reparation for them by a vehement rejection of the sordid in life and by regret for her impatient, uncharitable behavior. In the end, not only the girl but the world itself becomes the temple of the Holy Ghost.

Miss O'Connor, however, can and repeatedly does highlight the negative, despite these examples of a positive response to the divine invitation. She looks at her world with wide-open eyes and speaks about both the crude and the ugly, as did Christ in His parables, and she avoids any sentimental, *deus ex machina* endings. Her most celebrated story, "A Good Man Is Hard to Find," illustrates these traits. Her distortions are intended to "break through" to those who see the grotesque as normal (e.g., exponents of racism in twentieth-century America or the adulation of entertainment stars). Unlike Anderson's use of the grotesque, whereby one truth is stressed at the expense of Truth itself, Flannery O'Connor's grotesques correspond to dictionary meanings of the word: *distorted* (and we think of the one-legged atheist Hulga); *incongruous* (Hazel Motes with his queer hat in *Wise Blood*); *ugly in appearance* (Sabbath Lily in the same novel). A secondary meaning of *grotesque* refers to fantastic combinations of human and animal figures. One regular feature of Miss O'Connor's style is picturing human beings in terms of animal imagery: *large bug, wheezing horse, hyena, sheep, crab, goat, dog, buzzard, monkey.* Sometimes she goes almost as far as Steinbeck in this technique, although no concept of the nature of man could be more different than his from hers. Whereas he builds his fiction on a deterministic basis, she underscores above all the freedom of the will. It is the latter which makes her stories so very exciting for those who see: the high stal-es elevate the trivial to cosmic proportions.

The reason she often chooses grotesques is that these are the characters she can make live. She believes in the parable of the talents as related by Christ. Writing in *The Living Novel,* she asserts that all initial gifts are from God, and not even the least must be destroyed by using it outside its proper sphere.[14] Almost all her characters are either evangelical Protestants or men without faith; living in Milledgeville, Georgia, located in the Bible Belt, Flannery O'Connor knew best these people and their conscious or unconscious distortions of the face of Christ. Catholicism is a minority report in her environment. "The Enduring Chill," a *Harper's Bazaar* story (1958),[15] was the first specifically Catholic fiction she ever published. In *The Living Novel,* Miss O'Connor makes the statement: "My own feeling is that writers who see by the light of their Christian faith will have, in these times, the sharpest eyes for the grotesque, for the perverse, and for the unacceptable." [16]

The prophecies Catholics are most familiar with are the ones prefiguring Christ: the Books of Isaiah and Daniel. Miss O'Connor concentrates on the less-publicized prophets (Amos, Osee, Jonah, Obadiah) who endeavored to make their contemporaries see how far they were departing from what God wanted. Each had his own individuality, and yet they tend in our imaginations to join their voices under the typical term *prophet*. Men like Jeremiah were flesh and blood, real people, not just names on a scroll or printed page. Flannery O'Connor's characters also have this two-fold identity, the individual and the type. James G. Murray, writing for *The Critic*, says: "They have the look of people who walk on earth, and yet their voice is one of prophecy—the kind of prophecy which derives from a penetrating absorption in, not a divorcement or alienation from, this world." [17]

"Parker's Back," her last story to appear during her lifetime in magazine form,[18] may prove in time her very greatest. O. E. Parker, upon fiery cross-examination by the woman he is courting, turns out to be Obadiah Elihue: Obadiah, after the sixth-century B.C. minor prophet, and Elihue after Elihu, a visitor to Job in the thirty-second chapter of that account. As is not unusual in this writer, O. E. fails to convert the heathen but himself undergoes an everlasting metamorphosis. His wife (they eventually do marry, though he cannot see how he ever came to find himself bound to so repulsive a person as Sarah Ruth Cates) forever flings the judgment of God in his face and scorns the one thing which nourishes his ego: his collection of tattoos covering his whole body except for his back, where, since he could not see them, would give him no pleasure. He decides to add a religious tattoo in this undecorated area, to interest his highly moral wife. Before selecting the design, O. E. is given his apocalyptic vision, one which comes upon him as he is baling hay on the farm where he does day-labor for an elderly woman:

> As he circled the field his mind was on a suitable design for his back. The sun, the size of a golf ball, began to switch regularly from in front to behind him, but he appeared to see it both places as if he had eyes in the back of his head. All at once he saw the

tree reaching out to grasp him. A ferocious thud propelled him into the air, and he heard himself yelling in an unbelievably loud voice, "GOD ABOVE!" [*Everything,* 232].

The tractor, his shoes, and the tree burst into flame. "Parker did not allow himself to think on the way to the city. He only knew that there had been a great change in his life, a leap forward into a worse unknown, and that there was nothing he could do about it" (*Everything,* 233).

No drawing in the artist's collection suits him except the face of a Byzantine Christ, which pulls him toward its magnetic, "all-demanding eyes," insistent that it be chosen. Even after the vision described above, O. E. fails to acknowledge any need for Redemption. To the artist's query as to whether he has "got religion," he says bitterly: "A man can't save his self from whatever it is he don't deserve none of my sympathy" (*Everything,* 238). The men in the pool hall to which he goes are eager to see O. E.'s new decoration and yank off his shirt; in the fight that follows a weird silence, during which they gaze incredulously at the face of Christ, Obadiah Elihue lashes out at the scoffers as fearlessly as might the sternest of Old Testament prophets. "Then a calm descended on the pool hall as nerve-shattering as if the long barn-like room were the ship from which Jonah had been cast into the sea" (*Everything,* 241).

Perhaps it is this episode of violence that turns the main character toward a perception of the truth. As he sits on the ground in the alley behind the pool hall, he examines the "spider web of facts and lies" that is his soul. He discovers that he belongs to Christ: "The eyes that were now forever on his back were eyes to be obeyed. He was as certain of it as he had ever been of anything" (*Everything,* 241). Love plays no part in this certainty. Driving home, he finds the familiar countryside entirely strange and himself alien to it. Until he whispers through the keyhole his prophet's name, his shrew of a wife will not open the locked door. When she does, instead of recognizing the fresh tattoo as a picture of God, she begins to beat him over the shoulders with a broom, screaming at him that she will have no idolator in her house. The closing sentence suggests a crucifixion scene: "There he was—who called himself Obadiah Elihue—leaning against the tree, crying like a baby" (*Everything*, 244).

In "Parker's Back," as in other stories, prophecy is equated with fire. Writing to the author about this identification in January, 1960, Miss O'Connor said:

> I have been reading what St. Thomas has to say in the *De Veritate* on prophecy. He says prophecy depends on the imaginative and not the moral faculty. It's a matter of seeing. Those who, like Tarwater, see, will see what they have no desire to see and the vision will be the purifying fire. I think I am not done with prophets.[19]

Prophecy like poetry is often symbolic to a marked degree; there was very little imagination in Sarah Ruth Parker, and there is very little in many another character created by Miss O'Connor to contrast with her prophets and those imaginative enough to enter with good will into the purifying fire, a fire corresponding to Eliot's in *Little Gidding* but even more like that of Dante's great vision in the effect which his purgatorial revelations had on the pilgrim through eternal distances, the distances Miss O'Connor portrays under the guise of temporal realities.

Even though Flannery O'Connor seems to have believed with Emerson that "the soul is no traveller," it is foolish to call her a regional writer. Her South, like Frost's country north of Boston, is much more than its literal self. Analogically, it is as wide as the universe: it ultimately includes the realm envisioned by Teilhard de Chardin, whose words she borrowed for the title of a late story, "Everything That Rises Must Converge," also the name of her posthumous collection (1965). Recalling Saint Paul's designation of Greek cities, where his converts lived, as colonies of Heaven, places where they lived as if on a visit, their true country being elsewhere, so Flannery O'Connor's setting (there is fundamentally only one) is an "eternal and absolute" [20] country, not a colony. More by what is absent in her fiction than by what is present, her country resembles even here and now the country of perfect love centered in Christ and foreseen by Teilhard de Chardin.

Robert Frost once remarked: "All an artist needs is samples." The important thing is to look vertically into a certain setting, not to enlarge that setting. Once vision reaches the required depth, "moral judgment will be implicit." [21] "A View of the Woods" (*Everything*, 54-81), is a prime example. But even more important than the appearance of the country outside is its inner meaning, its symbolism. The woods in the story have a rich prophetical significance. They represent those moments of grace, of inspiration, which come to all of us from time to time, but which are in many cases rejected, as by the grandfather in "A View of the Woods." Looking out at these woods on the afternoon of his death, he rejects their warning. For the old man, the woods are first of all a vision of hell and as the story mounts to its climax, even more. In the beginning, they are pictured as walking in a line around the red-soil pit being gouged out to make a fishing resort. On the last afternoon the grandfather sees them thus:

> The third time he got up to look at the woods, it was almost six o'clock and the gaunt trunks appeared to be raised in a pool of red light that gushed from the almost hidden sun setting behind them. The old man stared for some time, as if for a prolonged instant he were caught up out of the rattle of everything that led to the future and were held there in the midst of an uncomfortable mystery he had not apprehended before. He saw it, in his hallucination, as if someone were wounded behind the woods and the trees were bathed in blood [*Everything*, 71].

It is the grandfather's vicious plan to sell the woods in order to spite Mr. Pitts, his daughter's husband; to sell them to a man whose name Tilman suggests someone who will destroy the

wilderness (one thinks of Faulkner's "The Bear"). To his favorite granddaughter, Mary Fortune, whom he mistakenly considers a second self, the woods symbolize all that is beautiful.
After murdering her in a fit of rage the old man suffers a fatal
heart attack during which he imagines himself swallowed up by
the red-soil pit, the gaunt dark trees marching off in disdain, re-
fusing to rescue him.

More important still is "the country within." From the knowledge of self arises humility because all sorts of weaknesses will
be uncovered, weaknesses requiring not only a need for Redemption but also an Absolute to be measured against. Even
deficiencies within the author are revealed to herself as the
work progresses. In "The Displaced Person," Mrs. Shortley's
initial attitude is just exactly the opposite of humility. Religion
to her was for the weak, not the strong, among whom she
placed herself. By the end of the story her eyes "seemed to
contemplate for the first time the tremendous frontiers of her
true country" (280).

False prophets are present in Flannery O'Connor's fiction
just as in the Old Testament. During the reign of Jezebel the
royal house maintained a staff of 850 "prophets" of pagan gods.
Madam Zoleeda, fortune teller in "A Stroke of Good Fortune,"
is ironically kept out of the class of false prophets, through no
fault of her own, by the circumstance that middle-aged Ruby's
unborn and unwanted child, newly discovered by her in the
"funeral urn" of her body, may just possibly be a stroke of good
fortune, bringing happiness into a selfish marriage.

Mrs. Shortley is another false prophet upon whom centers
the longest and last in Miss O'Connor's first collection of short
stories. An anti-religious emphasis is prepared for early in the
work when Mrs. Shortley's friend Mrs. McIntyre refers to
Christ as just another D.P. Before Mrs. Shortley's vision one
Sunday afternoon, she has undergone an intense and prepara-
tory reading from the Apocalypse and the Prophets, an activity
instigated by the addition, to the farm where her husband
works, of a refugee laborer from Europe, who has arrived with

his family. Mrs. Shortley would be ready to do, when the time came, what had to be done. Though earlier she prays to be delivered from the "stinking power of Satan," one suspects that her intuitions about her own part as the "valiant woman" in the mystery of the world's meaning may be of diabolical inspiration.

Her vision is prophetic, all right: a gigantic figure in the sky, indefinite in shape, with fiery wheels starred by fierce dark eyes and spinning rapidly all around it. The "monster" then turns blood-red as she gazes and the wheels turn white. "A voice, very resonant, said the one word, 'Prophesy'" (277). It is somehow significant that her eyes are shut tight as she responds: " 'The children of wicked nations will be butchered.' " The falsity in her prophecy is that adjective *wicked*. The rest of the words come true in the murder of "the displaced person," a crime committed by Mrs. McIntyre, Mr. Shortley, and a Negro servant. They let a truck run over the innocent farmer from Europe who had built up her property even as Helton does Thompson's in Katherine Anne Porter's "Noon Wine."

Real prophets always believe what they are saying, which is always true, and they keep their own lives in accordance with this truth. Tom Shiftlet, on the contrary, in "The Life You Save May Be Your Own," is a drifter who, like so many of Miss O'Connor's characters, used to be a Gospel singer, and can talk like an angel though he acts like a devil. The reader is almost grateful for the hitchhiker's coarse reply to Tom's moral apothegms. It is Tom's feeble-minded, child-wife whom he has abandoned who is the true prophet; yet Shiftlet's prayer which ends the story may be an act of genuine repentance. Grace is treated here with an ambiguity proper to its mystery.

As in *Oedipus the King*, where the action pivots around the prophet Tiresias, sight and blindness are predominant themes in Flannery O'Connor. In "Greenleaf," Mrs. May respects but disbelieves in religion. Church is merely a social occasion for her two sons to meet nice girls. In her death agony, after the Greenleaf bull has gored her, she has "the look of a person whose sight has been suddenly restored but who finds the light unbearable." *Wise Blood* uses sight-blindness imagery to tie the whole book together. In "The River," this figure climaxes the preacher's exhortation:

> "Listen," he sang, "I read in Mark about an unclean man, I read in Luke about a blind man, I read in John about a dead man! Oh you people hear! The same blood that makes this River red, made that leper clean, made that blind man stare, made that dead man leap! You people with trouble," he cried "lay it in that River of Blood, lay it in that River of Pain, and watch it move away toward the Kingdom of Christ" [151].

Many of the O'Connor characters wear spectacles, as if to extend sight beyond the ordinary. Such a prophet is Mary Fortune Pitts in "A View of the Woods," who rebukes her grandfather after he has called her father a fool: "He who calls his brother a fool is subject to hell fire." Later developments bear out her words. This extension of sight was explained in Miss O'Connor's talk at the College of Saint Teresa. "It is one of the functions of the Church to transmit the prophetic vision that is good for all time, and when the novelist has this as a part of his own vision, he has a powerful extension of sight." [22] Elsewhere she has commented on the blindness which is really sight (faith) and the loss of this prophetical character in modern society.[23]

Deafness is employed but not in any major way. Rayber's deafness in *The Violent Bear It Away* is one such symbol. At the Carmody Bible revival meeting, the girl-preacher, seeing Rayber looking in at the window, screams out before the crowd: "Listen, you people . . . I see a damned soul before my eye! I see a dead man Jesus hasn't raised. His head is in the window but his ear is deaf to the Holy Word!" (385).

The devil has his role to play in much of this fictional prophecy. To novelist John Hawkes Miss O'Connor wrote: "I suppose the devil teaches most of the lessons that lead to self-knowledge." [24] Although Hawkes seems unable to penetrate the real meaning of this statement, other readers will find it illuminating. Mr. Paradise in "The River" is a Satan-figure: his ridicule of the itinerant preacher only makes the small boy who longs for Baptism more determined to achieve it. Another such *persona* is the lunatic girl in "Revelation," who in a fit staged in a doctor's waiting room spouts out a prophecy which begins the smug Mrs. Turpin's awakening to spiritual life. In *The Violent Bear It Away* the devil takes on a voice, remaining unseen by Tarwater, an invisible companion who tempts the boy as he digs his great-uncle's grave. Tarwater perceives that he must choose either Jesus or the devil, but his tempter, denying his own existence, says: "It ain't Jesus or the devil. It's Jesus or *you*" (326). Actually, as the novel—an analogy to life—intends to imply, this second dichotomy is what the choice amounts to: self, or the other. *Wise Blood,* the earlier novel, has as its secondary hero Enoch Emery, who experiences all kinds of temptation, some of which are apparently the work of the devil. After his trip with Enoch to see the "substitute jesus" (a three-foot mummy housed in a museum), the real hero, Hazel Motes, hits Emery on the head with a rock. "Then he knew that whatever was expected of him was only just beginning" (58). When Enoch sends the stolen "jesus" to Hazel through Hazel's paramour Sabbath Lily, Motes destroys it in the manner of an Old Testament Jew destroying an idol.

In contrast with the diabolical are the portraits of sanctity, at least incipient. Mrs. Greenleaf, despite the strange ritual of her worship, is a true woman of prayer, as Mrs. May's two irreligious sons realize. In "A Temple of the Holy Ghost," the child, reminiscent of J. F. Powers' Father Urban in his novel *Morte D'Urban,* is a saint-like character. After cataloguing in her own mind why she can never be what she really wants to be—a saint (reasons which are really only evidence of a high sense of humor and are certainly indicative of "the examined life")—the child concludes: "She could never be a saint, but she thought she could be a martyr if they killed her quick" (189).

Flannery O'Connor, besides presenting the child as a type of holiness, sometimes selects a child to fulfill the prophetic function. This designation of the child as prophet has already been referred to in the Carmody revival episode of *The Violent Bear It Away*. In "A Circle in the Fire," Mrs. Cope's daughter (the surname here connotes religion in an ironic fashion) sees more deeply than anyone else into the disaster which serves as her mother's salvation. Complacent in her own rich real estate, Mrs. Cope ignores the sufferings of others by placing between them and herself a veil of hypocritical platitudes. Whatever the meanness exhibited by the three boys whom she piously helps (they end by setting her woods afire), at least these children do not worship the golden calf, nor do they soil holy things by proud and pseudo-religious comments. It takes the setting of the Benedictus of the Old Testament, a circle of fire (symbol of Eternal Love) to bring home to Mrs. Cope how agony unites us all. At this moment of crisis she herself is not able to see into this profundity, but her unnamed daughter, reacting like a true prophet, feels the metamorphosis even if she does not fully understand what is occurring: "The child came to a stop beside her mother and stared up at her face as if she had never seen it before. It was the face of the new misery she felt, but on her mother it looked old and it looked as if it might have belonged to anybody, a Negro or a European or to Powell [one of the three boys] himself" (231-32).

The child as prophet is not always recognized as such by adults. Mr. Fortune in "A View of the Woods" does not suspect it in his cherished granddaughter Mary Fortune Pitts, who, he thinks wrongly, hates her family as much as he does. Bent upon selling the woods where Mary Fortune's father grazes his calves, the old man reflects: "The dissatisfaction it caused Pitts [Mary's father] would be permanent, but he could make it up to Mary Fortune by buying her something. With grown people, a road led either to heaven or hell, but with children there were always stops along the way where their attention could be turned away with a trifle" (*Everything*, 71).

To prophesy to those who do not see that they need Redemption is to prophesy to the wind. Such a view of temporal existence coincides well with the theory of the author from whom the title of Miss O'Connor's last book is taken: *Everything That Rises Must Converge,* the Jesuit Teilhard de Chardin. Teilhard is also mentioned by Miss O'Connor in her introduction to *A Memoir of Mary Ann.*[25] In the title story of her last short story collection, Julian in the beginning compares himself to the martyr Sebastian. Later, when his mother collapses on the sidewalk after they get off the street car which has been taking them to her reducing class, he regrets bitterly his unkindness to her. "The tide of darkness seemed to sweep him back to her, postponing from moment to moment his entry into the world of quiet and sorrow" (*Everything,* 23). Yet it is in just this world that he will forge his spiritual destiny, as will Mr. Head after his cruelty toward his grandson Nelson in "The Artificial Nigger."

Julian, at least so the ending implies, profits by the "vision" God offers him. Not every O'Connor character, however, seizes upon his chance when offered. Mrs. McIntyre's encounter with the priest as pictured in "The Displaced Person"—a holy and sensitive man—comes to nothing but exasperation. Another example of fruitlessness is The Misfit. In the title story of the collection *A Good Man Is Hard to Find,* The Misfit has the opportunity to be merciful. Scornfully, he rejects the hysterical old woman's plea that he pray. " 'I don't want no hep,' he said. 'I'm doing all right by myself' " (141). The grandmother, on the other hand, after a superficially religious life, responds to a final insight and forgives her assailant. The whole story clearly illustrates the absence of love in the modern world, especially in family situations. In fact, the closest feeling one gets is to *The American Dream* by Edward Albee. The humor (Pitty Sing the cat's precipitation of the accident, the descriptive touches here and there) lightens the macabre quality of the Gothic plot. Here is a writer who can join laughter and pain simply, in images as everyday as a tear or sun-splattered knife, who knows that tragicomedy and life are synonymous, as she portrays in stylized yet at the same time realistic prose. Words are used carelessly by the grandmother, for example *conscience* (she does not scruple at a lie). Ironically, the character who says that a good man is hard to find (Red Sammy, tavern owner) is the man whose wife tells her customers that there isn't a soul in this green world of God's that one can trust.

The Misfit has something about him of John Gay or Bertolt Brecht relating the adventures of the underworld. The incongruity results from the fact that despite his crimes or abnormalities he is trying to live the "examined life," as his father long ago discerned, whereas the "average" family satirized by Miss O'Connor couldn't care less about an examined life. Evidently, like Chaucer's Pardoner, he is a fallen idealist, since at one time he was a Gospel singer though now he is the most heartless of killers. The grandmother in all her exhortations to him to pray never turns to Christ herself; she wants others to practice religion while ignoring it herself. Actually, The Misfit has more faith than she does, faith in the Resurrection. Her attempts to get him to acknowledge God are clearly motivated by self-preservation.

Like Parker and Mrs. Shortley in the first part of their stories, The Misfit will not acknowledge any need for Redemption. He feels that life has already punished him more than he deserves, whereas others who deserved far more have got off without any punishment. Here he summarizes an important aspect of the problem of evil. When efforts to make him "get religion" will not save her from his gun, the old lady tries bribery and flattery. After the first four members of the family have been murdered, The Misfit admits that Jesus raised the dead, destroying balance in the world thereby, thus making it necessary to embrace or reject Him. Even though believing, The Misfit has rejected Him. His polite veneer begins to crack as he says in anger that he should have been an eyewitness to the miracles of Christ so that he could have followed Him. It is here that the grandmother, despite all her mediocrity, much of which is a condition common to us all, reaches out to him in compassion, calling him one of her children and trying to comfort him as she might have her son Bailey when he was a small boy. This instant is the prophetic moment. The Misfit, however, is in command: he does not need compassion. Springing back at her touch, he shoots her three times through the chest, then remarks to one of his assistants: "She would of been a good woman . . . if it had been somebody there to shoot her every minute of her life" (143). She dies smiling.

Like Father Urban of Powers' novel, who is converted by a golf ball (hit by a bishop) which strikes him on the head, the grandmother has taken the last part of her life to turn away from self and think of others. She realizes that Hell, even in this world, is not as Sartre says "other people," but as Tennessee Williams says: "When you ignore other people completely, that is Hell." The truths about crises' bringing out our best, and the correlation that if life were to consist of brushes with death it would always be "examined," lend poignancy and depth to this story. It is a narrative meditation on family relationships (the pitiless but typical dialogue of the children on the universal desire to have others be good, and on the change in our lives which constant awareness of death, as in existentialism, would effect).

"Revelation," one of the very last stories, shows that Flannery O'Connor believed in justice, not racial justice, as the best way of handling questions of prejudice in the South. In a letter written about a month before she died she said:

> Justice is justice and should not be appealed to along racial lines. The problem is not abstract for the Southerner, it's concrete; he sees it in terms of persons, not races—which way of seeing does away with easy answers. I have tried to touch this subject by way of fiction only once—in a story called "Everything That Rises Must Converge." [26]

The prophecy in the story referred to in the letter is not directly concerned with the Negro woman and her son but rather with Julian's relationship to his mother. In "Revelation" (*Everything*, 191-218), however, written after this, she uses prophecy to bring out her insistence on true charity if races are to live together in peace. Complacent people seem especially to have annoyed Flannery O'Connor.

Mrs. Turpin, the leading character, is such a person. In view of all her virtues, she simply cannot understand how Jesus could let a lunatic girl publicly prophesy to her: "Go back to hell where you came from, you old wart hog" (*Everything*, 207). Once home, obsessed by the incident, she tries to get rid of her irritation by hosing down the pig parlor, but the sun stares at her out of a fiery sunset, like a farmer inspecting his own hogs. The dying light takes on the figuration of a path into eternity:

> She raised her hands from the side of the pen in a gesture hieratic and profound. A visionary light settled in her eyes. She saw the streak as a vast swinging bridge extending upward from the earth through a field of living fire. Upon it a vast horde of souls were rumbling toward heaven. There were whole companies of white-trash, clean for the first time in their lives, and bands of black niggers in white robes, and battalions of freaks and lunatics shouting and clapping and leaping like frogs. And bringing up the end of the procession was a tribe of people whom she recognized at once as those who, like herself and Claud [her husband], had always had a little of everything and the God-given wit to use it right. She leaned forward to watch them closer. They were marching behind the others with great dignity, accountable as they had always been for good order and common sense and respectable behavior. They all were on one key. Yet she could see by their shocked and altered faces that even their virtues were being burned away [*Everything*, 217–18].

All along in the novella, the writer has been underscoring Saint Paul's warning that the greatest of virtues is charity. Mrs. Turpin's attitude toward her husband's Negro employees shows how far she is from practicing charity. What has appeared to her throughout life to be virtue is really selfishness. What Mrs. Turpin does with this revelation the story does not say.

Sometimes Flannery O'Connor works the actual Biblical prophets into her fiction. In "The Lame Shall Enter First"

(*Everything*, 143-90), Rufus Johnson, a juvenile delin-
quent, eats a page of the Bible to prove to the motherless son
of his social-worker "secular saviour" that the Bible is really
true: "'I've eaten it like Ezekiel and it was honey to my
mouth!'" (*Everything*, 185). His own name suggests a de-
scendant of John the Baptist. The title is in itself a prophecy
by Christ. Another example of references to real prophets occurs in *The Violent Bear It Away*: young Tarwater's great-uncle
has given him as companions to his spirit "Abel and Enoch and
Noah and Job, Abraham and Moses, King David and Solomon,
and all the prophets, from Elijah who escaped death, to John
whose severed head struck terror from a dish" (313).

In her first novel, *Wise Blood*, Hazel Motes stands as a figure
for the moderns who hate religion, as Miss O'Connor describes
them to a French correspondent Anne Taillefer: "They are at
pains to establish a religion without teeth, a Church without
Christ." [27] Like Oedipus and Lear, however, prophets Hazel
Motes and later Francis Marion Tarwater come to the truth
through suffering, or at least to a realization of where faith will
lead them. They reach this state by a non-intellectual road:

> The Dionysiac complex, in which rests the basic religious impulse
> to tragic utterance, is made of impulses, which are of "music," "in-
> toxication," "enchantment," "transformation"; it is full of wisdom
> and knowledge, but its knowledge is passionate, intuitive, poetic
> —folk-knowledge, or blood-knowledge, rising out of a deep union
> with earth and time. [28]

The earlier versions of *Wise Blood*, parts of which came out
in magazines, were more farcical than the finished form. "It is
a comic novel," Miss O'Connor wrote, "about a Christian
*malgré lui*, and as such, very serious, for all comic novels that
are any good must be about matters of life and death" (8). It
would be easier not to be a Christian, let alone not to be a
prophet. But in the end one does what one has to: faces the
reality of a vocation, which is Tarwater's case in the second
novel. It is also the predicament of their creator.

At no other point in her fiction does Flannery O'Connor develop the function of the prophet so thoroughly as in *The Violent Bear It Away*. Like Auden in his use of Billy Budd's stammer in the elegy for Melville, she pictures contemporary evil as being quite ordinary to indiscriminate eyes, and the call to eradicate it she shows to be equally ordinary. Before the "murder" or baptism of his little cousin Bishop, Tarwater has a spiritual experience which overwhelms him:

> Tarwater clenched his fists. He stood like one condemned, waiting at the spot of execution. Then the revelation came, silent, implacable, direct as a bullet. He did not look into the eyes of any fiery beast or see a burning bush. He only knew, with a certainty sunk in despair, that he was expected to baptize the child he saw and begin the life his great-uncle had prepared him for. He knew that he was called to be a prophet and that the ways of his prophecy would not be remarkable [357].

He sees the handwriting on the wall, though his reluctance remains. His great-uncle, also a prophet, mirrors Flannery O'Connor's own convictions about religion. The uncle, in an omniscient flashback, dramatizes his maker's point of view in that he regards the cosmos as not to be disturbed prematurely by any apocalyptic upheaval but rather to exist as a setting for those who suddenly, through prophecy, see into themselves and recognize that the country they must evangelize is there. Such is the meaning of what old Tarwater endured in youth:

> It [the sun] rose and set and he despaired of the Lord's listening. Then one morning he saw to his joy a finger of fire coming out of it and before he could turn, before he could shout, the finger had touched him and the destruction he had been waiting for had fallen in his own brain and his own body. His own blood had been burned dry and not the blood of the world [306].

The younger Tarwater, before undergoing initiation into his vocation, vividly feels the evil pulsating in the city to which he has traveled from the farm, but instead of rejecting it, he delights in it: "He saw in a burst of light that these people were hastening away from the Lord God Almighty. It was to the city that the prophets came and he was here in the midst of it. He was here enjoying what should have repelled him" (318-19). The sun imagery throughout the story is the eye of God watching how His creatures carry out His will.

The old uncle accepts mystery, particularly the mystery of suffering, just as the Old Testament prophets did. When the Lord commanded Ezekiel not to mourn externally for his beautiful young wife, who was destined to die that very night, the prophet accepts, knowing that God has His own reasons. Not so Rayber, city-relative of the uncle and boy, and not so The Misfit. Rayber tells the uncle to ask the Lord why He made his only son an idiot. In answer the old man thunders: "Yours not to ask! . . . Yours not to question the mind of the Lord God Almighty" (323).

No one familiar with Christ's parables could come upon this sentence toward the close of the novel and not be aware that the writer was speaking in trope: "The sun, from being only a ball of glare, was becoming distinct like a rare pearl, as if sun and moon had fused into a brilliant marriage" (435). Even at this point, however, the boy Tarwater is unwilling to accept the Divine. It takes an introduction not into evil (he had known that before) but into a special kind of evil soiling his own flesh to bring him to grips with his prophetic future. Back at the farm, he resigns himself grimly to his vocation:

> He knew that he could not turn back now. He knew that his destiny forced him on to a final revelation. His scorched eyes no longer looked hollow or as if they were meant only to guide him forward. They looked as if, touched with a coal like the lips of the prophet, they would never be used for ordinary sights again [442].

The vision at the grave of his uncle wherein the real significance of Christ as the Bread of Life rushes in upon him seals his determination.

In an *America* essay,[29] James F. Farnham advances the idea that Flannery O'Connor considers Tarwater so warped by his disavowal of grace that she cannot conceive of his being saved.

This view in a sympathetic article indicates that utterances of prophets are not always easy to understand. The Tarwater who goes off to bring salvation to the sleeping city as the book closes is not the materialist of the opening chapters. Even The Misfit has more faith than Tarwater when the book begins. But he is quite a different person because of having lived at his uncle's house in the city, where already he starts to exercise his gift by telling Rayber that in him, baptized, the seed has fallen on bad ground. Rayber, sensing no need of Redemption, is content to be "born again" through his own intelligence.

Finally, young Tarwater succeeds both in drowning and in baptizing his uncle's child. When he returns to the cabin site and decides to follow in the footsteps of his great-uncle, he is accepting a vocation. Talking at Marillac College in Saint Louis, Miss O'Connor commented on how easy it was for the sisters there to understand this, because they understood what a vocation was. One of the many good outcomes of such addresses was that she could reveal to her auditors how familiar words function in her work. One may understand concepts and not connect them with their illustrations.

Father Leonard Mayhew, an Atlanta priest, writing a eulogy of Miss O'Connor for *Commonweal*,[30] stresses her work as resembling what the Middle Ages meant by the anagogical sense of Scripture. Because of her subtlety, many will not know they are reading chapters from an apocalypse. Father Mayhew's conclusion coincides with the estimate shared by all who knew Flannery O'Connor: "Truth—the living God—is a terrifying vision, to be faced only by the stout of heart. Flannery O'Connor was such a seer, of stout heart and hope." [31] She accepted in a very down-to-earth way the problems as well as the advantages of her faith. As she once wrote this writer:

> I feel the tension between the demands of art and the demands of faith but I believe that it is a tension which serves to deepen both and which is probably given us for just that purpose. Struggling to meet the necessities of the work does throw light on the spiritual life, though I am not articulate enough to see how.[32]

To understand Flannery O'Connor one must read and meditate upon the Bible. In talking with Joel Wells, Miss O'Connor regretted the fact that Catholics as a whole were so ignorant of Scripture but she saw no reason to "write down" because of this unpreparedness on their part to perceive her fictional intentions. She was writing for the future, not just for the present, a future when the needed revival in Scripture would have become a reality. To Mr. Wells she said: "The Bible is what we share with all Christians, and the Old Testament we share with all Jews." [33]

In her talk to the College of Saint Teresa students, Miss O'Connor concluded thus: "The poet is traditionally a blind man, but the Christian poet is like the blind man cured in the gospels, who looked then and saw men as if they were trees, but walking. This is the beginning of vision." [34] Only a realist of distances could have the insight that men symbolically have many of the properties of trees but in addition powers natural and supernatural. Faith is a light enabling a writer to discern form and motion while still retaining the essential mystery of existence. Even Saint Paul saw through a glass darkly. The cured blind man was courageous enough to stand up to the enemies of Christ. He used the prophetic vision well. So did Flannery O'Connor.

## Notes

1. "Flannery O'Connor's Campaign for Her Country," *Sewanee Review*, LXXII (Autumn, 1964), 555.

2. "The Role of the Catholic Novelist," *Greyfriar* [Siena Studies in Literature], VII (1964), 9.

3. *Funk and Wagnall's Standard College Dictionary* (New York: Funk and Wagnall, 1963), p. 1080.

4. *Sewanee Review*, LXXII (Spring, 1964), 178-202.

5. Sister Bede Sullivan, *Today*, XV (March, 1960), 36.

6. Joel Wells, "Off the Cuff," *Critic*, XXI (August-September, 1962), 72.

7. "The Role of the Catholic Novelist," p. 9.

8. Notre Dame: University of Notre Dame Press, 1964, p. 19.

9. Robert Drake, "The Harrowing Evangel of Flannery O'Connor," *Christian Century*, LXXXI (September 30, 1964), 1200.

10. *Critic*, XIX (February-March, 1961), 20-23, 82-85.

11. *Ibid.*, p. 83.

12. *Ibid.*, p. 85.

13. Katherine Fugin, Faye Rivard, and Margaret Sieh, "An Interview with Flannery O'Connor," *Censer* (Fall, 1960), 30.

14. "The Fiction Writer and His Country," in *The Living Novel, a Symposium*, edited by Granville Hicks (New York: Macmillan, 1957), pp. 158-59.

15. *Harper's Bazaar*, XCI (July, 1958), 44-45, 94, 96, 100-02, 108.

16. "The Fiction Writer and His Country," p. 162. Miss O'Connor connects this insight with prophecy by stating on the next page: "Those who believe that art proceeds from a healthy, and not from a diseased, faculty of the mind will take what he [the artist] shows them as a revelation . . . under given circumstances; that is, as a limited revelation but a revelation nevertheless."

17. "Southland à la Russe," *Critic*, XXI (June-July, 1963), 27.

18. *Esquire*, LXIII (April, 1965), 76-78, 151-55.

19. In the same letter Miss O'Connor says: "Baptism is just another idiocy to the general intelligent reader and the idea of anyone's having a vocation to be a prophet doesn't commend itself to his sense of the fitness of things in the 20th century."

20. "The Fiction Writer and His Country," p. 158.

21. *Ibid.*, p. 160.

22. "The Role of the Catholic Novelist," p. 9.

23. Introduction to *A Memoir of Mary Ann*, by the Dominican Nuns of Our Lady of Perpetual Help Home (New York: Farrar, Straus and Cudahy, 1961), p. 19.

24. "Flannery O'Connor's Devil," *Sewanee Review*, LXX (Summer, 1962), 406.

25. Introduction to *A Memoir of Mary Ann*, p. 15.

26. Letter to the writer, July 27, 1963.

27. "A Memoir of Flannery O'Connor," *Catholic Worker*, XXXI (December, 1964), 2.

28. B. L. Reid, *William Butler Yeats: The Lyric of Tragedy* (Norman, Oklahoma: University of Oklahoma Press, 1961), p. 27.

29. "The Grotesque in Flannery O'Connor," *America*, CV (May 13, 1961), 277, 280-81.

30. "Flannery O'Connor, 1925-1964," *Commonweal*, LXXX (August 21, 1964), 563.

31. *Ibid.*

32. Letter to the writer.

33. "Off the Cuff," p. 5.

34. "The Role of the Catholic Novelist," p. 12.

# Flannery O'Connor's Clarity of Vision

HAROLD C. GARDINER, S.J.

"Blessed Are the Merciful: for They Shall Obtain Mercy."
—Matthew V, 7

"Pity essentially depends on clarity of vision; you become most truly merciful when you become clean of heart. But you must be able to see the two things with equal clarity; the nature of sin in itself, and the immaturity of evil in the human heart." [1]

IN ONE SENSE, *A Memoir of Mary Ann* is the slightest of Flannery O'Connor's books. In fact, it is hardly her book at all, for she wrote only the introduction to it; yet it reveals quite clearly one of the deeper aspects of her work.

It came about this way: "Last spring," wrote Miss O'Connor,

I received a letter from Sister Evangelist, the Sister Superior of Our Lady of Perpetual Help Free Cancer Home in Atlanta. "This is a strange request," the letter read, "but we will try to tell our story as briefly as possible. In 1949, a little three-year-old girl, Mary Ann, was admitted to our Home as a patient. She proved to be a remarkable child and lived until she was twelve. Of those nine years, much is to be told. Patients, visitors, Sisters, all were influenced in some way by this afflicted child. Yet one never thought of her as afflicted. True she had been born with a tumor

184

on the side of her face; one eye had been removed, but the other eye sparkled, twinkled, danced mischievously, and after one meeting one was never conscious of her physical defect, but recognized only the beautiful brave spirit and felt the joy of such contact. Now Mary Ann's story should be written but who is to write it?"

Not me, I said to myself.

"We have had offers from nuns and others but we don't want a pious little recital. We want a story with a real impact on other lives as Mary Ann herself had that impact on each life she touched. . . . This wouldn't have to be a factual story. It could be a novel with many other characters but the outstanding character, Mary Ann."

A novel, I thought. Horrors.[2]

Miss O'Connor then goes on to recount that Sister Evangelist ended by inviting her to write Mary Ann's story and suggested that she come to the Home in Atlanta to "imbibe the atmosphere." Miss O'Connor did not want to imbibe the atmosphere —much less to write the story, mainly because, as she says,

Stories of pious children tend to be false. This may be because they are told by adults, who see virtues where their subjects would see only a practical course of action; or it may be because such stories are written to edify and what is written to edify usually ends by amusing. . . . I have never cared to read about little boys who build altars and play they are priests, or about little girls who dress up as nuns, or about those pious Protestant children who lack this equipment but brighten the corners where they are.[3]

One may be pardoned, I trust, a passing sigh that Flannery O'Connor's talents did not run in the channels of hagiography —what remarkably vivid and realistic lives of saints she could have produced—but this was one corner that she did not feel called upon to brighten.

At any rate, after reading the letter that offered her this rather distasteful opportunity, she picked up a photo of Mary Ann that had been enclosed.

It showed a little girl in her first Communion dress and veil. . . .

> Her small face was straight and bright on one side. The other side was protuberant, the eye was bandaged, the nose and mouth crowded slightly out of place. The child looked out at her observer with an obvious happiness and composure. I continued to gaze at the picture long after I had thought to be finished with it.[4]

Now it happens that the founder of the work in which Sister Evangelist was engaged was Rose Hawthorne, the daughter of one of Miss O'Connor's favorite authors, Nathaniel Hawthorne. She had become a Dominican nun and early devoted herself to working with incurable cancer cases. This connection quite naturally led Flannery O'Connor to recall and reread two marvelous episodes in Hawthorne's life, one in his creative life, the other in his actual experience. In what Miss O'Connor calls a "wonderful section of dialogue" in the story, "The Birthmark" (1846), Alymer hesitantly mentions to his wife for the first time that the slight blemish on her lovely face could be removed. When she responds smilingly that many have considered it a "charm," he bursts out: "upon another face perhaps it might [be], but never on yours. . . . you came so nearly perfect from the hand of Nature that this slightest defect, which we hesitate whether to term a defect or a beauty, shocks me, as being the visible mark of earthly imperfection." She thereupon bursts into tears: "Shocks you, my husband! . . . Then why did you take me from my mother's side? You cannot love what shocks you!"[5]

The second episode is recounted in *Our Old Home* (1863). It tells how a fastidious gentleman, going through a Liverpool workhouse, "was followed by a wretched and rheumy child, so awful-looking that he could not decide what sex it was. The child followed him about until it decided to put itself in front of him in a mute appeal to be held. The fastidious gentleman, after a pause that was significant for himself, picked it up and held it." Commenting on this, Hawthorne remarked that his fastidious gentleman obviously went through a considerable struggle to conquer his natural reserve and the feeling of revulsion that arose unbidden, and he concludes: "[I] am seriously of the opinion that he did a heroic act and effected more than he dreamed of toward his final salvation when he took up the loathsome child and caressed it as tenderly as if he had been its father." [6]

Flannery O'Connor then goes on to say that "what Hawthorne neglected to add is that he was the gentleman who did this." [7] This we discover in the notebooks published by his wife after his death. It is a most touching account, and ends: ". . . this little sickly, humor-eaten fright . . . expressed such perfect confidence that it was going to be taken up and made much of, that it was impossible not to do it. It was as if God had promised the child this favor on my behalf, and that I must needs fulfill the contract. . . . I should never have forgiven myself if I had repelled its advances." [8]

Despite these deeply moving literary connections between Mary Ann, the Sisters who wanted Miss O'Connor to write her story, and her favorite author, Miss O'Connor stuck to her decision that she would not be the one to tell Mary Ann's story: "Bad children are harder to endure than good ones, but they are easier to read about, and I congratulated myself on having minimized the possibility of a book about Mary Ann by suggesting that the Sisters do it themselves." [9] But the Sisters called her bluff, so to speak. They wrote the story of Mary Ann, and "there was everything about the writing to make the professional writer groan. . . . Yet when I had finished reading, I remained for some time, the imperfections of the writing forgotten, thinking about the mystery of Mary Ann. [The Sisters] had managed to convey it." [10] This is Flannery O'Connor's final direct statement about both the book and Mary Ann:

> The story was as unfinished as the child's face. Both seemed to have been left, like creation on the seventh day, to be finished by others. The reader would have to make something of the story as Mary Ann had made something of her face.
>
> She and the Sisters who had taught her had fashioned from her unfinished face the material of her death. The creative action of the Christian's life is to prepare his death in Christ. It is a continuous action in which this world's goods are utilized to the fullest, both positive gifts and what Père Teilhard de Chardin calls

"passive diminishments." Mary Ann's diminishment was extreme, but she was equipped by natural intelligence and by a suitable education, not simply to endure it, but to build upon it. She was an extraordinarily rich little girl.[11]

And, I think we may say, Mary Ann shared her riches. We have the nuns' witness that she shared them with those who came into contact with her, and Miss O'Connor has stated that her thinking about the little girl and her reading of the nuns' account "opened up for me a new perspective on the grotesque." [12] She explains this new perspective:

Most of us have learned to be dispassionate about evil, to look it in the face and find, as often as not, our own grinning reflections with which we do not argue, but good is another matter. Few have stared at that long enough to accept the fact that its face too is grotesque, that in us the good is something under construction. The modes of evil usually receive worthy expression. The modes of good have to be satisfied with a cliché or a smoothing down that will soften their real look. When we look into the face of good, we are liable to see a face like Mary Ann's, full of promise.[13]

This leads Miss O'Connor on to a deeper reflection, which, I fully believe, is a key to the understanding of all her work. She continues:

One of the tendencies of our age is to use the suffering of children to discredit the goodness of God, and once you have discredited His goodness, you are done with Him. . . . In this popular pity, we mark our gain in sensibility and loss in vision. If other ages felt less, they saw more, even though they saw with the blind, prophetical, unsentimental eye of acceptance, which is to say, of faith. In the absence of this faith now, we govern by tenderness. It is a tenderness which, long since cut off from the person of Christ, is wrapped in theory. When tenderness is detached from the source of tenderness, its logical outcome is terror. It ends in forced labor camps and in the fumes of the gas chamber.[14]

However harsh this conclusion may sound, Flannery O'Connor's line of thought in all the above quotations is clear. Her vision of the grotesque in life (the grotesque in evil *and* in good, be it recalled) is rooted in the vision that was opened up for the world in the Beatitude prefixed to this essay: "Blessed are the merciful"—*not*, let it be underlined, "blessed are the sentimental." Miss O'Connor pities, has mercy, in the only real sense precisely because of her clarity of vision. For her pity— or mercy—is not condescension, it is redemptive. She herself remarked, in a lecture given at the College of Saint Teresa:

> The novelist cannot choose what he is able to make live. The Catholic novelist in the South is forced to follow the spirit into strange places and to recognize it in many forms not totally congenial to him. But the fact that the South is the Bible Belt increases rather than decreases his sympathy for what he sees. His interest will in all likelihood go immediately to those aspects of Southern life where the religious feeling is most intense and where its outward forms are farthest from the Catholic. This is not because in the felt superiority of his orthodoxy, he wishes to subtract one theology from another, but because, descending within himself to find his region, he discovers that it is with these aspects of Southern life that he has a feeling of kinship strong enough to spur creation.[15]

The words "sympathy" and "kinship" are operative in this remark.

*You cannot love what shocks you.* A large portion of Flannery O'Connor's work essentially consists of an implicit statement that one can, and indeed often must, love what shocks. She recounts that when some of the nuns from the Home came to visit her, one of them asked her why she wrote about such grotesque characters and "why the grotesque (of all things) was my vocation" (it seems that the nuns had been delving into some of her writing before asking her to undertake the Mary Ann assignment). "I was struggling to get off the hook she had me on when another of our guests supplied the one answer that would make it immediately plain to all of them. 'It's your vocation, too,' he said to her." [16]

It is generally the sentimental who are shocked by the grotesque, and in Flannery O'Connor's artistic makeup there is not the slightest trace of sentimentality. Her pity is not sentimental, because it springs from the double view pointed out by Father Vann: it sees clearly the "nature of sin itself," and the "immaturity of evil in the human heart." The most obvious incarnation of evil in all her work is probably The Misfit in "A Good Man Is Hard to Find." His cold-eyed, wanton butchery of the grandmother and the five others is the act of one apparently hardened in crime; it is a heinous sin. But yet—but yet, who are we to judge, Miss O'Connor seems to say. What forces have warped these minds so that they come almost as it were to play with murder? Are they mature humans? Is their grotesquerie only ours writ large?

> "Turn to the right, it was a wall," The Misfit said, looking up again at the cloudless sky. "Turn to the left, it was a wall. Look up it was a ceiling, look down it was a floor. I forget what I done, lady. I set there and set there, trying to remember what it was I done and I ain't recalled it to this day. Oncet in a while, I would think it was coming to me, but it never come" [140].

When the old grandmother, sensing her impending murder, begins to cry upon Jesus:

> "Yes'm," The Misfit said as if he agreed. "Jesus thown everything off balance. It was the same case with Him as with me except He hadn't committed any crime and they could prove I had committed one because they had the papers on me. . . . I call myself The Misfit . . . because I can't make what all I done wrong fit what all I gone through in punishment" [142].

And as the murders continue down in the woods, The Misfit concludes:

> "Jesus was the only One that ever raised the dead . . . and He shouldn't have done it. He thown everything off balance. If He

did what He said, then it's nothing for you to do but thow away
everything and follow Him, and if He didn't, then it's nothing for
you to do but to enjoy the few minutes you got left the best way
you can—by killing somebody or burning down his house or
doing some other meanness to him. No pleasure but meanness,"
he said and his voice had become almost a snarl [142].

As we rise from The Misfit and his companions in this story to
the other characters in Miss O'Connor's unforgettable gallery
of grotesques, we come more and more frequently across those
who are not, as far as we can see them in her limning, so much
sinful as stupidly and deludedly groping for release from their
immaturity in evil—for redemption. They are driven by some
twisted theology; so many of them are "preachers," fanatical,
rabid, bigoted, blind. Such are the Reverend Bevel Summers in
"The River," and, pre-eminently, Fancis Marion Tarwater and
his "prophet" uncle in The Violent Bear It Away. Others, such
as Mrs. Shortley in "The Displaced Person"; Hazel Motes in
Wise Blood, the preacher of the "Church Without Christ," who
blinds himself in an effort to see what he thought the fake
preacher Hawks saw in the depths of his supposedly blind eyes;
the schoolteacher Rayber in The Violent Bear It Away—all are
driven by some awful religious or anti-religious compulsion
that truly keeps them immature in evil. But it would be a
mistake to think that all these horrendous characters are portrayed in tones of theological judgment—this itself might be
a species of sentimentalism, all the more to be reprobated because of its apparent profundity. On the contrary, as has been
remarked, "Miss O'Connor's insight into what is left of Chis-
tianity in the backcountry Bible-reading sections [of the South]
is profoundly empathic and satiric at the same time. Mrs.
Shortley [in "The Displaced Person"] belongs to a great company
of O'Connor revivalists and visionaries who are funny but by
no means figures of fun." [17]

When one passes from these more spectacularly fanatical
characters to those who occupy a sort of middle ground, we
meet those whose fanaticism, though not religiously inspired, is
nonetheless an index of stunted immaturity. Such are Mr. Shift-

let in "The Life You Save May Be Your Own," Ruby Hill in "A Stroke of Good Fortune" (perhaps Flannery O'Connor's most purely comic story), General George Poker Sash in "A Late Encounter with the Enemy," and Mr. Head and Nelson in "The Artificial Nigger." Each of these calls forth in their creator a steady-eyed pity that in turn opens up for them the wellsprings of the reader's mercy—the mercy of understanding how these fantastic characters come to be as they are and the consequent mercy of suspended judgment of them as individuals.

A similar lack of sentimentality is to be discovered in Miss O'Connor's attitude toward the Negroes who so richly populate her pages. She does not flinch in these days of integration to have the white characters simply and bluntly refer to them as "niggers." One believes that Flannery O'Connor herself would not have used the term, but she refuses in her stories to gloss over the harsh fact from any concession to a sentimental revulsion to the word. And what understanding of the cultural immaturity of the Negroes comes through their cryptic mumblings, their averted eyes, and shuffling feet. Flannery O'Connor says more quite unemotionally about the degradation of their lot, imposed and shackled upon them by the unthinking immaturity of their white masters, than could have been said in many a page of impassioned pleading for their betterment.

Perhaps Flannery O'Connor's clear-eyed lack of sentimentality is nowhere more evident than in her treatment of children, and this aspect of her work takes on deeper significance in view of her experience with the story of Mary Ann. Apart from the several mentally-retarded children, such as Bishop in *The Violent Bear It Away*, most of her young characters are seen with a vision that is clear because it encompasses the reality of Original Sin. When Sheppard tries vainly to cope with clubfooted and almost demoniacally fanatical Rufus Johnson, whom he is trying to tame and rehabilitate, he "felt a momentary dull despair as if he were faced with some elemental warping of nature that had happened too long ago to be corrected now" (*Everything*, 150). And Miss O'Connor does not mean that such warping was the result of mere environment (though that undoubtedly has a lot to do with the shaping of character); she sees clearly (and therefore pities truly and profoundly) that long before environment begins its work, the human soul is caught up, as Cardinal Newman said, in some cataclysmic catastrophe, and to make her vision of this fact clear and even shocking, she does not "hesitate to distort appearance in order to show a hidden truth." [18] Similarly, Star's corruption (basically the distortion of Original Sin), in "The Comforts of Home," is, paradoxically enough, "the most unendurable form of innocence" (*Everything*, 124). Robert Fitzgerald's perceptive remark has relevance here: "She sees the South . . . as populated by displaced persons. Almost all her people are displaced and some are either aware of it or become so." [19]

This attitude toward her child-characters (they are never "the poor little things" in her conception) certainly brought her face to face with the "peculiar problem of transmitting an enlarged vision of reality to a reader who not only does not understand or accept it, but is positively hostile to it. . . . For the modern reader, moral distinctions are usually blurred in hazes of compassion." [20] This blight of compassion was well exemplified in an article in *Commonweal* (March 7, 1958), by William Esty, who accused Miss O'Connor of engaging in a cult of the "gratuitous grotesque." Refuting this charge in "The Grotesque in Flannery O'Connor" (*America*, May 13, 1961), James F. Farnham quotes Miss O'Connor: "you have to make your vision apparent by shock—to the hard of hearing you shout, and for the almost blind you draw large and startling figures." [21] And certainly, for a culture that is so largely child-centered as ours, shock is necessary to bring home the reality of Original Sin, especially in its effects on the young.

It may seem strange to consider any creative writer as being concerned in his writing with the exercise of what the Catholic Church has called the "works of mercy." Such an approach certainly flies in the face of the sort of criticism that holds that the literary creative act is an end in itself, that the author is, and must be, if he be truly an artist, interested in, devoted to, merely and simply the production of the work itself, with no ultimate ulterior interest or concern. He writes a book and there it stands, complete, integral in itself, meaning nothing more than itself, looking to no further horizons or implications, above all having no further "meaning."

But there is another way in which to view literature, and using this approach it can be fairly said that every literary work of art is actually, at least on the purely natural plane, without calling on the truths of revelation, a work of mercy. The author's intrinsic purpose, which he himself may not realize or even suspect, is to bring some healing to the disorder of the world. His vision sees some center of unity, and even if his novel or his play cannot be expected to map the road to harmony and unity, even his depiction of disharmony and confusion implies that there is somewhere, somehow, a universe of harmony and love that is here and now in his concrete work only dimly glimpsed. But his work—if not the author himself—does tend to bind up the wounds of dissension, misunderstanding, bigotry, hatred, and all the other ills that beset the human race. As Denis de Rougemont has put it:

> It is evident that a classical work of art, a work of Bach, for example, creates order in man, evokes the order of the world, renders its laws comprehensible and even lovable. But some entirely different works, which seem to have no purpose other than that of evoking the present disorder, chaos, and absurdity. . . . I am thinking of certain parts of Joyce's works, or *The Waste Land* of T. S. Eliot, or the stories of Faulkner, the painting of Picasso—these works, dialectically, nostalgically, in revolt and defiance, carry still a witness to the lost order of the world—because art, all art worthy of the name, never has had and never can have any other object.[22]

Flannery O'Connor's grotesque world is a world that is desperately, even violently, seeking to rediscover such a lost order. As Robert Fitzgerald remarks in concluding his essay already alluded to: "[Flannery O'Connor's] stories not only imply, they as good as state again and again, that estrangement from

Christian plenitude is estrangement from the true country of man."[23] Miss O'Connor is able to say this effectively and powerfully because she refuses, as St. Thomas says some people do, "to withdraw [herself] from works of mercy lest they be involved in others' misery"; because she writes with a profound concern that eschews sentimentality to view with mercy —the mercy of those who are clean of heart.

## Notes

1. Gerald Vann, O.P., *The Divine Pity* (London: Sheed and Ward, 1945), p. 146.

2. Flannery O'Connor, in her introduction to *A Memoir of Mary Ann* (New York: Farrar, Straus and Cudahy, 1961), pp. 3-5.

3. *Ibid.*, p. 3.

4. *Ibid.*, pp. 5-6.

5. Quoted by Miss O'Connor, pp. 6-7.

6. Quoted by Miss O'Connor, p. 8.

7. Introduction to *A Memoir of Mary Ann*, p. 9.

8. Quoted by Miss O'Connor, pp. 9-10.

9. Introduction to *A Memoir of Mary Ann*, p. 13.

10. *Ibid.*, p. 14.

11. *Ibid.*, pp. 14-15.

12. *Ibid.*, p. 17.

13. *Ibid.*, pp. 17-18.

14. *Ibid.*, pp. 18-19.

15. "The Role of the Catholic Novelist," *Greyfriar* [Siena Studies in Literature], VII (1964), 8.

16. Flannery O'Connor, in her introduction to *A Memoir of Mary Ann*, p. 17.

17. Robert Fitzgerald, "The Countryside and the True Country," *Sewanee Review*, LXX (Summer, 1962), 388.

18. "The Role of the Catholic Novelist," p. 9.

19. "The Countryside and the True Country," p. 394.

20. "The Role of the Catholic Novelist," p. 10.

21. Originally written by Miss O'Connor in "The Fiction Writer and His Country," in *The Living Novel, a Symposium*, edited by Granville Hicks (New York: Macmillan, 1957), p. 163.

22. "Religion and the Mission of the Artist," in *The New Orpheus: Toward a Christian Poetic*, edited by Nathan A. Scott, Jr. (New York: Sheed and Ward, 1964), p. 68.

23. "The Countryside and the True Country," p. 394.

# Flannery O'Connor's Sacred Objects

MELVIN J. FRIEDMAN

THERE ARE few writers as free from experimentation as Flannery O'Connor. She has diligently avoided the literary fashions of her time. She has maintained, in several interviews, that her work springs from an oral tradition; indeed one notices in the two collections of her stories and in her two novels that the "spoken" seems always to triumph over the "written."

The only peculiarly twentieth-century technique she uses with any regularity is what critics have labeled indirect interior monologue: Miss O'Connor penetrates the minds of her characters but usually preserves the objectivity of the third person and the correctness of the syntax. There is nothing of Flannery O'Connor's consciousness in these monologues, only the consciousness of her characters, yet the sober controls exerted on the language are her own. A characteristic example is this third-person "quotation" from Tanner's mind in her story "Judgement Day."

> He laid his head on the back of the chair for a moment and the hat tilted down over his eyes. He had raised three boys and her. The three boys were gone, two in the war and one to the devil and there was nobody left who felt a duty toward him but her, married and childless, in New York City like Mrs. Big and ready

when she came back and found him living the way he was to take him back with her. She had put her face in the door of the shack and had stared, expressionless, for a second. Then all at once she had screamed and jumped back.[1]

The digressiveness and absence of logical development in the third sentence is especially close to the milder forms of stream-of-consciousness used by many of Flannery O'Connor's contemporaries. We notice the objective narrative of the first sentence gradually giving way to an approximation of Tanner's idiom in the somewhat transitional second sentence—which could represent the point of view of either the omniscient author or the character.

The narrative procedures of this passage are evident in all of Miss O'Connor's fiction from her first published story, "The Geranium" (1946).[2] The devices are so natural to her that it would probably be wrong to connect them with any of the revolutions in fiction which we normally associate with the twenties or thirties. It may be the haunting and obtrusive presence of the Southern oral tradition which explains these near-monologues, often in local idiom, breaking into passages of description.

There is still another element in her fiction which seems to connect her stories and novels with the practices of certain of her contemporaries. This is her reliance on "a literature of Things."[3] Dorothy Van Ghent has admirably explained this phenomenon in an essay on Dickens' *Great Expectations*:

> People were becoming things, and things (the things that money can buy or that are the means for making money or for exalting prestige in the abstract) were becoming more important than people. People were being de-animated, robbed of their souls, and things were usurping the prerogatives of animate creatures —governing the lives of their owners in the most literal sense.[4]

This is as precise a statement as we are likely to find anywhere to explain a set of literary circumstances which have characterized so much of modern fiction and poetry.

The exalting of "things," however, is not something new. Plutarch, in his life of Demosthenes, wrote: ". . . for it was not so much by the knowledge of words that I came to the understanding of things, as by my experience of things I was enabled to follow the meaning of words." In book IV, chapter 32 of *Tristram Shandy*, Tristram speaks of writing a "chapter of Things" and laments the fact "that things have crowded in so thick upon me, that I have not been able to get into that part of my work, towards which I have all the way looked forwards, with so much earnest desire. . . ."

This Shandyean lament is carried into the twentieth century in a series of prose poems, *Tropismes*. Nathalie Sarraute, in this early work, echoes Sterne:

> Les choses! les choses! C'était sa force. La source de sa puissance. L'instrument dont elle se servait, à sa manière instinctive, infaillible et sûre, pour le triomphe, pour l'écrasement.
>
> Quand on vivait près d'elle, on était prisonnier des choses, esclave rampant chargé d'elles, lourd et triste, continuellement guetté, traqué par elles.[5]

This passage may be said to have launched a new group of writers, who are occasionally referred to as *chosistes*. The inheritance of "things" has made its presence felt decisively in the novels of Samuel Beckett, Alain Robbe-Grillet, and Nathalie Sarraute herself. (We should not forget the title of one installment of Simone de Beauvoir's autobiography, *La Force des Choses*.) Almost all of Beckett's characters own hats, umbrellas, and bicycles which they treat with a certain reverence. No theatregoer can forget the vaudevillean moment in *En attendant Godot* when Vladimir and Estragon pass the hats ritualistically back and forth. The heroes of Beckett's novels are almost all feverishly attached to their bicycles—to the point that they seem to offer a new creatural dimension, which Hugh Kenner has classified as "Cartesian centaur." [6] Robbe-Grillet's novels depend heavily on physical objects, like the watches and the figure eight in *Le Voyeur*, the eraser in

*Les Gommes.* While Beckett's characters are fond of listing and cataloguing their "possessions," Robbe-Grillet's "narrators" describe objects in minute surface detail.

Flannery O'Connor's own reading probably did not include these "new novelists." Robert Fitzgerald mentions in his introduction to *Everything That Rises Must Converge*[7] that the only novels which she urged him to read during her stay in his Connecticut home were *Miss Lonelyhearts* and *As I Lay Dying.* Flannery O'Connor was evidently not drawn especially to French literature; as Fitzgerald reports: "Though she deprecated her French, now and again she would read some, and once carried off one of those appetizing volumes of Faguet from which I had learned about all I knew of old French literature" (*Everything,* xv). She would be unlikely to find out anything about *chosisme* (even in the broadest sense) from the pages of Emile Faguet. In the numerous interviews with Flannery O'Connor the only contemporary French novelist whose name turns up is François Mauriac. And he is as far from the practices of the *nouveau roman* as it is possible to be.

We must then look in another direction to understand Flannery O'Connor's preoccupation with physical objects, with "things." Very much to the point, I think, are some remarks made by Mircea Eliade in his *The Sacred and the Profane.* After defining elementary *hierophany* as the "manifestation of the sacred in some ordinary object, a stone or a tree," he goes on to say:

> It is impossible to overemphasize the paradox represented by every hierophany, even the most elementary. By manifesting the sacred, any object becomes *something else,* yet it continues to remain *itself,* for it continues to participate in its surrounding cosmic milieu. A *sacred* stone remains a *stone;* apparently (or, more precisely, from the profane point of view), nothing distinguishes it from all other stones. But for those to whom a stone reveals itself as sacred, its immediate reality is transmuted into a supernatural reality. In other words, for those who have a religious experience all nature is capable of revealing itself as

cosmic sacrality. The cosmos in its entirety can become a hiero-phany.[8]

The predominantly religious fiction of Flannery O'Connor, with its uneasy tension between the sacred and profane, seems to be an exact literary application of this theory.

There are few characters in Miss O'Connor's work who are not irresistibly tied to some commonplace object. Hazel Motes, the self-appointed preacher of the new "Church Without Christ" in *Wise Blood,* has as his equipment a suit of "glaring blue," "a stiff black broad-brimmed hat," a black Bible, and "a pair of silver-rimmed spectacles." He holds on to the in-congruously mated suit and hat almost as if they were religious objects, to the point at which (to use Dorothy Van Ghent's words again) they "were usurping the prerogatives of animate creatures—governing the lives of their owners in the most literal sense." The same can be said for the Bible and spectacles. They offer as ludicrous a combination as the suit and the hat. Hazel reads his Bible only when he is wearing the spec-tacles, despite the fact that "They tired his eyes so that after a short time he was always obliged to stop" (17). The "high rat-colored car" which he purchases later in the novel is treated with the same illogical reverence. Hazel Motes's "things" are perhaps the best illustration in Miss O'Connor's work of "immediate reality [being] transmuted into a super-natural reality" and of "nature [being] capable of revealing itself as cosmic sacrality."

Another character in *Wise Blood,* Enoch Emery, is char-acterized by Miss O'Connor as having "a certain reverence for the purpose of things." He presents Hazel with a shriveled-up mummy, stolen from a museum, to act as a new jesus for his Church Without Christ. A statement made by Paul Tillich in his *The Courage To Be* offers a gloss, perhaps, for Emery's action: "The man-created world of objects has drawn into itself Him who created it and who now loses His subjectivity in it."

Tarwater, the young hero of Flannery O'Connor's other novel, *The Violent Bear It Away*, shares Hazel Motes's regard for hats. When the novel reaches a kind of epiphany in the drowning-baptism of the mentally-retarded Bishop, we note that both Tarwater and Bishop are wearing hats. Bishop, just before the drowning, is ominously described by Miss O'Connor: "The small black-hatted figure sat like a passenger being borne by the surly oarsman across the lake to some mysterious destination" (420). This Dantesque moment is underscored by the reference to the hat. Several pages later we understand the talismanic importance of the hat:

> Bishop took off his hat and threw it over the side where it floated right-side-up, black on the black surface of the lake. The boy turned his head, following the hat with his eyes, and saw suddenly that the bank loomed behind him, not twenty yards away, silent, like the brow of some leviathan lifted just above the surface of the water. He felt bodiless as if he were nothing but a head full of air, about to tackle all the dead [431].

Despite the unpleasant symbolical reminders of Bishop's hat, Tarwater tenaciously holds on to his own through the final pages of *The Violent Bear It Away*.

Tarwater holds a corkscrew-bottleopener, which his uncle Rayber gives him, in the same awe: "He returned the corkscrew-bottleopener to his pocket and held it there in his hand as if henceforth it would be his talisman" (436). The hat and bottleopener are irresistibly linked to Tarwater and form part of a *Leitmotiv* which always identifies him.

Undoubtedly Rayber's hearing aid belongs in the same "hierophanic" category. The paradox is especially revealing here because of the two opposing views: Rayber treats the hearing aid as the commonplace object it is for most people who are continually aware of its function; Tarwater has transformed it into a miracle box with special powers. " 'What you wired for?' he drawled. 'Does your head light up?' " (366). Later he asks, with quite the same naive seriousness: "Do you

think in the box . . . or do you think in your head?" (367).
Eliade has an explanation for this: "By manifesting the sacred,
any object becomes *something else,* yet it continues to remain
*itself.* . . ." For Tarwater, with his developed awareness of the
sacred, it becomes *ganz Anderes.* For Rayber, with his firm roots
in the profane, it remains untransformed. If uncle and nephew
can be viewed as conflicting parts of the same personality, as
opposite sides of the same coin, their differing notions of the
same object make for an interesting union between sacred and
profane.

Flannery O'Connor's short stories offer the same reliance on
"things" as her novels. The plaster figure of a Negro manages
to exert a purging effect on the two main characters in "The
Artificial Nigger"; it acts as an epiphanic agent on the story
as it introduces a moment of illumination for both Nelson and
Mr. Head:

> They stood gazing at the artificial Negro as if they were faced
> with some great mystery, some monument to another's victory
> that brought them together in their common defeat. They could
> both feel it dissolving their differences like an action of mercy
> [212–13].

Hulga's artificial leg is one of the central concerns in "Good
Country People." The false Bible salesman makes off with it
triumphantly at the end of the story; he adds it to his collection
of unlikely objects which already includes a woman's glass eye.
Flannery O'Connor mentions, as he departs, that he is wearing
a "toast-colored hat"—a reminder of the hats which Tarwater
and Hazel Motes rarely remove from their heads and the hat
which Bishop throws in the water before he drowns. The
Bibles which the salesman carries are hollow but are otherwise
curiously similar to the Bible which Hazel reads with the
spectacles which betray his eyesight: the Biblical text emerges
with the same clarity in each instance. When Dorothy Van
Ghent speaks of "things" usurping the position of people and

governing their lives, readers of Flannery O'Connor should immediately think of "Good Country People."

"The Partridge Festival" begins with a mention of a "small pod-shaped car." Its physical appearance is obviously quite different from Hazel's "high rat-colored car," but it serves much the same evangelical function. Hazel preaches his new creed, in good revivalist fashion, standing up in his car. Calhoun and Mary Elizabeth try to rescue their "Christ-figure" Singleton from the asylum with Calhoun's car. Hazel's Essex ends fatefully as a policeman pushes it off an embankment, thus ending the self-appointed preacher's itinerant career. The pod-shaped car is connected with the failed mission of Calhoun and Mary Elizabeth as it transports them from the asylum; the car is given special analogical importance: ". . . the boy [Calhoun] drove it away as if his heart were the motor and would never go fast enough." [9]

Mrs. Greenleaf's special cult of "prayer healing" (in "Greenleaf") is filled with Flannery O'Connor's special brand of prophetic vitality. Mrs. Greenleaf has a daily ritual of clipping "morbid stories" from the newspaper, burying them, and mumbling inaudible prayers over them. She evidently found "manifestations of the sacred," which had been abused, in these scraps of newsprint; the sounds pronounced over them transformed them into Eliade's category of *something else*," another experience of the "hierophany."

Perhaps the best example of the importance of "things" in the shorter fiction is in "The Lame Shall Enter First." This story is filled with the same physical objects, with their sacred possibilities, which we have seen in the two novels, especially in *The Violent Bear It Away*—but in larger supply.

Rufus Johnson (the Tarwater of the story) has a club foot which is insistently returned to, especially by his self-appointed mentor, Sheppard. Sheppard is anxious to have him fitted with a new pair of shoes which Rufus stoutly opposes. The shoe-fitting scene (a mockery of the foot-washing scene in Homer or John 13?) is especially instructive: "Johnson was as touchy about the foot as if it were a sacred object. His face had been glum while the clerk, a young man with a bright pink bald head, measured the foot with his profane hands" (*Everything*, 162). Surely the sacred *vs.* the profane is in evidence here.

Rayber's hearing aid in *The Violent Bear It Away* has been turned into the telescope which Sheppard buys Rufus to dissuade him from his Bible-Belt superstitions. The telescope is used both symbolically and actually. It occasionally supplies a metaphorical function: "He appeared so far away that Sheppard might have been looking at him through the wrong end of the telescope" (*Everything*, 162). The telescope ends up as an object of betrayal, like so many of the objects in Flannery O'Connor's work; it proves to be the undoing of Sheppard's neglected son, Norton. "The tripod had fallen and the telescope lay on the floor. A few feet over it, the child hung in the jungle of shadows, just below the beam from which he had launched his flight into space" (*Everything*, 190).

Sheppard also purchases a microscope for Rufus: "Since Johnson had lost interest in the telescope, he bought a microscope and a box of prepared slides. If he couldn't impress the boy with immensity, he would try the infinitesimal" (*Everything*, 171). The telescope and microscope, however, prove ineffectual in the face of the ever-present Bible which Rufus insists on referring to with righteous defiance. He counters all of Sheppard's scientific thrusts with gentle parries from the Holy Scriptures. Rufus' Bible seems more real than its hollow counterpart in "Good Country People" or its counterpart mated with silver-rimmed spectacles in *Wise Blood*. Instead of Mrs. Greenleaf's "prayer healing," which involves the burial of scraps of morbid newsprint, we find a reference to Rufus' grandfather involved in a Bible-burying expedition.

"The Lame Shall Enter First" is a splendid example of Flannery O'Connor's "literature of Things." It is a good stopping-point for our discussion. There are certainly other works in her canon which use objects in the way we have described, but multiplying illustrations would now seem rather unnecessary. The tattoos in "Parker's Back," for example, symbolically echo such religiously-oriented objects as the Bibles, cars, and hats which abound in Miss O'Connor's fiction. Tanner's sitting "all day with that damn black hat on his head" ("Judgement Day") is still another reference to the special importance of hats (a preoccupation shared with Samuel Beckett).

Flannery O'Connor's work is thus a veritable community of objects.[10] She has made every effort (in Wylie Sypher's words, used in a different context) "to collaborate with things." It is tempting to connect her "objectal" bias with that of the *nouveau roman* but literary history would not go along with us here. The more likely explanation is a religious one, in the direction of the hierophany with its clash between the sacred and the profane.

## Notes

1. Found in Flannery O'Connor's posthumous collection of stories, *Everything That Rises Must Converge* (New York: Farrar, Straus and Giroux, 1965), p. 249. All subsequent references will be to this edition.

2. See, for example, the passage I quote from "The Geranium" in the introduction to the present volume.

3. See J. Robert Loy, "*Things* in Recent French Literature," *PMLA*, LXXI (March, 1956), 27.

4. Dorothy Van Ghent, *The English Novel: Form and Function* (New York: Harper Torchbooks, 1961), p. 128.

5. Nathalie Sarraute, *Tropismes* (Paris: Les Éditions de Minuit, 1957), p. 41. One might possibly think also of D. H. Lawrence's story "Things" in this connection, as well as Louis Simpson's poem "Things" (*The New Yorker*, May 15, 1965).

6. The connection between Beckett and Flannery O'Connor is not as farfetched as it might at first seem. In his "Le petit monde de Flannery O'Connor" (*Mercure de France*, January, 1964), Michel Gresset suggests the possibility: "On pense à Bosch, à Poe, à Beckett même" (p. 142). See also my "Les romans de Samuel Beckett et la tradition du grotesque," in *Un Nouveau Roman?*, edited by J. H. Matthews (Paris: Lettres Modernes, 1964), especially pp. 42-44.

7. The title of this posthumous collection of stories is taken from Pierre Teilhard de Chardin. Claude Cuénot, in his book *Teilhard de Chardin: A Biographical Study,* makes abundantly clear Teilhard's fascination with objects, especially with stones. Perhaps this renowned French archaeologist has proved to be somewhat of an inspiration here. On the more secular side, we can look to another modern declaration of a fondness for things—this time on the part of the great Italian *littérateur,* Mario Praz: "Things remain impressed in my memory more than people. Things which have no soul, or rather, which have the soul with which we endow them, and which can also disappoint us when one day the scales fall from our eyes . . ." (*The House of Life*; New York: Oxford University Press, 1964, p. 333). Mario Praz, by the way, wrote an early piece on *A Good Man Is Hard to Find* in the 1956 *Studi Americani* ("Racconti del Sud").

8. Mircea Eliade, *The Sacred and the Profane: The Nature of Religion,* translated from the French by Willard R. Trask (New York and Evanston: Harper Torchbooks, 1961), pp. 11, 12.

9. "The Partridge Festival," in *Critic,* XIX (February-March, 1961), 85. For an interesting discussion of Hazel Motes's automobile, see Jonathan Baumbach, "The Acid of God's Grace: *Wise Blood* by Flannery O'Connor" in *The Landscape of Nightmare* (New York: New York University Press, 1965), pp. 95-96.

10. For a discussion of imagery patterns and their significance in Flannery O'Connor's work see Irving Malin's excellent *New American Gothic* (Carbondale: Southern Illinois University Press, 1962); also his "Flannery O'Connor and the Grotesque" in this volume.

# "The Perplex Business": Flannery O'Connor and Her Critics Enter the 1970s

## MELVIN J. FRIEDMAN

GILBERT MULLER begins his *Nightmares and Visions: Flannery O'Connor and the Catholic Grotesque* (University of Georgia Press, 1972) with this revealing sentence: "I have been told that Flannery O'Connor read *The Pooh Perplex* with glee, and that subsequently she referred to the act of criticism as the perplex business." She did not live long enough to see the perplex business directed toward her own work turn into the "industry" it now threatens to become. The first gathering of this criticism took on serious proportions following her death, culminating in the pamphlets of Stanley Edgar Hyman and Robert Drake and in the first edition of the present collection. We are probably now in the midst of the second gathering of critical attention which was started by Josephine Hendin's naughtily irreverent study, *The World of Flannery O'Connor* (Indiana University Press, 1970). The two texts which seem central to this new interest in her work are Sally and Robert Fitzgerald's 1969 compilation, *Mystery and Manners: Occasional Prose*, and *The Complete Stories of Flannery O'Connor* which appeared in 1971. While these two collections offer rather little new material, they tend to focus our attention in a useful way to offer us a unique glance at the maturing of a remarkable talent.

We understand from *Mystery and Manners* how secondary, in her mind, the critical function was: it resulted in an "occasional" gesture which produced *aperçus* rather than final statements; it was a way of sorting out impressions on subjects as diverse as the raising of peacocks and the effective turning of a situation to produce a story; it was, finally, little more than an addendum to her practices as a fiction writer. Despite this almost negative aspect of *Mystery and Manners*, critics of O'Connor's work can ill afford to be without it. Indeed the elegance of her phrasing and her fine sense of the epigrammatic are always in evidence in this collection. No American writer of our time, with the possible exception of Katherine Anne Porter, could manage this economy of phrasing: "the prophet is a realist of distances"; "hazy compassion"; "the South is hardly Christ-centered, it is most certainly Christ-haunted"; "the writer's business is to contemplate experience, not to be merged in it"; "it is the business of fiction to embody mystery through manners." I could go on almost endlessly.

*The Complete Stories of Flannery O'Connor* makes available in a single volume all 31 of her shorter fictional pieces. Gathered together are the 19 stories from *A Good Man Is Hard to Find* and *Everything That Rises Must Converge*; the six stories which originally comprised her Master's thesis at the University of Iowa; early versions of chapters of *Wise Blood* and *The Violent Bear It Away*; a previously uncollected story, "The Partridge Festival"; and a brief section of a novel-in-progress. The arrangement is chronological according to date of composition. Thus we are allowed to see how the apprentice writer learned her craft and matured to the point of being able to write the superbly finished last stories like "Revelation" and "Judgement Day." In fact, the volume gains a kind of symmetry by beginning with "The Geranium" and ending with a later version of the same story, "Judgement Day." A close examination of the two reveals the differences in the narrative strategies of the O'Connor of 1946 and the O'Connor of 1964. *The Complete Stories* thus offers us a privileged glance into her workshop.

The notion of arranging the stories chronologically might prove unsettling to those who view the two collections, *A Good Man Is Hard to Find* and *Everything That Rises Must Converge,* as following some inviolable pattern or design. Indeed rearranging the stories might be likened by some critics to the heresy of reordering Joyce's *Dubliners* or Sherwood Anderson's *Winesburg, Ohio.* It does seem odd, for example, to place "A Stroke of Good Fortune" (the fourth story in *A Good Man Is Hard to Find*) between "The Heart of the Park" and "Enoch and the Gorilla," early versions of parts of *Wise Blood.* This gesture, determined entirely by chronology, breaks up a four-part narrative sequence ("The Train," "The Peeler," "The Heart of the Park," and "Enoch and the Gorilla") which traces Hazel's[1] train ride to Taulkinham, his first encounter with Enoch Emery, a subsequent meeting between the two, and Enoch's confrontation with "Gonga, Giant Jungle Monarch." Hazel dominates the first two stories, Enoch the latter two. Ruby Hill's unwillingness to face up to her pregnancy in "A Stroke of Good Fortune" clearly has no place between the two Enoch Emery–controlled stories.

Yet there is a certain value in having the chronological arrangement; it lets us in on the subtle and gradual maturing of a remarkable talent. When Flannery O'Connor remarks in *Mystery and Manners* that "a story really isn't any good unless it successfully resists paraphrase, unless it hangs on and expands in the mind," we have a reliable index for measuring her development. The possibilities for effective paraphrase are surely better in the early stories; the lines of their narrative strategies are much more clearly drawn. They do not, however, linger on quite so long. The vintage O'Connor story, as Carter Martin suggested in *The True Country: Themes in the Fiction of Flannery O'Connor* (Vanderbilt University Press,

1969), has the effect of good poetry with its oblique devices, with its economy of means, and with its density. An early story like "The Barber" has certain decisive regional and tall-story properties: the self-righteous liberal confronts the bigoted hangers-on at the local barber shop and loses control in the face of their mockery. The humor results partly from the incongruity between the intellectual's[2] precise speech and the regionalisms of his taunters. The taunters, predictably, win the day. The humor is much darker and grimmer in the later stories and the effects are arrived at through much less obvious devices. Our laughter is quite muted as Sarah Ruth screams "Idolatry!" when her husband bares his tattooed back to her ("Parker's Back"), or as Mrs. Turpin approaches the pig pen and "remained there with her gaze bent to them as if she were absorbing some abysmal life-giving knowledge" ("Revelation").

*The Complete Stories,* then, points to the subtle, slow, and not always obvious growth of a major short story writer who deserves a place beside her friend Katherine Anne Porter. The Flaubertian way in which Flannery O'Connor went about her work apparently prevented these startling and rather terrifying leaps from apprenticeship to early prime to full maturity to later manner—which so many writers go through. We are grateful for *The Complete Stories* also because it includes such a fine uncollected piece as "The Partridge Festival" which was previously available only in the pages of *The Critic.*

## II

Another sign of this second gathering of critical attention is *The Flannery O'Connor Bulletin,* published at Georgia College in Milledgeville. Its unprepossessing format and the low-keyed nature of many of the contributions seem precisely right for an annual which honors a writer who shied away from any form of pretense. We should glance briefly at the first issue which appeared in 1972. It contains four critical articles, a reminiscence, a review of Kathleen Feeley's *Flannery O'Connor: Voice of the Peacock* (Rutgers University Press, 1972), some photographs, and a description of the Flannery O'Connor Collection at Georgia College. The manuscript collection, outlined by its curator Gerald Becham, should offer an interesting detour for the literary faithful who visit Andalusia, the O'Connor farm outside Milledgeville, Georgia.

Many of Flannery O'Connor's admirers and commentators have made the trip and enjoyed the scenery, both literary and actual. We have, for example, the gracious reminiscence of Louise Hardeman Abbot, "Remembering Flannery O'Connor" (*Southern Literary Journal*, Spring 1970). Josephine Hendin briefly describes her visit in the early pages of *The World of Flannery O'Connor* but unlike most of the other pilgrims she notices such unpleasant things as "The squirrels have lately begun to eat her dogwood buds" (p. 6). Mrs. Hendin's is a tough-minded, warts-and-all approach. She refuses to accept the gospel according to Stanley Edgar Hyman, Robert Drake, Sister M. Bernetta Quinn, and other O'Connor critics who subscribe to the "religious interpretation." She proceeds almost immediately to force Flannery O'Connor on the psychiatric couch and raise questions about her personal life: Why did she leave New York to settle on the Connecticut farm of the Robert Fitzgeralds? Why could she only be "comfortable when alone in an insulated and protected world?" (p. 11). Why did she have to play the role of the Southern hick mocking the Northern "interleckchul"? Mrs. Hendin tries very hard to classify Flannery O'Connor's "essential malaise" before turning to the fiction.

The problem with all of this is that Josephine Hendin emerges from her book as the very type of the Northern "interleckchul" whom Flannery O'Connor felt so uncomfortable with. Mrs. Hendin keeps turning to *The New York Review of Books* for her solace: one of the few critical pieces on O'Connor which she responds to at all favorably is Irving Howe's review of *Everything That Rises Must Converge* in *The New*

*York Review of Books*; she gets the useful term "comic literalization" from F. W. Dupee's essay on *Zuleika Dobson* in *The New York Review of Books*. In a sense we have the feeling that she is playing Rayber to Flannery O'Connor's old Mason Tarwater. We might recall the appropriate passage from *The Violent Bear It Away*: " 'That's where he wanted me,' the old man said, 'and he thought once he had me in that schoolteacher magazine, I would be as good as in his head.' The schoolteacher's [Rayber's] house had had little in it but books and papers. The old man had not known when he went there to live that every living thing that passed through the nephew's eyes into his head was turned by his brain into a book or a paper or a chart."

The tone Josephine Hendin assumes strikes me as rather unfortunate. Yet *The World of Flannery O'Connor* is in many ways a valuable book. It offers a necessary corrective to the insistently religious interpretations Flannery O'Connor's work has been subjected to. There is surely a place for a critic who questions the old pieties and offers new readings of the *oeuvre*. One helpful suggestion Mrs. Hendin offers is that Flannery O'Connor's work falls somewhere between the symbolist novel of Joyce, Faulkner, and Virginia Woolf and the objectivist novel of Robbe-Grillet and Susan Sontag. This is a way of removing the emphasis from the theological and placing it more squarely on the aesthetic. The feeling is that if we apply the criteria of critical studies like Tindall's *The Literary Symbol*, Virginia Woolf's "Modern Fiction," or Forster's *Aspects of the Novel* to Flannery O'Connor we might begin to say useful things about the formal and technical aspects of her work.

The opening chapter of *The World of Flannery O'Connor*, revealingly called "In Search of Flannery O'Connor," revaluates the life and work. The biographical pages make some doubtful assertions, as I have indicated above, while the critical pages offer us valuable new optics for viewing the fiction. A self-consciously paradoxical statement like "Flannery

O'Connor seems to have lived out a fiction and written down her life" (p. 13) has limited value in understanding either the writer or her work, while a more straightforward judgment like "The great strength of O'Connor's fiction seems to me to spring from the silent and remote rage that erupts from the quiet surface of her stories and that so unexpectedly explodes" (p. 14) is quite worth preserving and taking seriously. Fortunately, there are more aesthetic than clinical assumptions made. Mrs. Hendin can, on occasion, walk an interesting literary tightrope and come up with conclusions as valuable as this: "Writing within an older literary framework of traditional symbols, she begins with a vague suggestion of depth that is not sufficiently developed to make her work symbolic but does provide a point of departure—a three-dimensional image which she can flatten out as the story progresses" (p. 27).

What seems most to turn Josephine Hendin off about Flannery O'Connor is her reversal of the roles of hero and villain; "secular missionaries" like Rayber and Sheppard receive most of the ill-treatment while the "murderers, psychic cripples, sometimes freaks" seem to be the heroes. In short, Flannery O'Connor becomes for Mrs. Hendin "the pure poet of the Misfit."

Chapter 2 offers a consideration of *Wise Blood* and *The Violent Bear It Away*. After the impressive amount of theorizing in chapter 1, one expects rather more attention and close reading than either of the two novels gets. The search to uncover the "real" Flannery O'Connor seems to suffer a disappointing letdown here. We are told that each novel is a sort of anti-Bildungsroman because neither Hazel Motes nor Tarwater ever grows up or comes of age; each enacts "a childhood role for a lifetime" (pp. 60–61).

Josephine Hendin, like most O'Connor critics, prefers the short stories to the novels. She reveals this bias by studying three of the stories from *A Good Man Is Hard to Find*—"The Life You Save May Be Your Own," "Good Country People," and "A Temple of the Holy Ghost"—in admirable detail. Her twenty-page discussion of "A Temple of the Holy Ghost," the most complete we are ever likely to get about this story, is slightly longer than the combined treatment given to the two novels. One perhaps wonders a bit about this curious disproportion. Yet one is grateful for the close and intelligent reading of a difficult story.

The fourth chapter does for *Everything That Rises Must Converge* very much what chapter three did for *A Good Man Is Hard to Find*. This time six stories are treated in some detail, with "Revelation" getting the lion's share of the attention. Josephine Hendin offers some useful background information on Père Teilhard de Chardin who suggested the title of the collection; she rightly insists that "O'Connor takes from Teilhard what she likes" (p. 98).

The final chapter places Flannery O'Connor in a literary context, by suggesting certain ties with other Southern writers. Mrs. Hendin's critical strategy here is enormously persuasive. She chooses five murder scenes from novels written by Southerners—Percy Grimm's murder of Joe Christmas in *Light in August*, Nat Turner's murder of Margaret Whitehead in *The Confessions of Nat Turner*, the Misfit's murder of the Grandmother in "A Good Man Is Hard to Find," Hazel's murder of Solace Layfield in *Wise Blood*, the murders of Nancy and Mr. Clutter in *In Cold Blood*—and proceeds rather brilliantly to distinguish among them. She finds Faulkner and Styron using symbolical and mythological machinery while Capote and Flannery O'Connor seem to retreat into "an historical void." She further distinguishes between Capote and O'Connor to demonstrate the uniqueness of the latter's special kind of violence. By using words like "demythologizing" and "depthless," Josephine Hendin describes a universe in which things and acts are of crucial importance. We seem to be perilously close, in certain ways, to the *nouveau roman* (which came in for some discussion in the opening chapter of *The World of Flannery O'Connor*). Even Mrs. Hendin's vocabulary resembles that which Robbe-Grillet makes such insistent use of in his collection of essays, *Pour un nouveau roman*. When she speaks of the conflict between body and mind in certain O'Connor fictions, we are perhaps obliquely reminded of the famous sixth chapter of Beckett's *Murphy*.

The reading Josephine Hendin offers in *The World of Flannery O'Connor* is far from traditional. She goes against the grain of virtually all existing O'Connor criticism. It is true that she rather tactlessly dismisses much first-rate commentary, like the pamphlets of Stanley Edgar Hyman and Robert Drake. Yet if her manner is occasionally unfortunate, her matter is not; she is worth listening to.

## III

Another critic who has benefited from the pilgrimage to Andalusia and environs is Kathleen Feeley. She has even been through the manuscript collection at Georgia College and has examined all the books in Flannery O'Connor's personal library. Her *Flannery O'Connor: Voice of the Peacock* makes its way through all of the fiction, often measuring aspects of it against passages marked by Miss O'Connor in her own reading. Frederick Asals, in his competent review of Kathleen Feeley's book in the first *Flannery O'Connor Bulletin*, suggests "that there are actually two books inside these covers," one "a series of 'readings' of virtually every work of fiction," the other an uncovering of her "thought." He feels that these two books never quite meet, that "the focus remains, in the end, divided." If this judgment is to be taken seriously—and I tend to believe that it should be—I still cannot quite share Mr. Asals' keen disappointment. Her book does so many useful things that I can forgive Sister Kathleen her divided focus.

Caroline Gordon prefaces *Flannery O'Connor: Voice of the Peacock* with a four-page appreciative foreword which throws accolades in the directions of both Kathleen Feeley and Flannery O'Connor. Sister Kathleen returns the favor by invoking the authority of Caroline Gordon on several crucial occasions.

Armed with the encouragement and wisdom of Caroline Gordon on the one hand and with *Mystery and Manners* and the impressive resources of Flannery O'Connor's library on the other, she meets the fiction head on.

Taking a cue from earlier critics Sister Kathleen makes a good deal of the notion: "In describing the cry of the peacock, Flannery [she persists in calling her by her given name] has most aptly described her own writing" (p. 17). She manages, interestingly, to show how the fascination with peacocks, revealed in the opening piece in *Mystery and Manners*, "The King of the Birds," informs the fiction—not only in the obvious way that the peacock is a central symbol in the long story "The Displaced Person." Thus, for example, Kathleen Feeley reasons with considerable perception: "Her [Flannery O'Connor's] mysterious attraction to strange birds that led finally to her acquisition of peacocks seems analogous to Parker's mysterious attraction to tattoos [in "Parker's Back"] that finally led to his total absorption in Christ" (p. 149).

To show how Sister Kathleen's critical strategies work at their best, we should look closely at the first half of chapter three which is devoted to *Wise Blood*. The chapter begins with a letter—quoted in its entirety—on the conflict between faith and reason, which turned up between the pages of a book in Flannery O'Connor's library. (Kathleen Feeley's exemplary research habits helped unearth a variety of inspired jottings in O'Connor's handwriting, both on scratch paper and in the margins of her books.) Then Sister Kathleen quotes marked passages from Anton Pegis' foreword to the *Introduction to St. Thomas Aquinas*, from de Tocqueville's *Democracy in America*, from volume two of Eric Voegelin's *Order and History*, and from Jacques Maritain's *Creative Intuition in Art and Poetry*—all of which illustrate "the extent to which her concept of reality affected other areas of thought" (p. 55). After quoting from a lecture Flannery O'Connor delivered at Sweetbriar in March 1963, Kathleen Feeley finally turns to the "comic romance" *Wise Blood*. Her perceptions of this novel seem the keener and the shrewder for her awareness of these background texts. Among other things, she views Mrs. Hitchcock and Mrs. Flood, who appear respectively at the beginning and the end of the narrative, as " 'normal' characters [who] frame this story of spiritual 'freaks' " (p. 57). This gives *Wise Blood* a design, accounted for by the clash between reason and faith, not generally noticed by O'Connor critics. One might be tempted at this point to liken the composition of Flannery O'Connor's first novel to the structure of a novel she much admired, *Madame Bovary* (see *Mystery and Manners*). Flaubert's work is framed by a "normal" character, Charles Bovary, who is present at the beginning and end. His numbing ordinariness—Flaubert, on one occasion, describes his conversation as being as flat as a sidewalk—is set against the eccentricities of the other characters and helps to give the novel its shape. There are certainly rougher edges in *Wise Blood* than in *Madame Bovary*, but it is interesting to note how an organizational principle they have in common offers the O'Connor novel a certain structural tidiness.

Sister Kathleen also works interestingly with the plot lines of the novel and their convergence in an attempt to explain how it develops narratively. Her discussion ends with a quotation of a marked passage from Richard Chase's *The American Novel and Its Tradition* and an excerpt from a Flannery O'Connor lecture on the way to explaining the form of the "comic romance." She finally puts the matter eloquently for *Wise Blood*: "Here comedy undercuts romance; laughter wins out" (p. 69).

There is something a bit suspect about this approach of counterpointing the closeted reading habits and tastes of a writer with her own finished stories and novels. But somehow the method works. We seem to understand the fiction better after Kathleen Feeley has gone through these elaborate gestures. We have known for some time how much Pierre Teilhard de Chardin, Romano Guardini, Henry James, and Nathaniel Hawthorne have mattered to her. But so many other writers and thinkers, like Edith Stein and C. G. Jung, now surface forcibly for the first time. We notice, for example, how Mircea Eliade's term "hierophany," used repeatedly in his great book *The Sacred and the Profane,* informs certain strategies in her work. (See my use of Eliade's concept in "Flannery O'Connor's Sacred Objects" found earlier in this volume. The essay was written over ten years ago, considerably before Kathleen Feeley unearthed Flannery O'Connor's reading habits and preferences.)

Sister Kathleen, unfortunately, never gives us a list of the complete holdings of the library; her bibliography at the end of *Flannery O'Connor: Voice of the Peacock* includes only those titles she makes use of. I must echo Frederick Asals' curiosity about the rest of them and his assertion of the need for a complete catalogue. While on the subject of the bibliography we should note that in the section called "Additional Sources" she lists only a handful of critical works. By my count there are fewer than 20 entries which might qualify as critical examinations of the stories and novels. Such talented critics of O'Connor's work as Louis Rubin, Walter Sullivan, Marion Montgomery, and John Hawkes are nowhere mentioned. There is, by the way, an error in one of these entries: the subtitle of Leon V. Driskell's and Joan T. Brittain's *The Eternal Crossroads* is *The Art of Flannery O'Connor* not *The Wit of Flannery O'Connor.* We should also note before leaving *Flannery O'Connor: Voice of the Peacock* that footnote 10 on p. 180 refers to a Granville Hicks review of *Everything That Rises Must Converge* instead of *A Good Man Is Hard to Find;* the 1965 date of the review should have alerted Sister Kathleen to this mistake.

One statement Kathleen Feeley makes would be looked at with suspicion by a good many critics: ". . . but Flannery O'Connor does not write allegory" (p. 173). David Eggenschwiler, for one, firmly believes that she does (see especially pp. 12–13 of his *The Christian Humanism of Flannery O'Connor* [Wayne State University Press, 1972]).

Eggenschwiler admits in his preface that he is intent on developing "a single thesis, that Flannery O'Connor consistently wrote from the point of view of a Christian humanist." He marshals all of his evidence in this direction as he closely examines the two novels and many of the stories. He manages successfully to rid her of the tag of provincialism which so many of the early commentators attached to her work.

Eggenschwiler takes the epigraph for his first chapter from Allen Tate's essay in the 1930 Fugitive manifesto, *I'll Take My Stand*. The most revealing sentence quoted goes like this: "The religious mind, on the other hand, has this respect; it wants the whole horse, and it will be satisfied with nothing less." This notion of the "whole horse," when applied to Flannery O'Connor—she who had "the religious mind" par excellence—brings out the range of her experience with a variety of disciplines and the resultant "integral universe" of her fiction. Eggenschwiler proceeds to illuminate the work with help from an impressive number of psychologists, theologians, philosophers, and even poets and playwrights. He leans most heavily on Kierkegaard and Freudian psychology. Words like *Angst*, Dionysian, fetishist, alter-ego, *eros, thanatos, animus, agon,* and *alazon* thread their way through the text. After a while Mr. Eggenschwiler, like Josephine Hendin before him, begins to emerge as one of those "interleckchuls" Flannery O'Connor was constitutionally ill-at-ease with. This is rather too bad because he does read the stories and novels with insight—once he brushes away the verbal cobwebs which he has allowed to accumulate about them.

One of Eggenschwiler's considerable strengths is his perseverance. He rarely leaves a story (I find him to be better with the stories than with the novels) until he has examined every last wrinkle of it. He studies in depth not only the principal characters but also the secondary and tertiary ones. Thus he has several revealing pages on Father Flynn in "The Displaced Person" (see pp. 78–81) as well as on the more central figures in that long story. He is very adept also at placing O'Connor's characters on the psychiatric couch and pointing out, for example, that Hulga Hopewell and Manley Pointer ("Good Country People") are "morbid fetishists" or that O. E. Parker ("Parker's Back") is a "most obvious case of sublimated will to believe" (p. 74).

By bringing various disciplines, like psychology, philosophy, and theology, to bear on Flannery O'Connor's work Eggenschwiler has made us respond to its "wholeness," its "Christian humanism." He succeeds to this extent. His manner, however, seems not in concert with the wide range of his matter. There is a certain narrowness about his method which seems intent on dismissing conflicting interpretations. He is very generous to Josephine Hendin's *The World of Flannery O'Connor* which he admits, in his first note, "offers the most detailed and interesting complement to my approach" (p. 141). But this gesture is not his usual practice. His text is liberally sprinkled with references to unnamed critics who have sinned in various ways by misinterpreting Flannery O'Connor. There are some two dozen vague allusions to "several critics," "several commentators," "a number of commentators," "some readers," and so forth. One wonders, for example, who "some readers" are who "have considered him [Tarwater] a terrifying madman and fanatic as he went off toward the defenseless children of God, an extreme response which sacrifices the whole structure of the novel for a few isolated images but which does recognize his violent prophetic power" (p. 134). This habit proves annoying after a while. Eggenschwiler offers four closely printed pages of notes at the back of his book (there is no bibliography) and might have expanded this section somewhat to let us in on who these unnamed "readers," "critics," and "commentators" are. But I do not want to leave *The Christian Humanism of Flannery O'Connor* on this negative note. Eggenschwiler offers some very perceptive readings of the work and analyzes O'Connor's characters with exceptional insight.

The opening paragraph of Gilbert Muller's preface to his

*Nightmares and Visions: Flannery O'Connor and the Catholic Grotesque* is agreeably self-effacing; he apologizes genuinely for adding to "the perplex business." We should say in fairness to *Nightmares and Visions* that it does not add at all to the confusion and indeed, in its modest way, should illuminate some of the remaining dark corners of Flannery O'Connor's work. Muller gets down in his opening chapter to the important matter of defining the word "grotesque" and distinguishing it from other terms often used interchangeably with it, like "gothic." The matter is handled with ease and dispatch and we come away understanding a good deal about the history and possible applications of the term. Muller prefixes the word Catholic to it and applies the concept neatly: "In promulgating an antidote to the absurd, Flannery O'Connor creates what properly should be termed an art of the Catholic grotesque. She maneuvers her characters through dark and impenetrable mazes which seemingly lead nowhere, but which unexpectedly reveal an exit into Christianity's back yard" (p. 18). Muller's opening chapter offers the best corrective we have to William Esty's unthinking dismissal of Flannery O'Connor's art as partaking of the "gratuitous grotesque" (see his "In America, Intellectual Bomb Shelters," *Commonweal*, March 7, 1958, pp. 586–588).

Muller is very effective in suggesting large categories for considering the work. Thus he finds that many of Flannery O'Connor's stories and her two novels partake of the narrative of quest and belong to a fictional type as old as the *Odyssey*. In their "grotesque" and "absurd" aspects they belong to a lineage which includes such distinguished modern fiction as *Ulysses, The Castle, Lolita, As I Lay Dying,* and *The Tin Drum*. He never views her work in a vacuum. He invariably brings it together in interesting confrontation with something else in American literature: he suggests that the family trip in "A Good Man Is Hard to Find" might be thought of as "a parody of Wilder's 'The Happy Journey to Trenton and Camden'" (p. 31); he thinks of Guizac in "The Displaced Person" as "one of the two most convincing Christ figures in American short fiction" along with Melville's Bartleby (p. 35); he describes "The Artificial Nigger" as "perhaps the most perfect allegory of quest in American literature since Hawthorne wrote 'My Kinsman, Major Molineux'" (p. 74); he distinguishes the typical O'Connor characters from the Hemingway heroes on the basis that they "rarely seek social justification for their destructive acts" (p. 85).

Gilbert Muller has clarified an aspect of her work which has long been muddled and confused. His unpretentiousness would surely have delighted Flannery O'Connor. There is little to find fault with in this readable and intelligent study.

## IV

Miles Orvell's *Invisible Parade: The Fiction of Flannery O'Connor* (Temple University Press, 1972) is one of the few O'Connor studies which devote much attention to style and narrative. After a rather too cute geographical introduction to Flannery O'Connor's farmhouse and environs—which favors unfortunate poetic turns like "what brave old world was this, what Eden?"—and after the expected glance at the Southern and Catholic aspects of the work, Orvell gives us a close and convincing reading of the two novels and a representative sampling of the stories. He is very good, for example, in his explanation of how "multiple viewpoints" function in *The Violent Bear It Away* and how her prose is "deliberately flattened" to gain certain stylistic advantages in the stories. The following judgment about *The Violent Bear It Away* is worth taking seriously: "The total effect is that of a statue being rotated on a pedestal: with each turn, the observer perceives some new plane, some new relationship between the planes, until at last the whole pattern takes shape in the clarity of its meaning" (p. 101).

Orvell's first concern, rightly, is to give her work a context. He finds her roots in a variety of places: in the tradition of nineteenth-century American romance (Poe, Hawthorne, and Melville); in Jansenism ("without going so far as to call O'Connor a latter-day Jansenist"); in Nathanael West, Sherwood Anderson, Faulkner, and other twentieth-century acknowledgers of the "grotesque." He is surely not the first to indicate these affinities and influences but he manages to deepen his discoveries to the point that we are almost left believing that Miles Orvell has indeed unveiled them for the first time. There are certain risks, however, in his "comparatist" strategies. He brings too many writers and works in awkward confrontation with Flannery O'Connor. It does not help especially to call her short story "The Artificial Nigger" "a miniature Pilgrim's Progress" (p. 158). I can scarcely agree that ". . . the simplest way to define Flannery O'Connor might be to say she is the 'opposite' of Samuel Beckett" (p. 129). I do not understand Hazel Motes in *Wise Blood* any better by being told that he "would expire in Hemingway's universe" (p. 92). Orvell clearly works too hard at these rapprochements, producing rather strained effects. Gilbert Muller handles this kind of thing more effectively.

*Invisible Parade* is generally a very perceptive book. Its advantages far outweigh its defects. Perhaps "ironic"—surely Mr. Orvell's favorite word—is overused and occasionally even misused. He errs in speaking of Rufus Johnson's *father* in "The Lame Shall Enter First" as having "gone with a remnant to the hills" (see p. 41). Actually it is Johnson's grandfather. This is more important than it might at first appear as the grandchild–grandfather relationship is crucial in quite a number of O'Connor's works.

The most annoying aspect of Orvell's study is the too-frequent cuteness. He can change his accustomed serious tone quite abruptly and suddenly become very chatty: "I had not brought my camera for nothing: three clicks" (p. 4). Some of his stylistic effects become rather heavy-handed and wearying: ". . . whether or not Fortune [the grandfather in "A View of the Woods"] should be building a gas station qua gas station on a site that will block a view of the woods qua woods" (p. 16); or "Appearing from nowhere as an allegorical agency of grace, this deus ex machina proceeds to push off the road Hazel's well-worn deus in machina, his Essex" (p. 84).

Following Mr. Orvell's text are two appendices, one offering a chronological arrangement of Flannery O'Connor's fiction and the other a chronological list of her book reviews. The latter is made good use of in the first chapter of *Invisible Parade* when Orvell discusses some of these reviews in an attempt to account for the "shape" of O'Connor's belief. The book ends with a valuable ten-page bibliography.

## V

We tend often to undervalue Twayne books because of their introductory nature and because of their rather inflexible format. The feeling is that spontaneity and originality are stifled when a critic's movements are too rigidly prescribed. Yet the first book in Twayne's United States Authors Series, Frederick J. Hoffman's *William Faulkner,* is even now one of the handful of best books we have on the Mississippi writer. Earl Rovit's *Ernest Hemingway,* number 41 in the series, belongs in the elite company of the pioneering studies of Philip Young and Carlos Baker. And I am speaking now of books on writers who have been more responsible for crowding our shelves of criticism than any other twentieth-century American novelists. There has, of course, always been an acknowledged place for a Twayne book on an unknown or largely ignored writer. Flannery O'Connor is among neither the most studied American writers of this century (at least not yet) nor the neglected. She falls somewhere in between the Hemingways and Faulkners, on the one hand, and the Amélie Riveses on the other. Dorothy Walters, in a sense, reconfirms the versatility of the Twayne format by writing a quite useful study of a writer in this middle group.

Dorothy Walters sees as central to Flannery O'Connor's art

the "remarkable capacity to blend the *comic* and the *serious* in a single view of reality" (p. 13) on the way to realizing "Christian tragicomedy." She interestingly finds in the two novels a triadic "pattern of flight, apprehension, and capitulation" (p. 90). She sees a variation on Bergson's "snowball technique" working in many of the stories (p. 33). In speaking of the "restricted ranges" of the O'Connor characters, she suggests a connection with Ben Jonson's theory of "humours" (p. 29). She restlessly tries to account for the structural, technical, stylistic, and thematic elements in Flannery O'Connor by making reference to a wide variety of earlier artistic stratagems—and usually with considerable success.

She joins David Eggenschwiler in feeling that the "fiction tends always toward allegory" (p. 153). She echoes Flannery O'Connor's statement from *Mystery and Manners*—"Fiction writing is very seldom a matter of saying things; it is a matter of showing things."—by insisting that O'Connor's is an "art of *showing* as opposed to *telling*" (p. 153).

In the course of individually examining the 19 stories from *A Good Man Is Hard to Find* and *Everything That Rises Must Converge* as well as the two novels, Dorothy Walters manages both comprehensiveness and originality. She not only seems to touch all the bases but also comes up with a startling number of fresh insights. At the same time she does not allow her obvious admiration for Flannery O'Connor to get in the way of a fair and balanced appraisal of her work. She is quick to point out shortcomings, like the repetition of earlier themes and characters in the later stories—giving us something of the sensation of *déjà lu* as we turn from, say, "Good Country People" to "Revelation." She also listens attentively to the unpopular notion first expressed by John Hawkes that Flannery O'Connor "was on the devil's side." Despite O'Connor's categorical dismissal of the idea, Dorothy Walters finds it "intriguing" and explores its implications.

Dorothy Walters is clearly not at all stifled by the Twayne format. She works within its limitations and offers a penetrating study of the fiction. Her carefully annotated bibliography of secondary sources, which follows the fairly complete list of primary material, is a reliable index to the best O'Connor criticism.

A few lapses should be pointed out. When discussing the end of *Wise Blood*, Dorothy Walters refers to only a single "cop" being on the scene (see p. 60). Actually "two young policemen" are there. The number two has special importance when one recalls that two men appear to carry K. off and murder him at the end of Kafka's *The Trial*. There are, also, two detectives functioning in the last chapter of John Hawkes's *The Lime Twig*. Hawkes remarked in his *Sewanee Review* essay on Flannery O'Connor: "In *Wise Blood* two policemen turn out to be sadistic versions of Tweedledum and Tweedledee." *The Lime Twig* appeared nine years after *Wise Blood*. Hawkes may very well have gotten the inspiration for his two detectives from O'Connor's two policemen, just as O'Connor may have been thinking of the last chapter of *The Trial* when she wrote the ending of *Wise Blood*.

In her discussion of "A Circle in the Fire" Dorothy Walters mistakenly speaks of "Mrs. Hopewell's daughter, Sally Virginia" (p. 69). Actually she means Mrs. Cope instead of Mrs. Hopewell (who functions in "Good Country People"). The confusion between the two matrons is surely understandable; there is a certain sameness about them. When Dorothy Walters refers to the city Hazel Motes operates in she calls it Taulkingham instead of Taulkinham. David Eggenschwiler turns up in the bibliography as Effenschwiler. These and other minor lapses can easily be corrected in a second printing.

Martha Stephens is another critic who is willing to find fault with Flannery O'Connor's work. She refuses to accept many of the pious pronouncements mouthed by earlier commentators—who seemed too frequently to look on the novels and stories as sacred texts, as passageways to salvation through literary modes. *The Question of Flannery O'Connor* (Louisiana State University Press, 1973) is a usefully irreverent book which demands that we go through a kind of Cartesian purging of previous notions and start reading the work again. The appeal is to the reader who, Martha Stephens believes, has been shortchanged in a curious way: he has been left with ambivalent feelings and peculiar responses when confronted with Flannery O'Connor's fiction; it is about time that he face up to the problem and engage the work head on.

It is the "tonal dimension" which Martha Stephens believes should be our principal negotiating point. Critics have not worried enough about the tonal peculiarities of the work. The flawed aspects of the fiction are often directly ascribable to oddities in tone.

The other serious dilemma is with the matter of doctrine or belief. Flannery O'Connor's view of the world is too eccentric and repugnant to allow the reader anything but discomfort. Martha Stephens puts the case very well in her opening chapter; she deserves to be quoted at length:

> And one's own experience simply will not support such a view. With all one's admiration for the high technical brilliance of O'Connor's work, for her cunning selection of detail and delicate sense for nuance in speech and manners, and for the wonderfully controlled momentum with which her stories move— even with all this, one's pleasure is at least diminished by the fact that what the stories are moving *to* is a truth or hypothesis about life that sometimes seems hardly worth our consideration. We may feel that the stories would appear, seen from a certain point of view, nearly perfectly executed, but that that point of view is not ours, that—to restate the dilemma in Boothian terms —we cannot be the readers the stories require us to be [p. 11].

This problem has never been stated so persuasively and emphatically. Josephine Hendin, in The World of Flannery O'Connor, expressed her misgivings with a certain eloquence but in the end tried too hard to refashion the O'Connor universe by turning the Raybers into heroes and the Mason

Tarwaters into villains; in short, she tried to reverse the roles of O'Connor's creatures to suit her own fancies. Martha Stephens always takes this world on its own terms. She invariably understands what Flannery O'Connor is about but cannot always sympathize with its results. She feels duty-bound to point out the rough spots as well as the triumphs.

Martha Stephens wrestles throughout her book with the eccentricities and tonal oddities of the work. She walks a difficult tightrope, acknowledging at every turn "the philosophical and tonal dilemma" yet feeling the urgency to "redress the balance" in Flannery O'Connor's favor. Her herculean labors are amply rewarded; *The Question of Flannery O'Connor* is simply the best book we have on the Georgia writer.

With this said we should look at Martha Stephens' method. She eschews the more fashionable devices of the Structuralists and the Geneva School in favor of a close, quasi-formalist examination of texts. She avoids the special vocabulary which gets a good O'Connor critic like David Eggenschwiler into terminological difficulties. She does not expend her energies looking far and wide for sources and influences. She does not persist in bringing Flannery O'Connor into confrontation with other writers and works as Miles Orvell does rather irritatingly in his *Invisible Parade*. In short, hers is an unmediated view of the *oeuvre*, starting with the humble beginnings of the six Master's thesis stories and carrying through the mature last work.

Martha Stephens' concentration is on the two novels and four of the stories, with side glances at the rest of the fiction. She devotes a chapter each to *Wise Blood* and *The Violent Bear It Away*, offers an extended discussion of "A Good Man Is Hard to Find" in her rather theoretical opening chapter, and gives full-scale analyses of "A Temple of the Holy Ghost," "A Circle in the Fire," and "Parker's Back" in a final chapter. She joins the majority of O'Connor critics in believing that the stories are of a higher order than the novels. She is obviously more at ease with them as she heaves a kind of sigh of relief when she starts her last chapter: "It is a pleasure to turn finally to a part of O'Connor's work about which one need express few serious reservations: that is, to some nine or ten nearly perfect short stories" (p. 144).

It is tone, as I remarked above, which is her principal concern. The "tonal hybrid" *Wise Blood* proves a source of irritation. Martha Stephens will not accept the easy solutions offered by those earlier critics who think of it as an unrelievedly comic novel. Sister Kathleen Feeley, for example, feels keenly that "comedy undercuts romance; laughter wins out." Mrs. Stephens keeps seeing a tension set up between the frivolous and the serious which produces a "tonal problem." The "crazy shenanigans" of Sabbath Hawks and Enoch Emery, for example, never sit right tonally with the "bitter seriousness" of Hazel Motes.

The tonal difficulties have been more nearly resolved in *The Violent Bear It Away*. This novel is more of a piece than *Wise Blood*; it does not suffer from the often awkward counterpointing of two plots which informs the narrative strategy of the earlier book. (How different this position is from the one taken by Leon V. Driskell and Joan T. Brittain in their *The Eternal Crossroads: The Art of Flannery O'Connor* [The University Press of Kentucky, 1971]; they insist that *Wise Blood* "is a skillfully crafted work of prose fiction.") Yet Martha Stephens is wholly satisfied with only the first part of *The Violent Bear It Away*:

The rich invention and spontaneity of the Powderhead section are giving way to a too-mechanical working out of the O'Connor formula. The tendency of the story is to move, without the zest and marvelous conviction of Part One, from symbolic incident to symbolic incident—the sun's sudden illumination, for instance, of the head of the dim-witted child as Tarwater watches him in the pool of a fountain in the park; Rayber's perplexed discovery of Tarwater standing transfixed before an undressed bakery window where lies one forgotten loaf of bread. An almost unbroken succession of such scenes finally overwhelms the reader with a sense that the characters are being more and more fatally trapped in the author's narrow purpose for them—that O'Connor's artistry, however brilliant it could sometimes be, is knuckling under to the evangelist, intent on clearing out all possible ambiguities [pp. 131–132].

She admires what she calls the "tonal control" in this opening section and despairs of its absence in the remainder of the book.

One crucial observation Martha Stephens makes concerns the difference in tone between the six stories of the Master's thesis and the work which follows. Even though the last of these stories, "The Train," was refashioned into the first chapter of *Wise Blood,* it belongs to "the mild, warm, predictable mode of this earliest work" (p. 91) rather than to the grim and austere manner of the later fiction. Thus, as Mrs. Stephens convincingly demonstrates, an immense amount of reworking and refocusing took place in transforming "The Train" into a chapter of O'Connor's first novel while relatively little revision was needed to allow "The Peeler," "The Heart of the Park," and "Enoch and the Gorilla" to take their places in *Wise Blood.* Martha Stephens admits that "One does not know what in her private life helps to account for the fact that this writer who began so normally was to adopt so fierce and forbidding a mode of fiction in all her subsequent work . . ." (p. 95). Then she makes a stab at an explanation:

It may be a factor that it was during this early period that Miss O'Connor first left the South, her Catholic family and conservative hometown. Perhaps her deepening sense of how nearly alone she was, among American artists and intellectuals, in her strict commitment to a Christian view of life helped to drive her to the hostile and prophetic mode of her first novel. Her experiences at Iowa and her reading during these years—of West's *Miss Lonelyhearts,* for instance—may of course have played their parts as well [p. 96].

She leaves the final word to Flannery O'Connor's biographers. *The Question of Flannery O'Connor* does not pretend to offer solutions to all the problems. It raises all the right questions and gently punctures holes in the theories of many of the earlier critics who refused to see the forbidding side of Flannery O'Connor. David Eggenschwiler, for example, insisted "that Flannery O'Connor consistently wrote from the point of view of a Christian humanist." Martha Stephens' answer to this position is as forthright as possible:

> Christian art is not dead for us, and there would still seem to be a great deal of common ground between humanistic Christian thought and secular humanism for the Christian artist to occupy if he can. But perhaps the crucial word here is "humanistic." For certainly O'Connor's Christian faith was as grim and literalistic, as joyless and loveless a faith, at least as we confront it in her fiction, as we have ever seen in American letters—even, perhaps, in American theology [p. 41].

One can see after a while that Martha Stephens—who was an undergraduate at Georgia College in Milledgeville like Flannery O'Connor before her—does not enjoy this maverick role. She is not completely at ease in registering her doubts, in going against the grain of accepted opinion. The "inadequate tonal resolutions," as she calls them, keep her constantly off-balance in her judging of Flannery O'Connor; they offer her all the wrong vibrations. The result is that *The Question of Flannery O'Connor* is a completely honest book which airs all the reservations and uncertainties of its author. It was a difficult book to write but one which very much needed to be written.

Preston Browning, in his *Flannery O'Connor* (Southern Illinois University Press, 1974), sympathetically considers the position of the various nay-sayers like John Hawkes and Josephine Hendin—not Martha Stephens because her book appeared too late for him to acknowledge—and opts for the

more widely accepted "mystery and manners" approach. H
sets forth his position clearly in his opening chapter:

> Briefly, my conclusions are that Flannery O'Connor's work ma'
> be conceived as an effort to recover the idea of the Holy in a1
> age in which both the meaning and the reality of this concep
> have been obscured; that she perceived that loss of the Holy
> involved for contemporary man a concomitant loss of "depth'
> and a subsequent diminution of being; and that she furthe1
> understood that in reclaiming depth and being . . . contemporary
> man might very well become involved in a journey through
> the radically profane, embracing evil in order to rediscover good,
> pursuing the demonic in order finally to arrive at the Holy
> [pp. 13–14].

This statement is not likely to unsettle any of Flannery O'Connor's apologists. It is an honest, forthright judgment on the
part of a critic who has written an unpretentious and low-
keyed book about a writer whom he admires a great deal.

After an introductory chapter which considers biography,
fictional patterns, and reputation, Browning turns to detailed
examinations of the work. He proceeds chronologically, with
chapters given over to *Wise Blood, A Good Man Is Hard to
Find, The Violent Bear It Away*, and *Everything That Rises
Must Converge* in that order.

He sees *Wise Blood* as functioning through a series of con-
frontations between opposites; the resulting tension gives the
novel its structure and determines the direction of Hazel
Motes's quest. The controlling theme of the novel, we are told,
is "mystery"—a word which appears almost as frequently in
Browning's text, by the way, as it does in *Mystery and Manners*. He also manages some interesting comments about two
of the characters in *Wise Blood*: about Asa Hawks he notes,
". . . after Haze, Hawks is the most spiritually aware person
in the novel" (p. 32); about the landlady he observes, ". . .
Mrs. Flood has been granted a spiritual awakening which,

no matter how limited, in a sense validates Haze's own journey . . ." (p. 38).

In his chapter on *A Good Man Is Hard to Find*, he defines three types which recur in the fiction: the positivist, the positive thinker, and the criminal-compulsive. These three sometimes appear in the same story. Browning discusses four of the stories from O'Connor's first collection in detail, "Good Country People," "A Circle in the Fire," "A Good Man Is Hard to Find," and "The Artficial Nigger."

The chapter on *The Violent Bear It Away* is less remarkable for its insights than the previous two chapters. Browning is at his best in the final section which is concerned with the posthumous collection, *Everything That Rises Must Converge*. He sees in this volume preoccupations which readily distinguish it from the earlier *A Good Man Is Hard to Find*: an awareness of the breaking down of established class and racial distinctions in the South; "an almost clinical understanding of certain forms of neurosis" (p. 100). Three of the stories are examined at length, "Everything That Rises Must Converge," "A View of the Woods," and "The Lame Shall Enter First."

The book ends with a brief selected bibliography, followed by a detailed and very useful index which even lists names of characters. Browning's attention to detail is as noticeable in his bibliography and index as it is in his study proper. His scholarly habits are exemplary.

*Flannery O'Connor*, however, is not a very exciting book. Its focus is unduly narrow and it goes over too much familiar terrain. Occasionally Browning will venture outside of O'Connor's work and come up with a valuable comparison with something, say, in Faulkner or Dostoevsky: he suggests a certain kinship between Julian of "Everything That Rises Must Converge" and the Quentin Compson of *Absalom, Absalom!*; he brings Rufus Johnson of "The Lame Shall Enter First" in interesting juxtaposition with Raskolnikov. But his usual manner is to remain firmly rooted in O'Connor's work and insistently account for its theological dimension. He rarely says anything of any consequence about her use of language, her narrative techniques, her stylistic habits. These are matters which require our attention a good deal more than the much-studied concerns with the demonic and the holy.

Louise Gossett commented in the course of reviewing two books about Flannery O'Connor in the November 1972 *American Literature*: "... we still need a fuller assessment of the *how*, the art, of this commanding writer." This need is now partially met by some of the better studies which I have been discussing, like Miles Orvell's *Invisible Parade* and Martha Stephens' *The Question of Flannery O'Connor*. There is still some way to go. Still I must be encouraged by recent developments in Flannery O'Connor criticism. The second gathering of critical attention does not present too many of the storm warnings Flannery O'Connor found in the distressing "perplex business" which she believed literary criticism to be.

### Notes

1. He is called Hazel Wickers in "The Train," Hazel Motes in "The Peeler," and Hazel Weaver in "The Heart of the Park." He does not appear in "Enoch and the Gorilla."

2. The intellectual is called Rayber and he is clearly the model for the character of the same name in *The Violent Bear It Away*.

# Bibliography

This bibliography includes: 1) separate publication of stories and of chapters of novels; 2) chronology of editions of books; 3) book reviews; and 4) critical articles. Since Miss O'Connor's second collection of short stories, *Everything That Rises Must Converge*, was only recently published,* the list of book reviews for that collection will necessarily be incomplete. I am indebted to George F. Wedge, who compiled the first bibliography of Miss O'Connor's work for *Critique*, II (Fall, 1958), 59-63. I am also indebted to many friends of Miss O'Connor's work who supplied information that would have otherwise eluded me. For the errors that have inevitably crept in, I alone am responsible.

LEWIS A. LAWSON

*At the time the Bibliography was compiled.

SEPARATE PUBLICATION OF STORIES AND OF CHAPTERS
OF NOVELS

I. Alphabetical Order

"The Artificial Nigger" (*A Good Man Is Hard to Find*)
"The Capture" (*Mademoiselle*)
"A Circle in the Fire" (*A Good Man Is Hard to Find*)
"The Comforts of Home" (*Everything That Rises Must Converge*)
"The Displaced Person" (*A Good Man Is Hard to Find*)
"The Enduring Chill" (*Everything That Rises Must Converge*)
"Enoch and the Gorilla" (*Wise Blood,* after modification)
"Everything That Rises Must Converge" (*Everything That Rises Must Converge*)
"The Geranium" (*Accent*)
"Good Country People" (*A Good Man Is Hard to Find*)
"A Good Man Is Hard to Find" (*A Good Man Is Hard to Find*)
"Greenleaf" (*Everything That Rises Must Converge*)
"The Heart of the Park" (*Wise Blood,* after modification)
"Judgement Day" (*Everything That Rises Must Converge*)
"The Lame Shall Enter First" (*Everything That Rises Must Converge*)
"A Late Encounter with the Enemy" (*A Good Man Is Hard to Find*)
"The Life You Save May Be Your Own" (*A Good Man Is Hard to Find*)
"Parker's Back" (*Everything That Rises Must Converge*)
"The Partridge Festival" (*Critic*)
"The Peeler" (*Wise Blood,* after modification)
"Revelation" (*Everything That Rises Must Converge*)
"The River" (*A Good Man Is Hard to Find*)
"A Stroke of Good Fortune" (*A Good Man Is Hard to Find*)
"A Temple of the Holy Ghost" (*A Good Man Is Hard to Find*)
"Train" (*Wise Blood,* after modification)

237

"A View of the Woods" (*Everything That Rises Must Converge*)
"Why Do the Heathens Rage?" (*Esquire*)
"The Woman on the Stairs" (later retitled "A Stroke of Good Fortune")
"You Can't Be Any Poorer Than Dead" (*The Violent Bear It Away*, after modification)


II. Chronological Order

1946   "The Geranium," *Accent*, VI (Summer, 1946), 245-53.
1948   "The Capture," *Mademoiselle*, XXVIII (November, 1948), 148-49, 195-96, 198-201.
     Abels, Cyrilly, and Margarita G. Smith, eds. *Best Stories from Mademoiselle*. New York: Popular Library, 1961. Pp. 343-54.
     "Train," *Sewanee Review*, LVI (April, 1948), 261-71. (*Wise Blood*)
1949   "The Heart of the Park," *Partisan Review*, XVI (February, 1949), 138-51. (*Wise Blood*)
     "The Peeler," *Partisan Review*, XVI (December, 1949), 1189-1206. (*Wise Blood*)
     "The Woman on the Stairs," *Tomorrow*, VIII (August, 1949), 40. Retitled "A Stroke of Good Fortune," it appeared in *Shenandoah*, IV (Spring, 1953), 7-18.
1952   "Enoch and the Gorilla," *New World Writing*, I (April, 1952), 67-74. (*Wise Blood*)
1953   "A Good Man Is Hard to Find," *Modern Writing I*. William Phillips and Philip Rahv, eds. New York, 1953. Pp. 186-99. Paperback.
     Gordon, Caroline, and Allen Tate, *The House of Fiction*, second edition. New York: Charles Scribner's Sons, 1960. Pp. 370-81.
     "A Late Encounter with the Enemy," *Harper's Bazaar*, LXXXVII (September, 1953), 234, 247, 249, 252.
     "The Life You Save May Be Your Own," *Kenyon Review*, XV (Spring, 1953), 195-207.
     Engle, Paul, and Hansford Martin, eds. *Prize Stories 1954: The O. Henry Awards*. Garden City: Doubleday, 1954. Pp. 194-204.
     *Perspectives USA*, XIV (1956), 64-75.

*Prospetti*. Rome: Casa Editrice Sansoni, 1956. (In Italian)

"The River," *Sewanee Review*, LXI (Summer, 1953), 455-75.

"A Stroke of Good Fortune," *Shenandoah*, IV (Spring, 1953), 7-18. See also "The Woman on the Stairs," 1949.

1954 "A Circle in the Fire," *Kenyon Review*, XVI (Spring, 1954), 169-90.

Engle, Paul, and Hansford Martin, eds. *Prize Stories 1955: The O. Henry Awards*. Garden City: Doubleday, 1955. Pp. 35-52. (Second Prize Story)

Foley, Martha, ed. *The Best American Short Stories of 1955*. Boston: Houghton Mifflin, 1955. Pp. 230-48.

"The Displaced Person," *Sewanee Review*, LXII (October, 1954), 634-54.

"A Temple of the Holy Ghost," *Harper's Bazaar*, LXXXVIII (May, 1954), 108-09, 162-64.

1955 "The Artificial Nigger," *Kenyon Review*, XVII (Spring, 1955), 169-92.

Foley, Martha, ed. *The Best American Short Stories of 1956*. Boston: Houghton Mifflin, 1956. Pp. 264-84.

Gold, Herbert, ed. *Fiction of the Fifties*. Garden City: Doubleday, 1959. Pp. 283-304.

"Good Country People," *Harper's Bazaar*, LXXXIX (June, 1955), 64-65, 116-17, 121-22, 124, 130.

"You Can't Be Any Poorer Than Dead," *New World Writing*, VIII (October, 1955), 81-97. (*The Violent Bear It Away*)

1956 "Greenleaf," *Kenyon Review*, XVIII (Summer, 1956), 384-410.

Engle, Paul, and Constance Urdang, eds. *Prize Stories 1957: The O. Henry Awards*. Garden City: Doubleday, 1957. Pp. 15-36. (First Prize Story)

*First Prize Stories, 1919-1957*, from the O. Henry Memorial Awards. Introduction by Harry Hansen. Garden City: Doubleday, 1957. Pp. 533-52.

Foley, Martha, ed. *The Best American Short Stories of 1957*. Boston: Houghton Mifflin, 1957. Pp. 241-63.

*First Prize Stories, 1919-1963*, from the O. Henry Memorial Awards. Introduction by Harry Hansen. Garden City: Doubleday, 1963. Pp. 533-52.

1957   "A View of the Woods," *Partisan Review*, XXIV (Fall, 1957), 475-96.

     Engle, Paul, Curt Harnack, and Constance Urdang, eds. *Prize Stories 1959: The O. Henry Awards*. Garden City: Doubleday, 1959. Pp. 234-56.

     Foley, Martha, and David Burnett, eds. *The Best American Short Stories of 1958*. Boston: Houghton Mifflin, 1958. Pp. 192-212.

1958   "The Enduring Chill," *Harper's Bazaar*, XCI (July, 1958), 44-45, 94, 96, 100-02, 108.

1960   "The Comforts of Home," *Kenyon Review*, XXII (Fall, 1960), 523-54.

1961   "Everything That Rises Must Converge," *New World Writing*, XIX (1961), 74-90.

     *First Prize Stories, 1919-1963*, from the O. Henry Memorial Awards. Introduction by Harry Hansen. Garden City: Doubleday, 1963. Pp. 669-81.

     Foley, Martha, and David Burnett, eds. *The Best American Short Stories of 1962*. Boston: Houghton Mifflin, 1962. Pp. 324-39.

     Poirier, Richard, ed. *Prize Stories 1963: The O. Henry Awards*. Garden City: Doubleday, 1963. Pp. 1-16. (First Prize Story)

     Germann, Leonore, ed. *Exkursionen*. Munich, 1964. (In German)

     "The Partridge Festival," *Critic*, XIX (February-March, 1961), 20-23, 82-85.

1962   "The Lame Shall Enter First," *Sewanee Review*, LXX (Summer, 1962), 337-79.

1963   "Why Do the Heathens Rage?" [Excerpt from planned third novel], *Esquire*, LX (July, 1963), 60-61.

1964   "Revelation," *Sewanee Review*, LXXII (Spring, 1964), 178-202.

     Poirier, Richard, and William Abraham, eds. *Prize Stories 1965: The O. Henry Awards*. Garden City: Doubleday, 1965. Pp. 1-20. (First Prize Story)

1965   "Parker's Back," *Esquire*, LXIII (April, 1965), 76-78, 151-55.

     "Judgement Day," in *Everything That Rises Must Converge*, ed. and intro. by Robert Fitzgerald. New York: Farrar, Straus & Giroux, 1965. Pp. 245-69.

**1952**

*Wise Blood.* New York: Harcourt, Brace and Company, 1952.
————. Toronto: McLeod, 1952.

**1953**

————. New York: New American Library, 1953.

**1955**

————. London: Neville Spearman Company, 1955.
————. Toronto: Burns and MacEachern, 1955.
*A Good Man Is Hard to Find and Other Stories.* New York:
Harcourt, Brace and Company, 1955. Contents: "A Good
Man Is Hard to Find," "The River," "The Life You Save
May Be Your Own," "A Stroke of Good Fortune," "A Tem-
ple of the Holy Ghost," "The Artificial Nigger," "A Circle
in the Fire," "A Late Encounter with the Enemy," "Good
Country People," "The Displaced Person."

**1956**

————. New York: New American Library, 1956.

**1957**

*The Artificial Nigger and Other Tales* (same contents as *A
Good Man Is Hard to Find and Other Stories*). London:
Neville Spearman Company, 1957.

**1959**

*La Sagesse dans le sang* (*Wise Blood*). Roman trad. et préf. par
M. E. Coindreau (Collection du Monde Entier). Paris:
Gallimard, 1959.

1960

*Wise Blood.* London: Longacre Press, 1960.

*The Violent Bear It Away.* New York: Farrar Straus and Cudahy, 1960.

————. London: Longmans, Green and Company, 1960.

————. London: Ambassador, 1960.

1961

*Ein Kreis im Feuer* (*A Circle in the Fire*). Erzählungen. Übertr. aus dem Amerikan. von Elisabeth Schnack. Hamburg: Claassen Verlag, 1961. Contents: "Ein Kreis im Feuer" ("A Circle in the Fire"); "Ein letztes Treffen mit dem Feind" ("A Late Encounter with the Enemy"); "Brave Leute vom Lande" ("Good Country People"); "Ein guter Mensch ist schwer zu finden" ("A Good Man Is Hard to Find"); "Es kostet vielleicht das eigene Leben" ("The Life You Save May Be Your Own"); "Der Fluss" ("The River"); "Der künstliche Nigger" ("The Artificial Nigger"); "Leute von drüben" ("The Displaced Person"). Omitted were "A Stroke of Good Fortune" and "A Temple of the Holy Ghost."

*The Violent Bear It Away.* New York: New American Library, 1961.

*A Memoir of Mary Ann.* Introduction by Flannery O'Connor. By the Dominican Nuns of Our Lady of Perpetual Help Home, Atlanta, Georgia. New York: Farrar, Straus and Cudahy, 1961.

1962

*Wise Blood,* Second Edition. With an Introduction by the Author. New York: Farrar, Straus and Cudahy, 1962.

*A Good Man Is Hard to Find.* London: New English Library, 1962.

*Death of a Child* (*A Memoir of Mary Ann*). London: Burns and Oates, 1962.

*Das brennende Wort* (*The Violent Bear It Away*). Übertr. aus

d. Amerikan. von Leonore Germann. Munich: C. Hanser Verlag, 1962.

——. Munich: Hanser Broschüren, 1962.


## 1963

*Les braves gens ne courent pas les rues* (*A Good Man Is Hard to Find*). Nouvelles. Trad. par Henri Morisset (Collection du Monde Entier). Paris: Gallimard, 1963. Contents: "Les braves gens ne courent pas les rues" ("A Good Man Is Hard to Find"); "Le fleuve" ("The River"); "C'est peut-être votre vie que vous sauvez" ("The Life You Save May Be Your Own"); "Un heureux événement" ("A Stroke of Good Fortune"); "Les temples du Saint-Esprit" ("A Temple of the Holy Ghost"); "Le nègre factice" ("The Artificial Nigger"); "Un cercle dans le feu" ("A Circle in the Fire"); "Tardive rencontre avec l'ennemi" ("A Late Encounter with the Enemy"); "Braves gens de la campagne" ("Good Country People"); "La personne déplacée" ("The Displaced Person").


## 1964

*Three.* New York: New American Library, 1964. Contents: *Wise Blood, A Good Man Is Hard to Find,* and *The Violent Bear It Away.*


## 1965

*Everything That Rises Must Converge.* New York: Farrar, Straus and Giroux, 1965. Introduction by Robert Fitzgerald. Contents: "Everything That Rises Must Converge," "Greenleaf," "A View of the Woods," "The Enduring Chill," "The Comforts of Home," "The Lame Shall Enter First," "Revelation," "Parker's Back," "Judgement Day."

*Kai i viastai arpazousi aftin* . . . (*The Violent Bear It Away*). Trans. by Alexander Kotzias. Athens: G. Fexis, 1965.

BOOK REVIEWS

(Since I have not seen all the reviews listed below I have not in every case been able to supply complete bibliographical information.)

*Wise Blood* (first edition)

*Atlanta Journal and Atlanta Constitution*, May 18, 1952, p. 7F.
*Commonweal*, LVI (June 27, 1952), 297-98 (J. W. Simons).
*Hudson Review*, VI (Spring, 1953), 144-50 (R. W. B. Lewis).
*Kenyon Review*, XV (Spring, 1953), 320-26 (Joe Lee Davis).
*Kirkus*, XX (May 1, 1952), 285.
*Library Journal*, LXXVII (May 15, 1952), 894-95 (Milton S. Byam).
*New Republic*, CXXVII (July 7, 1952), 19 (Isaac Rosenfeld).
*Newsweek*, XXXIX (May 19, 1952), 114-15.
*New York Herald Tribune Book Review*, May 18, 1952, p. 3 (Sylvia Stallings).
*New York Times Book Review*, May 18, 1952, p. 4 (William Goyen).
*New Yorker*, XXVIII (June 14, 1952), 106.
*Saturday Night*, LXVII (July 19, 1952), 22-23.
*Saturday Review*, XXXV (May 24, 1952), 22 (Oliver LaFarge).
*Time*, LIX (June 9, 1952), 108, 110.
*Times Literary Supplement*, September 2, 1955, p. 505.
*U. S. Quarterly Book Review*, VIII (Summer, 1952), 256.
*Western Review*, XVII (Autumn, 1952), 76-80 (Carl Hartman).

*Wise Blood* (second edition)

*Christian Century*, LXXXVI (August 14, 1963), 1008-09 (Dean Peerman).
*Commonweal*, CXXX (February 22, 1963), 576 (Leonard F. X. Mayhew).
*Critic*, XXI (November, 1962), 95 (Doris Grumbach).
*Jubilee*, X (December, 1962), 47 (Paul Levine).

## A Good Man Is Hard to Find

*Accent*, XV (Autumn, 1955), 293-97 (Thomas H. Carter).
*Best Sellers*, XV (June 1, 1955), 59.
*Booklist*, LI (June 15, 1955), 428.
*Bookmark*, XIV (July, 1955), 246.
*Books*, XIV (December, 1955), 187 (F. Steggert).
*Bulletin Critique du Livre Français*, XVIII (1963), 595-96.
*Catholic World*, CLXXXII (October, 1955), 55 (Riley Hughes).
*Chicago Sunday Tribune Magazine of Books*, July 3, 1955, p. 3 (Fanny Butcher).
*Commonweal*, LXII (July 22, 1955), 404 (J. Greene). Reply, August 12, 1955, 471 (D. Francis).
*Grail*, XXXVIII (January, 1956), 59.
*Hudson Review*, VIII (Winter, 1956), 630 (R. M. Adams).
*Kenyon Review*, XVII (Autumn, 1955), 661-70 (Walter Elder).
*Kirkus*, XXIII (April 5, 1955), 290.
*Library Journal*, LXXX (May 15, 1955), 1217 (J. D. Marshall).
*Newsweek*, XLIV (December 26, 1955), 68, 70.
*New York Herald Tribune Book Review*, June 5, 1955, p. 1 (Sylvia Stallings).
*New York Times*, June 10, 1955, p. 23 (Orville Prescott).
*New York Times Book Review*, June 12, 1955, p. 5 (Caroline Gordon).
*New Yorker*, XXXI (June 18, 1955), 105.
*San Francisco Chronicle*, July 10, 1955, p. 19 (Lewis Vogler).
*Saturday Review*, XXXVIII (June 4, 1955), 15 (J. C. Wyllie).
*Sewanee Review*, LXIII (Autumn, 1955), 671-81 (Louis D. Rubin, Jr.).
*Shenandoah*, VII (Autumn, 1955), 71-81 (Fred Bornhauser).
*Studi Americani*, II (1956), 212-18 (Mario Praz).
*Time*, LXV (June 6, 1955), 114.
*Today*, XI (October, 1955), 30-31 (John A. Lynch).
*Wisconsin Library Bulletin*, LI (July, 1955), 11.

## The Violent Bear It Away

*America,* CII (March 5, 1960), 682-83 (Harold C. Gardiner).

*Antioch Review,* XX (Summer, 1960), 256 (Nolan Miller).

*Arizona Quarterly Review,* XVI (Autumn, 1960), 284-86 (Donald C. Emerson).

*Atlanta Journal and Atlanta Constitution,* February 28, 1960 (Marjory Rutherford).

*Augusta Chronicle and Augusta Herald,* March 13, 1960 (W. G. Rogers).

*Ave Maria,* XCII (July 2, 1960), 25 (Pat Somers Cronin).

*Best Sellers,* XIX (March, 1960), 414-15 (John J. Quinn).

*Booklist,* LVI (April 1, 1960), 478.

*Catholic Library World,* XXXI (May-June, 1960), 518-21 (Sister Bede Sullivan).

*Catholic World,* CXC (February, 1960), 280-85 (P. Albert Duhamel).

*Censer,* Spring, 1960 (Sarah Walter).

*Chicago Sunday Tribune Magazine of Books,* March 6, 1960, p. 4 (Paul Engle).

*Christian Century,* LXXVII (June 1, 1960), 672.

*Clearing House,* XXXVI (November, 1961), 188 (Frederick S. Keley).

*Commentary,* XXX (October, 1960), 358-62 (Algene Ballif).

*Commonweal,* LXXII (April 15, 1960), 67-68 (James Greene).

*Critic,* XVIII (May, 1960), 45 (Francis X. Canfield).

*Crux,* XXXVII (May 29, 1962), 3 (Noel Coman).

*English Journal,* XLIX (April, 1960), 275.

*Esprit,* VII (Winter, 1963), 28-31 (John J. Quinn).

*Etudes,* CCCXVIII (September, 1963), 295 (A. Lauras).

*Extension,* LV (July, 1960), 26 (John J. Traynor).

*Font Hill Dial,* XXXVII (May, 1960), 38 (Kathleen E. Sullivan).

*Harper's,* CCXX (April, 1960), 114 (Paul Pickrel).

*Hochland,* LV (December, 1962), 174.

*Hudson Review,* XIII (Autumn, 1960), 449-56 (Vivian Mercier).

*Information,* LXXIV (April, 1960), 57.

*Jackson Daily News-Clarion Ledger,* March 27, 1960, p. 6D (Louis Dollarhide).

*Jubilee,* VIII (May, 1960), 52 (Paul Levine).

*Kansas City Star,* March 5, 1960.

*Kenyon Review,* XXIII (Winter, 1961), 170-72 (Edward M. Hood).
*Kirkus,* XXVII (December 15, 1959), 931.
*Library Journal,* LXXXV (January 1, 1960), 85 (Dorothy Nyren).
*Modern Age,* IV (Fall, 1960), 428-30 (Robert Drake).
*National Review,* VIII (April 9, 1960), 240-41 (Joan Didion).
*New Leader,* XLIII (May 30, 1960), 20-21 (Hubert Creekmore).
*New Republic,* CXLII (March 14, 1960), 18 (Frank J. Warnke).
*New Statesman,* LX (September 24, 1960), 445-46 (Gerda Charles).
*New York Herald Tribune Book Review,* February 28, 1960, p. 13
   (Coleman Rosenberger).
*New York Post,* February 12, 1960.
*New York Times,* February 24, 1960, p. 35 (Orville Prescott).
*New York Times Book Review,* February 28, 1960, p. 4 (Donald
   Davidson).
*New Yorker,* XXXVI (March 15, 1960), 179.
*Nexus,* October, 1960 (Ben Czaplewski).
*Partisan Review,* XXVII (Spring, 1960), 378 (R. W. Flint).
*Punch,* CCXXXIX (October 5, 1960), 505.
*Renascence,* XIII (Spring, 1961), 147-52 (Robert O. Bowen).
*San Francisco Chronicle,* February 25, 1960, p. 31 (William Hogan).
*Saturday Review,* LXIII (February 27, 1960), 18 (Granville Hicks).
*Savannah Morning News,* February 21, 1960 (A. C. H.).
*Sewanee Review,* LXIX (Winter, 1961), 161-63 (Arthur Mizener).
*Sign,* XL (March, 1961), 46-48 (Robert Donner).
*Southwest Review,* XLVI (Winter, 1961), 86-87 (Thomas F. Gos-
   sett).
*Springfield Republican,* March 6, 1960, p. 50 (H. B. H.).
*Tablet,* CCXIV (December 17, 1960), 1175 (David Lodge).
*Time,* LXXV (February 29, 1960), 118.
*Times Literary Supplement,* October 14, 1960, p. 666.
*Today,* XV (March, 1960), 36-37 (Sister Bede Sullivan).
*Virginia Quarterly Review,* XXXVI (Summer, 1960), lxxii-lxxiii.

## Everything That Rises Must Converge

*America,* CXII (June 5, 1965), 821-22.
*Atlantic Monthly,* CCXVI (July, 1965), 139 (W. Barrett).
*Best Sellers,* XXV (June 1, 1965), 124 (John J. Quinn).

*Booklist,* LXI (July, 1965), 1015.

*Boston Sunday Herald,* June 13, 1965, Section VI, p. 8 (Sister Bernetta Quinn, O.S.F.).

*Catholic World,* CCII (October, 1965), 54 (R. A. Dupray).

*Chicago Sunday Tribune,* June 6, 1965, Book Section, p. 5 (Lillian Smith).

*Choice,* II (September, 1965), 387.

*Christian Century,* LXXXII (May 19, 1965), 656 (R. Drake).

*Christian Science Monitor,* LVII (June 17, 1965), 7 (Robert Kiely).

*Commonweal,* LXXXII (July 9, 1965), 510-11 (James P. Degnan).

*Critic,* XXIII (June-July,1965), 58-60 (Sister Mariella Gable, O.S.B.).

*Critique,* VIII (Fall, 1965), 85-91 (Patricia Kane).

*Esquire,* LXIII (May, 1965), 46, 48 (Malcolm Muggeridge).

*Harper's,* CCXXXI (July, 1965), 112 (Katherine Gauss Jackson).

*Hudson Review,* XVIII (Autumn, 1965), 444 (P. Cruttwell).

*Library Journal,* XC (May 1, 1965), 2160 (L. E. Bone).

*Nation,* CCI (September 13, 1965), 142-44 (W. Schott).

*National Observer,* IV (June 28, 1965), 19 (R. Ostermann).

*National Review,* XVII (July 27, 1965), 658 (Guy Davenport).

*New Leader,* XLVIII (May 10, 1965), 9-10 (Stanley Edgar Hyman).

*New York Herald Tribune* (also *Washington Post* and *San Francisco Examiner*) *Book Week,* May 30, 1965, 1, 13 (Theodore Solotaroff).

*New York Herald Tribune,* CXXV (May 25, 1965), 23 (A. Pryce-Jones).

*New York Review of Books,* V (September 30, 1965), 16 (Irving Howe).

*New York Times,* CXIV (May 27, 1965), 35 (Charles Poore).

*New York Times Book Review,* LXX (May 30, 1965), 6 (Richard Poirier).

*New Yorker,* XLI (September 11, 1965), 220-21 (Naomi Bliven).

*Newsweek,* LXV (May 31, 1965), 85-86.

*Saturday Review,* XLVIII (May 29, 1965), 23-24 (Granville Hicks).

*Time,* LXXXV (June 4, 1965), 92.

*Times Literary Supplement,* March 24, 1966, p. 242.

*Virginia Quarterly Review,* XLI (Summer, 1965), lxxxiv.

*Wall Street Journal,* XLV (July 9, 1965), 6 (E. Lloyd).

*Yale Review,* LV (Autumn, 1965), 144 (S. Trachtenberg).

CRITICAL ARTICLES

Alice, Sister Mary, O.P. "My Mentor, Flannery O'Connor," *Saturday Review*, XLVIII (May 29, 1965), 24-25. [Letters]

Alice, Sister Rose, S.S.J. "Flannery O'Connor: Poet to the Outcast," *Renascence*, XVI (Spring, 1964), 126-32.

Allen, Walter. "Flannery O'Connor—a tribute," *Esprit*, VIII (Winter, 1964), 12.

Antoninus, Brother, O.P. "Flannery O'Connor—a tribute," *Esprit*, VIII (Winter, 1964), 12-13.

Bassan, Maurice. "Flannery O'Connor's Way: Shock, with Moral Intent," *Renascence*, XV (Summer, 1963), 195-99, 211.

Baumbach, Jonathan. "The Acid of God's Grace: The Fiction of Flannery O'Connor," *Georgia Review*, XVII (Fall, 1963), 334-46. Republished, with alterations, as "The Acid of God's Grace: *Wise Blood* by Flannery O'Connor," in *The Landscape of Nightmare: Studies in the Contemporary American Novel* (New York: New York University Press, 1965), pp. 87-100. This volume developed from a dissertation, "The Theme of Guilt and Redemption in the Post Second World War Novel," Stanford University, 1961.

Bishop, Elizabeth. "Flannery O'Connor, 1925-1964," *New York Review of Books*, III (October 8, 1964), 21. Reprinted in *Esprit*, VIII (Winter, 1964), 14-16.

Boyle, Kay. "Flannery O'Connor—a tribute," *Esprit*, VIII (Winter, 1964), 16.

Brady, Charles A. "Flannery O'Connor—a tribute," *Esprit*, VIII (Winter, 1964), 16-17.

Breit, Harvey. "Flannery O'Connor—a tribute," *Esprit*, VIII (Winter, 1964), 17.

Brooks, Cleanth. "Flannery O'Connor—a tribute," *Esprit*, VIII (Winter, 1964), 17.

Cargill, Oscar. "Flannery O'Connor—a tribute," *Esprit*, VIII (Winter, 1964), 17.

Cheney, Brainard. "Flannery O'Connor's Campaign for Her Country," *Sewanee Review*, LXXII (Autumn, 1964), 555-58.

———. "Miss O'Connor Creates Unusual Humor Out of Ordinary Sin," *Sewanee Review*, LXXI (Autumn, 1963), 644-52.

Clarke, John J. "The Achievement of Flannery O'Connor," *Esprit*, VIII (Winter, 1964), 6-9.

Coffey, Warren. "Flannery O'Connor," *Commentary*, XL (November, 1965), 93-99.

———. "Flannery O'Connor—a tribute," *Esprit*, VIII (Winter, 1964), 18.

Connolly, Francis X. "Flannery O'Connor—a tribute," *Esprit*, VIII (Winter, 1964), 18.

Connolly, John. "The Search," *Esprit*, VIII (Winter, 1964), 66-68.

Daniel, Frank. "Good Writer Must Set His Book in a Region Which is Familiar," *Atlanta Journal*, March 28, 1960, p. 27.

Davis, Barnabas. "Flannery O'Connor: Christian Belief in Recent Fiction," *Listening* (Autumn, 1965), 5-21.

Dowell, Bob. "Grace in the Fiction of Flannery O'Connor," *College English*, XXVII (December, 1965), 235-39.

Drake, Robert. "The Harrowing Evangel of Flannery O'Connor," *Christian Century*, LXXXI (September 30, 1964), 1200-02. Reprinted in *Esprit*, VIII (Winter, 1964), 19-22.

Duhamel, P. Albert. "Flannery O'Connor—a tribute," *Esprit*, VIII (Winter, 1964), 22-23.

Enright, Elizabeth. "Flannery O'Connor—a tribute," *Esprit*, VIII (Winter, 1964), 23.

Esty, William. "In America, Intellectual Bomb Shelters," *Commonweal*, LXVII (March 7, 1958), 586-88.

Fancher, Betsy. "Authoress Flannery O'Connor Is Evidence of Georgia's Bent to Female Writer," *Atlanta Constitution*, April 21, 1961, p. 27.

Farnham, James F. "The Grotesque in Flannery O'Connor," *America*, CV (May 13, 1961), 277, 280-81. Reprinted in *Esprit*, VIII (Winter, 1964), 23-25. [An answer to Esty.]

Ferris, Sumner J. "The Outside and the Inside: Flannery O'Connor's *The Violent Bear It Away*," *Critique*, III (Winter-Spring, 1960), 11-19.

Fitzgerald, Robert. "The Countryside and the True Country," *Sewanee Review*, LXX (Summer, 1962), 380-94.

Freeman, Warren Eugene, S.J. "The Social and Theological Implica-

tions in Flannery O'Connor's *A Good Man Is Hard to Find*,"
Unpublished M.A. Thesis, University of North Carolina, 1962.

Friedman, Melvin J. "Flannery O'Connor: Another Legend in Southern Fiction," *English Journal*, LI (April, 1962), 233-43. Reprinted in *Recent American Fiction*, edited by Joseph J.
Waldmeir. (Boston: Houghton Mifflin, 1963), pp. 231-45.

――――. "Flannery O'Connor," *Kleines Lexikon der Weltliteratur im
20. Jahrhundert* (Freiburg: Verlag Herder, 1964), pp. 260-61.

――――. "Les romans de Samuel Beckett et la tradition du grotesque,"
in *Un nouveau roman? Recherches et tradition. La critique
étrangère*, edited by J. H. Matthews. (Paris: Lettres Modernes,
1964), pp. 31-50, esp. pp. 42-44.

Gable, Sister Mariella, O.S.B. "The Ecumenic Core in the Fiction
of Flannery O'Connor," *American Benedictine Review*, XV
(June, 1964), 127-43.

――――. "Flannery O'Connor—a tribute," *Esprit*, VIII (Winter,
1964), 25-27.

Gardiner, Harold C., S.J. "Flannery O'Connor—a tribute," *Esprit*,
VIII (Winter, 1964), 27-28.

Gordon, Caroline. "Flannery O'Connor—a tribute," *Esprit*, VIII
(Winter, 1964), 28.

――――. "Flannery O'Connor's *Wise Blood*," *Critique*, II (Fall, 1958),
3-10.

――――, and Allen Tate. *The House of Fiction*. Second Edition. New
York: Charles Scribner's Sons, 1960. Pp. 382-86 [on "A Good
Man Is Hard to Find"].

Gossett, Louise Y. "Violence in Recent Southern Fiction," Doctoral
Dissertation, Duke University, Durham, 1961 [contains a
chapter on Flannery O'Connor]. Published, with the same title,
by Duke University Press, 1965. Pp. 75-97.

Gresset, Michel. "Le petit monde de Flannery O'Connor," *Mercure
de France*, No. 1203 (January, 1964), 141-43.

Griffith, A. "Flannery O'Connor," *America*, CXIII (November 27,
1965), 674-75.

Hale, Nancy. "Flannery O'Connor—a tribute," *Esprit*, VIII (Winter, 1964), 28.

Hallinan, Paul J. "Archbishop's Notebook," *Georgia Bulletin*, August 6, 1964 [Obituary].

Hardwick, Elizabeth. "Flannery O'Connor, 1925-1964," *New York
Review of Books*, III (October 8, 1964), 21, 23.

Hart, Jane. "Strange Earth, The Stories of Flannery O'Connor," *Georgia Review*, XII (Summer, 1958), 215-22.

Hassan, Ihab. "The Existential Novel," *Massachusetts Review*, III (Summer, 1962), 795-97 [Attempts to place Miss O'Connor in existential tradition].

————. *Radical Innocence*. Princeton: Princeton University Press, 1961. *Passim*.

Hawkes, John. "Flannery O'Connor—a tribute," *Esprit*, VIII (Winter, 1964), 30.

————. "Flannery O'Connor's Devil," *Sewanee Review*, LXX (Summer, 1962), 395-407.

————. "Notes on The Wild Goose Chase," *Massachusetts Review*, III (Summer, 1962), 784-88 [praises Djuna Barnes, Nathanael West, and Flannery O'Connor for creativeness].

————. "Scholars, Critics, Writers and the Campus," *Wisconsin Studies in Contemporary Literature*, VI (Summer, 1965), 146-47 [remarks similar to "Flannery O'Connor's Devil"].

Hicks, Granville. "Flannery O'Connor—a tribute," *Esprit*, VIII (Winter, 1964), 30.

————. "Southern Gothic with a Vengeance," *Saturday Review*, LXIII (January 2, 1960), 18.

Hoskins, Frank. "Editor's Comments," *Studies in Short Fiction*, II (Fall, 1964), iii-iv. Reprinted in *Esprit*, VIII (Winter, 1964), 31.

Jeremy, Sister, C.S.J. "*The Violent Bear It Away*: A Linguistic Education," *Renascence*, XVII (Fall, 1964), 11-16.

Jacobsen, Josephine. "A Catholic Quartet," *Christian Scholar*, XLVII (Summer, 1964), 139-54 [Also Spark, Greene, and Powers].

Jones, Bartlett C. "Depth Psychology and Literary Study," *Midcontinent American Studies Journal*, V (Fall, 1964), 50-56.

Joselyn, Sister M., O.S.B. "Flannery O'Connor—a tribute," *Esprit*, VIII (Winter, 1964), 31-32.

————. "Thematic Centers in 'The Displaced Person,'" *Studies in Short Fiction*, I (Winter, 1964), 85-92.

Judge, John F. "The Man Under the Microscope," *Esprit*, VIII (Winter, 1964), 65.

Kermode, Frank. "Flannery O'Connor—a tribute," *Esprit*, VIII (Winter, 1964), 33.

Kevin, Sister Mary, O.S.B. "Flannery O'Connor: In Memory of a Vision Unlimited," *Censer*, Winter, 1965, 37-42.

Kunkel, Francis L. "Flannery O'Connor—a tribute," *Esprit*, VIII (Winter, 1964), 33.

Lawson, Lewis A. "Flannery O'Connor and the Grotesque: *Wise Blood*," *Renascence*, XVII (Spring, 1965), 137-47, 156.

Levine, Paul. "The Violent Art," *Jubilee*, IX (December, 1961), 50-52 [on the use of the grotesque].

Lowell, Robert. "Flannery O'Connor—a tribute," *Esprit*, VIII (Winter, 1964), 33.

Ludwig, Jack B. *Recent American Novelists*, University of Minnesota Pamphlets on American Writers, No. 22. Minneapolis: University of Minnesota Press, 1962. Pp. 36-37.

Lytle, Andrew. "Flannery O'Connor—a tribute," *Esprit*, VIII (Winter, 1964), 33-34.

McCown, Robert M. "The Education of a Prophet: A Study of Flannery O'Connor's *The Violent Bear It Away*," *Kansas Magazine*, 1962, 73-78.

———. "Flannery O'Connor and the Reality of Sin," *Catholic World*, CLXXXVIII (January, 1959), 285-91.

Macauley, Robie. "Flannery O'Connor—a tribute," *Esprit*, VIII (Winter, 1964), 34.

Malin, Irving. *New American Gothic*. Carbondale: Southern Illinois University Press, 1962. *Passim*.

"May 15 is Publication Date of Novel by Flannery O'Connor, Milledgeville," *Milledgeville Union-Recorder*, Milledgeville, Georgia, April 25, 1952.

Mayhew, Leonard F. X. "Flannery O'Connor, 1925-1964," *Commonweal*, LXXX (August 21, 1964), 562-63. Reprinted in *Esprit*, VIII (Winter, 1964), 34-36.

———. "Flannery O'Connor's People, Authentic and Universal," *Georgia Bulletin*, August 6, 1964.

Meeker, Richard K. "The Youngest Generation of Southern Fiction Writers," in *Southern Writers*, edited by Rinaldo C. Simonini, Jr. (Charlottesville: The University Press of Virginia, 1964), pp. 186-87.

Merton, Thomas. "Flannery O'Connor," *Jubilee*, XII (November, 1964), 49-53.

———. "Flannery O'Connor—a tribute," *Esprit*, VIII (Winter, 1964), 36.

Meyers, Sister Bertrande, D.C. "Flannery O'Connor—a tribute," *Esprit,* VIII (Winter, 1964), 13-14.

———. "Four Stories of Flannery O'Connor," *Thought,* XXXVII (Autumn, 1962), 410-26 ["A View of the Woods," "The Enduring Chill," "The Comforts of Home," and "The Partridge Festival"].

Montgomery, Marion. "The Sense of Violation: Notes Toward a Definition of 'Southern' Fiction," *Georgia Review,* XIX (Fall, 1965), 278-87. *Passim.*

Murray, J. Franklin, S.J. "Flannery O'Connor—a tribute," *Esprit,* VIII (Winter, 1964), 37.

Nolde, Sister M. Simon, O.S.B. "*The Violent Bear It Away*: A Study in Imagery," *Xavier University Studies,* I (Spring, 1962), 180-94.

Nyren, D. *A Library of Literary Criticism.* New York: F. Ungar, 1960. Pp. 361-63.

O'Connor, William Van. "Flannery O'Connor—a tribute," *Esprit,* VIII (Winter, 1964), 37-39.

Peden, William. *The American Short Story: Front Line in the National Defense of Literature.* Boston: Houghton Mifflin, 1964. Pp. 127-30.

———. "Flannery O'Connor—a tribute," *Esprit,* VIII (Winter, 1964), 39.

Perrine, Laurence. "Flannery O'Connor—a tribute," *Esprit,* VIII (Winter, 1964), 39-40.

Porter, Katherine Anne. "Gracious Greatness," *Esprit,* VIII (Winter, 1964), 50-58.

Powers, J. F. "Flannery O'Connor—a tribute," *Esprit,* VIII (Winter, 1964), 40.

Prescott, Orville. "Flannery O'Connor—a tribute," *Esprit,* VIII (Winter, 1964), 40-42. Reprinted from an earlier review in the *New York Times,* June 10, 1955, p. 23.

———. "Flannery O'Connor—a tribute," *Esprit,* VIII (Winter, 1964), 42. Reprinted from the *New York Times,* February 24, 1960, p. 35.

*Publishers Weekly,* CLXXXVI (August 17, 1965), 28 [Obituary].

Quinn, Sister M. Bernetta, O.S.F. "Flannery O'Connor—a tribute," *Esprit,* VIII (Winter, 1964), 42-44.

———. "View from a Rock: The Fiction of Flannery O'Connor and J. F. Powers," *Critique,* II (Fall, 1958), 19-27.

Ragan, Marjorie. "Southern Accent," *Raleigh Times,* April 18, 1965, p. III-3.

Ragan, Sam. "Southern Accent," *Raleigh Times,* August 16, 1964.

Rechnitz, Robert M. "Passionate Pilgrim: Flannery O'Connor's *Wise Blood,*" *Georgia Review,* XIX (Fall, 1965), 310-16.

Roseliep, Raymond. "Flannery O'Connor, 1925-1964," *Georgia Review,* XIX (Fall, 1965), 368 [Poem].

Rubin, Louis D., Jr. *The Faraway Country: Writers of the Modern South.* Seattle: University of Washington Press, 1963. Pp. 195-96, 238-40.

———. "Flannery O'Connor: A Note on Literary Fashions," *Critique,* II (Fall, 1958), 11-18.

———. "Flannery O'Connor—a tribute," *Esprit,* VIII (Winter, 1964), 44.

———. "Two Ladies of the South," *Sewanee Review,* LXIII (Autumn, 1955), 671-81 [also treats Eudora Welty].

Rupp, Richard H. "Fact and Mystery: Flannery O'Connor," *Commonweal,* LXXIX (December 6, 1963), 304-07.

"Saturday Review Tells of Milledgeville as Well as of Writer Flannery O'Connor," *Milledgeville Union-Recorder,* May 17, 1962.

Scharper, Philip. "Flannery O'Connor—a tribute," *Esprit,* VIII (Winter, 1964), 45.

Scott, Nathan A., Jr. "Flannery O'Connor—a tribute," *Esprit,* VIII (Winter, 1964), 45-46.

Sessions, William. "Flannery O'Connor, a Memoir," *National Catholic Reporter,* October 28, 1964, p. 9.

Snow, Ollye Tine. "The Functional Gothic of Flannery O'Connor," *Southwest Review,* L (Summer, 1965), 286-99.

Spivey, Ted R. "Flannery O'Connor—a tribute," *Esprit,* VIII (Winter, 1964), 46-48.

———. "Flannery O'Connor's View of God and Man," *Studies in Short Fiction,* I (Spring, 1964), 200-06.

Stelzmann, Rainulf. "Shock and Orthodoxy: An Interpretation of Flannery O'Connor's Novels and Short Stories," *Xavier University Studies,* II (March, 1963), 4-21.

———. "Der Stein des Anstosses: Die Romane und Erzählungen Flannery O'Connors," *Stimmen der Zeit,* CLXXIV (1964), 286-96.

Stern, Richard. "Flannery O'Connor: A Remembrance and Some Letters," *Shenandoah,* XVI (Winter, 1965), 5-10.

Sullivan, Walter. "Flannery O'Connor, Sin, and Grace: *Everything That Rises Must Converge,*" *Hollins Critic,* II (September, 1965), 1-8, 10.

Tate, Allen. "Flannery O'Connor—a tribute," *Esprit,* VIII (Winter, 1964), 48-49.

Thomas, Esther. "Flannery O'Connor Helps Nuns Write Child's Story," *Atlanta Journal,* August 10, 1961 [*A Memoir of Mary Ann*].

Thorp, Willard. "Suggs and Sut in Modern Dress," *Mississippi Quarterly,* XIII (Fall, 1960), 169-75 [discussion of similarity of Miss O'Connor's characters to those of Old Southwest humorists].

Townend, Joseph C. "The Inner Country," *Esprit,* VIII (Winter, 1964), 70.

Turner, Margaret. "Brenda Award and Missiles to Orbit at Theta Sig Fete," *Atlanta Journal and Atlanta Constitution,* April 24, 1960. P. 15G [award to Miss O'Connor].

Voss, Victor. "A Study in Sin," *Esprit,* VIII (Winter, 1964), 60-63.

Walter, Sarah. "Strange Prophets of Flannery O'Connor," *Censer* (Spring, 1960), 5-12.

Warren, Robert Penn. "Flannery O'Connor—a tribute," *Esprit,* VIII (Winter, 1964), 49.

Wedge, George F. "Two Bibliographies: Flannery O'Connor and J. F. Powers," *Critique,* II (Fall, 1958), 59-70.

Wells, Joel. "Flannery O'Connor—a tribute," *Esprit,* VIII (Winter, 1964), 49.

Welty, Eudora. "Flannery O'Connor—a tribute," *Esprit,* VIII (Winter, 1964), 49.

West, Ray B., Jr. "Flannery O'Connor—a tribute," *Esprit,* VIII (Winter, 1964), 49.

# Index

## FLANNERY O'CONNOR'S WRITINGS

# GENERAL INDEX